510

KS3

Collins

Total Revision

KS3 Maths

D0281544

Kevin Evans
Keith Gordon

Series Editor: Jayne de Courcy

Contents

How this book will help you...   iii

Boosting your National Test score   vi

How this book will help you...

It doesn't matter whether you're facing school exams in Year 7 or 8, or in the final run-up to your National Test in Year 9 – **this book will help you to produce your very best.**

Whichever approach you decide to take to revision, this book will provide everything you need:

1 Total revision support
2 Quick revision check-ups
3 Exam practice

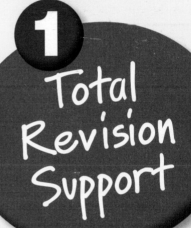

1

Total Revision Support

Everything you need to know

This book contains **all the maths topics you'll be studying** at school for each Attainment Target (Number; Shape, Space and Measure; Algebra; and Handling Data).

Short, easy-to-use chapters

This book is divided into short chapters. They're organised by level so that you can use the book wherever you are in your KS3 course. If you're facing exams in Year 7, you will probably revise the chapters at levels 4 and 5, and then revise the chapters at levels 6 and 7 in years 8 and 9.

Lots of worked examples

If, when you're revising, you need to go over something you haven't understood, you're bound to find it in this book. Each chapter has **lots of worked examples which show exactly what you need to do** to answer questions correctly.

...Turn over for QUICK REVISION CHECK-UPS and EXAM PRACTICE... →

Quick Revision Check-ups

Check yourself questions

It can be really hard knowing where to start when you're revising. Sitting down and wading through pages of notes isn't easy. You're probably asleep before the third page! This book makes it easy to stay awake – **because it makes revising ACTIVE.**

We came up with the idea of putting 'Check yourself' questions at the end of each chapter. **The questions test your understanding of the maths**. In this way, you can find out quickly and easily whether you really can do it.

If you get all the questions right, you can move straight on to the next chapter or the same topic at a higher level. If you get several of the questions wrong, you know you need to read through the worked examples really carefully.

Use the 'Check yourself' questions **to cut down on revision time – and help you focus on where you need to put most effort.**

You can 'cheat' if you want to!

If you want the 'Check yourself' questions to be a genuine test of how much you know, then use the flaps to cover up the answers. But, if you'd rather, you can read through a question, then the answer and then the '**tutorial**'. This will still do you a lot of good – and doesn't require quite as much effort!

Even more help – tutorials

We've included 'tutorials', as well as answers. The tutorials provide extra help if you're having problems getting an answer or if your answer is wrong. Look out for our hints!

3 Exam Practice

Test technique

Knowing your maths is important. But **it's even more important to know how to use it to answer Test questions properly.** The authors see hundreds of Test scripts a year and students very often lose marks because **they haven't understood how to tackle the questions.**

Practising mental maths

We've included two sample mental Tests for you to practise on. You'll need to ask someone to read each test to you. Remember you must work out the answers completely in your head although you can write down any workings to help you.

Examiner's comments

The answers to the past Test questions are at the back of the book. The authors have commented on every answer. **They show you the best way to answer the question and where you may have gone wrong if you didn't get the right answer.** They also tell you about common mistakes students make so that you can avoid making them!

Practise real Test questions

At the end of the chapters at each level, you'll find Test questions from previous years' papers.

If you're entered for the level 3-5 or 4-6 tier Test, try some of the questions at level 4 first. Once you're confident with these, move on to level 5 and so on.

If you're entered for the level 5-7 or 6-8 tier Test, start with the level 5 questions and move on.

Three final tips:

1. **Work as consistently as you can during your whole KS3 Maths course.** If you don't understand something, ask your teacher straight away, or look it up in this book. You'll then find revision much easier.

2. **Plan your revision carefully and focus on the areas you know you find hard.** The 'Check yourself' questions in this book will help you do this.

3. **Try to do some Test questions as though you were in the actual Test.** Time yourself and don't 'cheat' by looking at the answers until you've really had a good go at working out the answers.

Boosting your National Test score

The Mathematics National Curriculum explained

First, the technical information!
The Mathematics National Curriculum is divided into four *Attainment Targets*. These are called:

Ma1 Using and applying mathematics

Ma2 Number and algebra

Ma3 Shape, space and measures

Ma4 Handling data

Each Attainment Target is divided up into *level descriptions*, numbered from level 1 to level 8. (There is also a top level called Exceptional performance.) These describe what you should know and be able to do at each level.

By the end of Key Stage 3, the majority of students will be between levels 3 and 7. A typical Key Stage 3 student should be around levels 5 and 6.

Exceptional performance ●	} considerably better than the expected level
Level 8 ●	
Level 7 ●	} better than the expected level
Level 6 ●	} expected level for 14 year olds
Level 5 ●	
Level 4 ●	
Level 3 ●	} working towards the expected level
Level 2 ●	
Level 1 ●	
Age **14 years**	

Typical 14 year olds get a level 5 or 6 in the Mathematics National Test. This book will show you where you are and help you move up the levels.

What's in the Maths National Test?

The National Test papers for Maths that you will sit in May of year 9 have questions that cover Ma2, 3 and 4. Your teacher assesses *Using and applying mathematics* (Ma1) from your coursework.

You sit two Test papers. Both papers include questions on Number, Algebra, Shape, space and measures and Handling data.

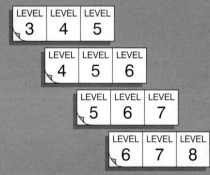

There are four tiers of Test papers – Tier 3–5, Tier 4–6, Tier 5–7 and Tier 6–8.

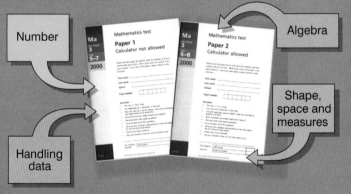

The Test papers are available at four different *tiers*. The first tier covers National Curriculum levels 3–5; the second tier levels 4–6; the third tier levels 5–7 and the final tier levels 6–8.

Everybody has to take their Tests in one of these tiers. Your teacher will decide which tier of papers is best for you to show what you know and understand about maths.

You have to take two Test papers and a mental Test. The Tests start with the easier questions and get harder as you work through. You are only allowed to use a calculator in Paper 2.

Chapter 1

The four operations of number

You should be able to use the four operations of addition, subtraction, multiplication and division in a range of mental and written problems. You should know your multiplication tables up to 10 × 10.

You should already know how to add and subtract numbers up to 20. You also need to know your 2, 5 and 10 times tables and how to use these in multiplication and division problems.

In this chapter we are going to look at the 'four rules' used with whole numbers – **addition**, **subtraction**, **multiplication** and **division**. You will need to add and subtract numbers of up to 3 digits and know all of your tables up to the 10 times table. If you do not know your tables and you find basic addition and subtraction difficult, you might not be able to do some of the problems.

Below is the standard multiplication table. You can use it to help you do multiplication and division problems. You need to know it!

×	1	2	3	4	5	6	7	8	9	10
1	1	2	3	4	5	6	7	8	9	10
2	2	4	6	8	10	12	14	16	18	20
3	3	6	9	12	15	18	21	24	27	30
4	4	8	12	16	20	24	28	32	36	40
5	5	10	15	20	25	30	35	40	45	50
6	6	12	18	24	30	36	42	48	54	60
7	7	14	21	28	35	42	49	56	63	70
8	8	16	24	32	40	48	56	64	72	80
9	9	18	27	36	45	54	63	72	81	90
10	10	20	30	40	50	60	70	80	90	100

1   Mary is trying to work out how far the trip is from her home in Leeds to Plymouth, if she goes via Birmingham. She knows that:

EXAMPLE

Leeds to Birmingham	158 miles
Birmingham to Plymouth	256 miles

Mary works out that the distance is over 500 miles.

(a)   How can you tell that Mary's answer is wrong without working out the correct total?

(b)   Work out the correct answer.

The four operations of number

(a) Leeds to Birmingham is about 150 miles. Birmingham to Plymouth is about 250 miles. Together that is about 400 miles. As both values were just over their estimates the distance is over 400 miles but not over 500 miles.

(b) 414 miles.

You do not need to show carry digits or other evidence. You will not be allowed to use a calculator on the paper that will ask this sort of question.

EXAMPLE **2** First class stamps used to cost 25p. Now they are 26p.

(a) Work out the total cost of 9 stamps that are 26p each.

(b) How much more is this than the cost of 9 stamps at 25p each?

ANSWER Think about this problem. There is a very easy way to do it.

(a) This is a short multiplication:

$$
\begin{array}{r}
26 \\
\times\ 9 \\
\hline
234
\end{array}
$$

There are lots of other ways. You can add 26 nine times or multiply 26 by 10 and take 26 away from the answer.

(b) $9 \times 25 = £2.25$

$£2.34 - £2.25 = £0.09$, or 9p

Or, each stamp is 1p more, so 9 stamps cost 9p more! You may be able to do this sum in your head. You do not need to show any working; just write the answer down.

EXAMPLE **3** Julie is organising a concert for Year 9. There are 232 pupils in Year 9. The caretaker tells Julie that there are only 178 chairs in the hall. Julie works out that they need another 146 chairs:

$$
\begin{array}{r}
232 \\
-\ 178 \\
\hline
146
\end{array}
$$

(a) Explain what she did wrong.

(b) Work out how many extra chairs are needed.

Your explanation does not need to be long – just a sentence.

ANSWER (a) Julie just took the smallest number from the biggest and not the bottom number from the top number.

(b)
$$
\begin{array}{r}
232 \\
-\ 178 \\
\hline
54
\end{array}
$$

**The four operations
of number**

4 6 pupils can sit at each table in the canteen. The canteen has 40 tables. After the inter-school cross-country race 162 pupils are expected for tea.

(a) Without doing an exact calculation, explain why you know there will be enough tables.

(b) If the smallest number of tables is to be used, how many will be needed?

(a) $6 \times 40 = 240$. This is bigger than 162.

(b) This is short division: $6\overline{)16^42}$ with 27 above   27 tables are needed.

Check yourself

QUESTIONS

Q1 Complete these multiplication squares:

×	7	6	3
2			
5			
10			

×	2	5	9
9			
4			
8			

×	3	7	6
4			
8			
6			

×	5	2	7
7			
9			
3			

Q2 There are 9 pots of yoghurt in a carton. How many pots of yoghurt are there in 7 cartons?

Q3 A piece of string is 147 centimetres long. It is cut into 7 pieces. How long is each piece?

ANSWERS AND TUTORIAL

A1

×	7	6	3
2	14	12	6
5	35	30	15
10	70	60	30

×	2	5	9
9	18	45	81
4	8	20	36
8	16	40	72

×	3	7	6
4	12	28	24
8	24	56	48
6	18	42	36

×	5	2	7
7	35	14	49
9	45	18	63
3	15	6	21

A2 63 pots

T2 This is the sum 9×7. There is an easy way to remember the 9 times table. Hold up the fingers of both hands facing you. Count across 7 fingers from the left and put that finger down.

There are 6 fingers before the gap and 3 fingers after it. $7 \times 9 = 63$!

A3 21 pieces

T3 This is short division $147 \div 7$ or $7\overline{)147}$.

ANSWERS AND TUTORIAL

QUESTIONS

A4   (a) He can catch the 07.45 or the 08.10
     (b) 08.54
     (c) 9 minutes

T4   Time problems are common in SATs. You are likely
to make mistakes if you do these with a calculator
as there are not 100 minutes in an hour!

A5   (a) 235 (b) 176 (c) 506
      -78 -97 -358
      157 79 148

T5   You will not be expected to show carries and
borrows but these make the sum easier for you.

A6   (a) He is wrong: there will be less than 300
       when the people get off but the guard has
       forgotten to count the people who got on.
     (b) $418 - 129 = 289$
       $289 + 58 = 347$

T6   Keep your explanation short and to the point.

A7

(a)	9	(f)	16	(k)	42
(b)	12	(g)	24	(l)	48
(c)	18	(h)	28	(m)	49
(d)	21	(i)	32	(n)	56
(e)	24	(j)	36	(o)	64

T7   We can easily remember the 1, 2, 5 and 10 times
tables. Cross these out of the multiplication table on
page 1 and also cross out one of the sums if there
are 2 the same, like 3×4 and 4×3. This leaves just
15 multiplication facts to learn. This is a lot less
than 100! These 'special' facts are the sums you
have just done in Question 7. Learn them!

Q4   This timetable shows the buses from Wath
to Doncaster.

Leave Wath	07.45	08.10	08.45	08.59	09.10
Arrive Doncaster	08.12	08.42	09.15	09.30	09.37

   (a) John needs to arrive in Doncaster by 09.05.
      Which buses could he catch?
   (b) Lauren has a five minute walk to the bus stop.
      What time should she leave home to catch the
      bus that gets into Doncaster at 09.30?
   (c) Kim is 5 minutes late for the 08.45. How
      long does she have to wait for the next bus?

Q5   Do these subtractions:
   (a) $235 - 78$
   (b) $176 - 97$
   (c) $506 - 358$

Q6   The train from Edinburgh to London leaves
Edinburgh with 418 passengers. At Newcastle
129 get off and 58 get on.
   (a) The guard estimates that there are now less
      than 300 people on the train. Without doing
      any calculations, explain how you can tell
      he is wrong.
   (b) How many passengers are there on the train
      when it leaves Newcastle?

Q7   Time yourself doing these 15 multiplication sums:

(a)	$3 \times 3 =$		(i)	$4 \times 8 =$
(b)	$3 \times 4 =$		(j)	$6 \times 6 =$
(c)	$3 \times 6 =$		(k)	$6 \times 7 =$
(d)	$3 \times 7 =$		(l)	$6 \times 8 =$
(e)	$3 \times 8 =$		(m)	$7 \times 7 =$
(f)	$4 \times 4 =$		(n)	$7 \times 8 =$
(g)	$4 \times 6 =$		(o)	$8 \times 8 =$
(h)	$4 \times 7 =$			

Chapter 2

Multiplying and Dividing by 10 and 100

You need to understand the place value of numbers. You should be able to multiply and divide whole numbers by 10 and 100.

You should already know which digits in a number represent the units, tens and hundreds. You should also know your ten times table. We now look at how to multiply and divide whole numbers by 10 and 100. This is easy and follows some rules. First, a reminder about **place value**.

Place value

In a number such as 453 (four hundred and fifty three), the 4 represents 4 hundreds, or 400; the 5 represents 5 tens, or 50; and the 3 represents 3 units, or 3. So: $453 = 400 + 50 + 3$

When we multiply a whole number by 10, we put a zero to the end. So:

H T U
  3 2 × 10
3 2 0 $32 \times 10 = 320$

When we multiply a whole number by 100, we put two zeros to the end. So:

Th H T U
    5 8 × 100
5 8 0 0 $58 \times 100 = 5800$

When we divide a number by 10, each digit moves one place to the right, or a zero is crossed off the end. So:

H T U
4 6 0 ÷ 10
  4 6 $460 \div 10 = 46$

When we divide a number by 100, each digit moves 2 places to the right, or two zeros are crossed off the end. So:

Th H T U
7 3 0 0 ÷ 100
    7 3 $7300 \div 100 = 73$

---

1 Jon picks three numbers from these cards:

1   **2**   **3**   **4**   **5**

(a) He picks three cards that make the biggest even number. Which three does he pick?

(b) He picks three cards that make the smallest odd number. Which three does he pick?

(a) **5** **4** **2**   An even number must end in 0, 2, 4, 6 or 8. Choose the biggest number you can to be the hundreds value. Choose the next biggest to be the tens value, then use the biggest even digit that is left.

(b) **1** **2** **3**   An odd number must end in 1, 3, 5, 7 or 9. Choose the smallest number you can to be the hundreds value. Choose the next smallest to be the tens value, then use the smallest odd digit that is left.

Multiplying and Dividing by 10 and 100

EXAMPLE

2 You have these cards:

| 3400 | 38 | 65 | 6500 | 380 | 340 | 308 | 650 |

(a) Pick two cards so that the number on one of them is 10 times the number on the other.

(b) Pick two cards so that the number on one of them is 100 times the number on the other.

ANSWER

(a) Any pair from 340 and 3400, 650 and 6500, 38 and 380, 65 and 650. The digits must be the same with an extra zero at the end.

(b) 65 and 6500. The digits must be the same with an extra two zeros at the end.

EXAMPLE

3 A chocolate bar costs 13p. How much are 10 chocolate bars?

ANSWER

10 x 13 = 130p. You can also write this as £1.30.

Answers can be in pounds or pence but you cannot use the two at the same time, so £1.30p is wrong.

EXAMPLE

4 A box of 100 chews costs £3. How much is each chew?

ANSWER

300 ÷ 100 = 3p

You need to make £3 into 300p.

Check yourself

ANSWERS AND TUTORIAL

A1
(a)	370	(e)	30700	(i)	9
(b)	6030	(f)	2100	(j)	43
(c)	780	(g)	49	(k)	6
(d)	5200	(h)	63	(l)	40

T1 You can multiply or divide whole numbers by 10 and 100 simply by adding or crossing off zeros.

A2 (a) £40 (b) £400

T2 This is just multiplying by 10 and 100.

QUESTIONS

Q1 Write down the answers to these sums:
(a)	37 × 10	(g)	490 ÷ 10
(b)	603 × 10	(h)	630 ÷ 10
(c)	78 × 10	(i)	90 ÷ 10
(d)	52 × 100	(j)	4300 ÷ 100
(e)	307 × 100	(k)	600 ÷ 100
(f)	21 × 100	(l)	4000 ÷ 100

Q2 A pair of socks costs £4. How much are:
(a) 10 pairs?
(b) 100 pairs?

QUESTIONS

Q3 Say if the following statements are true or false
(a) 600 is 6 tens
(b) 600 is 6 hundreds
(c) 600 is 60 tens
(d) 600 is 60 units

Q4 Match these cards in two sets of three that give the same number:

Q5 A box of 10 candles costs £4.50. How much does 1 candle cost?

Q6 22 000 people saw a recent Barnsley match.
(a) At half time, 1 person in 10 had a cup of tea. How many cups of tea were sold?
(b) At half time, 1 person in 100 had a snack . How many snacks were sold?

Q7 A rope 20 metres long is divided into 100 equal pieces. How long is each piece?

Q8 Harry has the following cards:

He picks three cards and makes the number 452.
(a) Make a smaller number than 452 with Harry's cards.
(b) Make a larger number than 452 with Harry's cards.
(c) Pick another card so that Harry can make a number 10 times as big as 452. What number does Harry make?

ANSWERS AND TUTORIAL

A3 (a) False   (c) True
(b) True   (d) False

T3 6 tens is 6 x 10 = 60 so (a) is false. 600 is 600 units, so (d) is false.

A4 The first set is 40 tens, 400 units and 400. The second set is 40 hundreds, 4 thousands and 4000.

T4 In Questions 2 and 3, be careful with the number of zeros at the end of a number.

A5 45p

T5 Make £4.50 into 450p before dividing.

A6 (a) 2200 cups of tea
(b) 220 snacks

T6 Be careful of the number of zeros. Take 1 off when dividing by 10 and 2 off when dividing by 100.

A7 20 cm

T7 Make 20 metres into 2000 centimetres.

A8 (a) 425 or 254 or 245
(b) 524 or 542
(c) Pick zero: The number is 4520

T8 You have to think which card represents the hundreds digit, which is the tens digit and so on.

Chapter 3

LEVEL 4
NUMBER

Addition and subtraction of decimals

You should be able to add and subtract decimals up to 2 decimal places. When solving problems with a calculator you should check that your answers are about the right size.

You should already know how to round off a number to the nearest 10 or 100. You should also know that the decimal point in a number separates the whole number parts from the fractions. As we have a decimal system of money, you should be used to adding and subtracting numbers up to 2 decimal places.

It is also important to check that your answers are about the right size. In this chapter we look at ways to do **decimal sums** and **estimate answers**.

EXAMPLE **1** Martin goes shopping and buys a shirt that costs £18, a tie that costs £4.65 and a pair of socks that are £3.99. How much does he spend altogether?

ANSWER £26.64

When adding decimals it is important to line up the decimal point. Remember that £18 must be written as £18.00. Your working should look like this:

$$
\begin{array}{r}
£18.00 \\
£4.65 \\
+ \underline{£3.99} \\
£26.64
\end{array}
$$

EXAMPLE **2** Owen cuts a piece of wood that is 3 metres long into two pieces. One of these is 1.65 metres long. How long is the other piece?

ANSWER 1.35 metres

When subtracting decimals it is important to line up the decimal point. So, write 3 metres as 3.00 metres.

$$
\begin{array}{r}
3.00 \\
- \underline{1.65} \\
1.35 \text{ metres}
\end{array}
$$

EXAMPLE **3** When doing the sum 378 ÷ 5 on his calculator, Sanjay gets the answer 147.6.

(a) Explain clearly why he is incorrect.

(b) What should the answer be, roughly?

ANSWER (a) 5 times 100 is 500, so 5 × 146 must well over 500. This is much bigger than the original number, 378. So, Sanjay must be wrong.

(b) About 80.

Make the sum easy by taking 378 as about 400.

4 Mr. Jones is buying a set of books for his class of 30 students. The books are £6.50 each. Mr. Jones estimates that the total cost will be £200. Explain clearly why this is a good estimate.

£6 × 30 = £180 and £7 × 30 = £210, so £6.50 × 30 must be between £180 and £210.

Explain answers like this using numbers that can be worked out easily <u>without</u> a calculator.

Check yourself

QUESTIONS

Q1 Do the following decimal sums:
(a) 1.63 + 5.24
(b) 2.05 + 1.87
(c) 4.56 – 3.81
(d) 3.08 – 2.16

Q2 Put the following decimals in order, smallest first:

| 1.23 | 1.20 | 1.3 | 1.02 | 1.00 |

Q3 Put the following decimals in order, largest first:

| 3.46 | 3.08 | 3.4 | 3.06 | 3.3 |

Q4 This is a picture of a child's toy train:

(a) **How long is the train?**
(b) **How high is the chimney?**

ANSWERS AND TUTORIAL

A1 (a) 6.87   (c) 0.75
(b) 3.92   (d) 0.92

T1 Don't forget to line up the decimal point. After that, just do it like a normal sum.

A2

| 1.00 | 1.02 | 1.20 | 1.23 | 1.3 |

T2 You must be careful that you do not take 1.20 as bigger than 1.3 because 20 is bigger than 3. 1.3 can also be written as 1.30. The trick is to add zeros so each number has the same number of decimal places.

A3

| 3.46 | 3.4 | 3.3 | 3.08 | 3.06 |

T3 If we add zeros as recommended in Question 2, the numbers are 3.46, 3.40, 3.30, 3.08 and 3.06.

A4 (a) 10.69 cm
(b) 0.78 cm

T4 Remember to line up the decimal point.
(a) The sum is 7.23 + 3.46
(b) The sum is 5.15 – 4.37

ANSWERS AND TUTORIAL

A5 (a) 3.2 and 5.8 added together are not bigger than 10.4, so they would not fit around a triangle.
(b) 22.1 cm

T5 Any two sides of a triangle added together must be bigger than the third side. This is really a shape question, but you may be asked to measure sides of a triangle or another shape.

A6 (a) £63.95
(b) £16.05

T6 Take £5 as 5.00 before you line up the point. Four £20 notes is £80, so take this as 80.00.

A7 (a) 2.3 cm
(b) 8.7 cm
(c) 6.1 cm
(d) 17.1 cm

T7 If you are asked to measure lines in SATs, you can be out by a millimetre and still get the marks for a correct answer.

A8 Sum (c) is wrong. 9 is about 10 so the answers should be about 57, 96 and 23. The actual answers will be a bit bigger as 9 is smaller than 10. 62 is too far out.

A9 She will probably have saved enough. 1840 × 10 ≑ 18400 so 1840 × 11 is a bit bigger than this, but she won't get much change!

QUESTIONS

Q5 Robin measures the sides of a triangle as 3.2 cm, 5.8 cm and 10.4 cm.

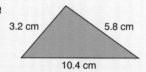

(a) Explain how you know he has made an error in his measuring.
(b) The correct measurements are 3.2 cm, 8.5 cm and 10.4 cm.
Add up these measurements to find the perimeter.

Q6 Ann buys some shoes for £35.50, a skirt for £23.45 and a belt for £5.
(a) How much does she spend altogether?
(b) If she pays with four £20 notes, how much change will she get?

Q7 What lengths are shown on these rulers?

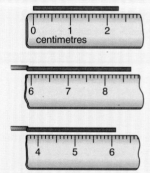

(d) Add your answers to parts (a), (b) and (c) together.

Q8 Two of these sums are correct and one is wrong:
(a) 567 ÷ 9 = 63   (b) 963 ÷ 9 = 107
(c) 234 ÷ 9 = 62
Explain, without using a calculator, which sum is wrong.

Q9 There are 1840 pupils at Wath Comprehensive School. To celebrate her retirement, the head takes them all to Alton Towers for the day. The cost is £11 per pupil. Will the £21 000 the head has put aside for the trip be enough? Do not use a calculator and explain your answer fully.

Chapter 4

Simple fractions, decimals and percentages

> You should be able to recognise proportions of a whole number and use simple fractions and percentages.

You should already know what a fraction is and what a decimal is. You should also know some of the easier percentages and their equivalent decimals and fractions. For example:

$$50\% = \tfrac{1}{2} = 0.5 \qquad 25\% = \tfrac{1}{4} = 0.25$$

In this chapter we look at how to estimate **fractions**, **percentages** and **decimals**. We also see how to do some problems using the easier fractions, percentages, and decimals.

A fraction is a part of a whole. A decimal is also part of a whole and a percentage is a measurement of a hundredth part of a whole. Basically, decimals, fractions and percentages are all the same thing.

At this level you need to learn some more of the common fractions and their equivalent percentages and decimals. For example:

$$20\% = \tfrac{1}{5} = 0.2 \qquad 75\% = \tfrac{3}{4} = 0.75 \qquad 33.3\% = \tfrac{1}{3} = 0.33$$

---

1 Approximately what percentage of these shapes is shaded?

EXAMPLE

a) 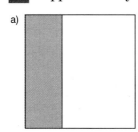 b) 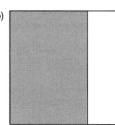 c)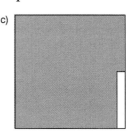

ANSWER

(a) 30% (b) 70% (c) 95%

An answer that is within 5% of the answer is OK. So, (a) could be any percentage between 25% and 35%.

---

2 Approximately what fraction of these shapes is shaded?

EXAMPLE

a) 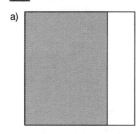 b) 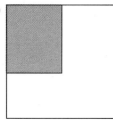 c)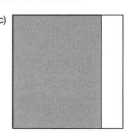

ANSWER

(a) $\tfrac{2}{3}$ or $\tfrac{3}{4}$ (b) $\tfrac{3}{10}$ or $\tfrac{2}{5}$ (c) $\tfrac{4}{5}$ or $\tfrac{9}{10}$

Fractions are difficult to see. Usually the shapes can be measured and they divide up easily. You can be a bit out on each one but all the fractions you are expected to find will have a simple denominator (the bottom number) like 2, 3, 4, 5 or 10.

EXAMPLE

3 If each of these squares represents one whole, approximately what decimal is shaded?

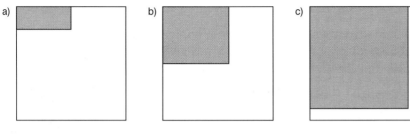

a)   b)   c)

ANSWER

(a)   0.1   (b)   0.3   (c)   0.8

Decimals are difficult to see. Usually the shapes can be measured and they divide up easily. You can be a bit out on each one but all the decimals you are expected to find will have one decimal place only, or will be 0.25 or 0.75.

Check yourself

ANSWERS AND TUTORIAL

A1   (a)   20%
        (b)   40%
        (c)   70%
        (d)   90%

T1   Most of the percentages you will be asked to estimate will be multiples of 5 or 10.

A2   (a) $\frac{1}{4}$ (b) $\frac{2}{3}$ (c) $\frac{1}{4}$ (d) $\frac{3}{5}$

T2   Remember the bottom number (the denominator) will always be 2, 3, 5 or 10.

QUESTIONS

Q1   Martin is painting a wall. These pictures show how much he has done at different times:

10.00 am   10.30 am   11.00 am   11.30 am

Approximately what percentage has he painted at each time?

Q2   Approximately what fraction of each flag is shaded:

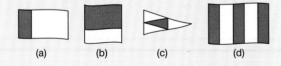

(a)   (b)   (c)   (d)

QUESTIONS

Q3 Copy this shape twice and shade in:
(a) $\frac{1}{5}$

(b) $\frac{3}{4}$

Q4 The picture shows how far up the scale of a 'Test your Strength' machine different people have hit the weight:

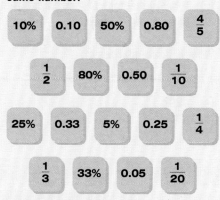

(a)   (b)   (c)   (d)

Approximately what fraction of the total distance is each weight from the bottom?

Q5 Match these cards into six sets that show the same number:

| 10% | 0.10 | 50% | 0.80 | $\frac{4}{5}$ |

| $\frac{1}{2}$ | 80% | 0.50 | $\frac{1}{10}$ |

| 25% | 0.33 | 5% | 0.25 | $\frac{1}{4}$ |

| $\frac{1}{3}$ | 33% | 0.05 | $\frac{1}{20}$ |

Q6 What is 10% of each of:
(a) £100?
(b) £300?
(c) £50?
(d) £10?

ANSWERS AND TUTORIAL

A3

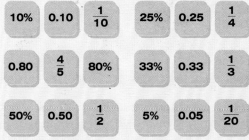

(a)   (b)

T3 The lines could go either way in both answers. You can be a little bit out from the exact answer. Try measuring the shape to see if it divides up exactly.

A4 (a) $\frac{3}{4}$ (b) $\frac{1}{4}$ (c) $\frac{1}{2}$ (d) $\frac{9}{10}$

T4 In Questions 1 to 4, there can be some differences in your answers and you will not be expected to give fractions percentages or decimals to greater accuracies than these.

A5

| 10% | 0.10 | $\frac{1}{10}$ | 25% | 0.25 | $\frac{1}{4}$ |

| 0.80 | $\frac{4}{5}$ | 80% | 33% | 0.33 | $\frac{1}{3}$ |

| 50% | 0.50 | $\frac{1}{2}$ | 5% | 0.05 | $\frac{1}{20}$ |

T5 It is worth learning some of the more common equivalent fractions and decimals. You might find the chart at the bottom of page 14 useful.

A6 (a) £10   (c) £5
(b) £30   (d) £1

T6 10% is the same as dividing by 10.

13

ANSWERS AND TUTORIAL

A7 (a) £1   (b) £100
     (c) £50   (d) £10

T7 One-third is a basic fraction. It is the only one that you have to learn at this level that doesn't have a simple percentage. It is 33.33333... %. usually we write this as 33% or 33.3%.

A8 (a) Sept – 40%, Oct – 55%, Nov – 65%, Dec – 90%
     (b) Sept – £12, Oct – £16.50, Nov – £19.50, Dec – £27
     (c) 10%

T8 Each division is 10% which is £3. Half a division is £1.50

A9 (a) 3   (b) 30   (c) 90   (d) 300

T9 Find a quarter then multiply it by 3.
This chart may help you to remember some of the equivalent fractions, percentages and decimals:

QUESTIONS

Q7 What is one-third of these amounts:
(a) £3?
(b) £300?
(c) £150?
(d) £30?

Q8 A class are trying to save £30 for a Christmas Party. This is the chart they keep over the term:

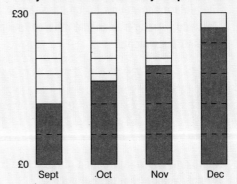

(a) What percentage of their target do they reach each month?
(b) How much money do they have each month?
(c) What percentage of their target are they down by in December?

Q9 What is three-quarters of:
(a) 4?
(b) 40?
(c) 120?
(d) 400?

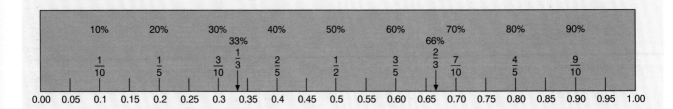

T E S T   Q U E S T I O N S

Answers with examiner's comments on page 237.

1. Kate is adding up the number of pupils in year 9 and the number of pupils in year 10.

Year 9	127 pupils
Year 10	154 pupils

Kate says that there is a total of 2711 pupils in years 9 and 10.

(a) How can you tell that Kate's total is wrong **before** you work out the correct total?
This is Kate's work:

$$\begin{array}{r} 127 \\ +\ \ 154 \\ \hline = 2711 \end{array}$$

(b) What do you think Kate did wrong?

(1993 paper 1)

2. A small chocolate bar costs 7p. Gill has 97p in her pocket.

(a) How many chocolate bars can she buy with 97p?
(b) How much money will she have left?

(1992 paper 3)

3. Tom has baked **50** small cakes for the school fair.
He wants to put them into bags of **4**. Tom says ⟨ I will need 200 bags ⟩

(a) You can tell that Tom must be wrong **before** you work out the right answer.
Explain why Tom must be wrong.
(b) Work out how many bags of 4 cakes Tom will have.
(c) How many cakes will Tom have left over.
(d) Lela needs **27** cakes for a party. Tom sell cakes in bags of **4**.
How many bags must Lela buy?

(1994 paper 2)

4. Derek is going from Croxton to Braytown by bus.

The bus Timetable shows what time buses leave Croxton and arrive at Braytown.

Bus Timetable: Croxton to Braytown					
Croxton depart:	08:30	08:45	09:20	09:45	10:30
Braytown arrive:	09:15	09:30	10:05	10:30	11:15

For example, the first bus leaves Croxton at 08:30 and arrives at Braytown at 09:15.

(a) Derek catches the 08:45 bus from Croxton. What time does he arrive at Braytown?
(b) How long does the bus journey take? Give your answer as a number of minutes.
(c) Derek caught the 08:45 bus from Croxton. He took 15 minutes to get from his house to the bus stop. He waited 5 minutes for the bus to come. What time did Derek leave his house?
(d) Ruth is going from Croxton to Braytown by bus as well. Ruth must get to Braytown by 10:20. Which buses could she catch?
(e) Ruth is 15 minutes late for the 08:45 bus from Croxton. She catches the next bus instead. How long does Ruth wait for the next bus?

(1996 paper 2)

5. By the end of term, a school had raised a total of **£976.85** in sponsorship. A local newspaper wrote about them. Fill in the space with a sensible amount. It should be a whole number of pounds.

> **The school has raised**
>
> **nearly £...............**

(1996 paper 2)

6. Here are some cards

Choose 2 cards. The number on one card must be **ten times** as big as the number on the other card. Write down the two cards you choose.

(1993 paper 2)

7. (a) Claire puts a 2 digit whole number into her calculator. She **multiplies** the number by **10**. Fill in **one** other digit which you **know** must be on the calculator display.
   (b) Claire starts again with the **same** 2 digit whole number. This time she **multiplies** it by **100**. Fill in **all** the digits that must be on the calculator display.

(1995 paper 2)

8. Here are some number cards

Samira picked these three cards:

5 2 4

She made the number 425 with her cards.

   (a) Make a **smaller** number with Samira's three cards.
   (b) Make the **biggest** number you can with Samira's cards.
   (c) Samira made the number 425 with her cards.
       What extra card should she pick to make her number **10 times** as big?
       What number is **10 times** as big as 425?

(1994 paper 2)

9. In a restaurant 4 people share 3 pizzas equally. How much pizza do they have each? Give your answer as a fraction of a pizza.

(1993 paper 1)

Chapter 5

Number patterns

You should be able to explore and describe number patterns.

You should already know how to work out the difference between two numbers. In this chapter we look at number patterns. A number pattern is a list, or series of numbers that are connected by a rule.

Describing patterns

You need to recognise a simple **number pattern** and describe how it builds up. Each of these is a number pattern:

(a)   2, 4, 6, 8, 10, 12.... This goes up in twos: it's the two times table.

(b)   3, 7, 11, 15, 19, 23.... This goes up in fours, but it isn't the four times table because it starts at 3.

(c)   6, 9, 12, 15, 18.... This goes up in threes and is part of the three times table, but it doesn't start at 3. Instead it starts at 6, the second number in the three times table.

(d)   2, 5, 9, 14, 20, 27.... This one is different from the others because it does not go up by the same amount each time. It is still a pattern though – from 2 to 5 is a jump of 3, from 5 to 9 is a jump of 4, from 9 to 14 is a jump of 5, and so on. It's a good idea to write down the 'jumps' under the pattern like this:

This makes it much easier to work out the next terms.

Next terms

In maths, there are lots of ways to write down how a pattern builds up. At this level you only have to find the next 2 or 3 terms in a pattern.

1   Find the next three terms in the number patterns shown in (a) to (d) above. Explain how you worked out your answers.

(a)   goes up in 2s, so we add 2s to get 14, 16 and 18.

(b)   goes up in 4s, so we add 4s to get 27, 31 and 35.

(c)   goes up in 3s, so we add 3s to get 21, 24 and 27.

(d)   goes up in jumps. Look at the diagram above. We need to add 8 to 27 and we get 35. Then we add 9 to 35 and get 44. Finally, we add 10 to 44 and get 54. So, the next three terms are 35, 44, 54. You can see this by extending the diagram:

Number patterns from diagrams

Very often, you need to explore number patterns shown in diagrams.
You usually have to count matches or squares to try to spot the pattern.

EXAMPLE

2 John is making matchstick patterns.
Here are his first three patterns:

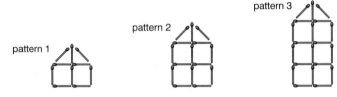

pattern 1   pattern 2   pattern 3

(a)   Draw the next pattern.

(b)   How many matches are needed for the 6th pattern?

ANSWER

(a)   One more layer of squares is added
each time. So, the next pattern is:

(b)   If you list the number of matches used in each pattern, you get
10, 15 and 20. This makes it really clear that the pattern goes up
in 5s. The next three numbers are 25, 30 and 35. So, you can
work out that 35 matches are needed to make the 6th pattern,
without drawing all the diagrams.

EXAMPLE

3 A company hires bikes. The cost is £10, plus £3 per hour. This
table shows how much it costs to hire a bike for different times.
Fill in the missing numbers.

Number of hours bike is hired	1	2	3	4	5	6	7	8
Cost (£)	13	16	19	22				

ANSWER

Number of hours bike is hired	1	2	3	4	5	6	7	8
Cost (£)	13	16	19	22	25	28	31	34

You can see that the cost is going up by £3 for every extra hour.
It is also possible to work out the time the bike was hired for, if
you know only the total cost.

Check yourself

QUESTIONS

Q1 Describe how each of these number patterns is building up:
  (a) 3, 6, 9, 12, 15....
  (b) 1, 3, 5, 7, 9....
  (c) 2, 5, 8, 11, 14, 17....
  (d) 2, 4, 7, 11, 16, 22....
  (e) 1, 4, 9, 16, 25....

Q2 For each of the number patterns in Question 1, write down the next three terms.

Q3 For each series of pictures below:

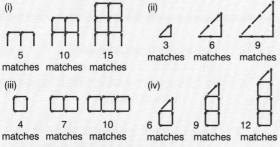

(i)
5 matches   10 matches   15 matches

(ii)
3 matches   6 matches   9 matches

(iii)
4 matches   7 matches   10 matches

(iv)
6 matches   9 matches   12 matches

  (a) Draw the next picture.
  (b) Write down (without drawing) how many matches you would need to make the 5th pattern.

Q4 A block of flats with five floors has the flats numbered like this:

5	10	15	20
4	9	14	19
3	8	13	18
2	7	12	17
1	6	11	16

  (a) Describe the number pattern for each floor.
  (b) What do all the patterns have in common?
  (c) The next block of flats has four floors and four flats on each floor. On which floor is flat number 7?

ANSWERS AND TUTORIAL

A1 (a) Up in 3s
  (b) Up in 2s
  (c) Up in 3s
  (d) Up by one more each time
  (e) Up by 2 more each time

A2 (a) 18, 21, 24 (c) 20, 23, 26 (e) 36, 49, 64
  (b) 11, 13, 15 (d) 29, 37, 46

T1/2 Don't forget to write down the number pattern and put down the differences.

A3 (a)

(i)   (ii)   (iii)   (iv)

  (b) (i) 25 (ii) 15 (iii) 16 (iv) 18

T3 These patterns all go up by a regular amount. Count on twice from the 3rd picture. In SATs you can lose marks if you do diagrams because the exam is trying to test if you can work things out using number patterns.

A4 (a) The ground floor numbers go up by 5, so do the 1st floor, 2nd floor, 3rd floor and 4th floor.
  (b) All the patterns go up by 5.
  (c) Flat 7 will be on the 2nd floor.

T4 You can work out part (c) by doing a sketch or by realising that flat 5 will now be on the ground floor and so 5, 6, 7 means that the 7th flat will be on the 2nd floor.

ANSWERS AND TUTORIAL

A5 (a)

(b) The pattern is increasing by 4 more each time.

(c) The sixth pattern will need 24 marbles.

A6 (a)

(b) The pattern is increasing by 1 more each time. It goes up 1, then 2, then 3 and so on.

(c) The sixth pattern will need 21 marbles.

T6 Write it out as a number pattern to see how it builds up.

A7 (a)

(b) The pattern is increasing by 2 more each time. It goes up by 3 then by 5 then by 7 and so on.

(c) The sixth pattern will need 36 marbles.

T7 These are called Square numbers and are dealt with on page 69.

QUESTIONS

Q5 Denise is making square patterns with marbles. These are her first 4 patterns:

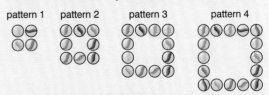

pattern 1   pattern 2   pattern 3   pattern 4

(a) Draw her next square.

(b) This list shows the numbers of marbles used for each pattern: 4, 8, 12, 16, ...
Describe how the pattern is building up.

(c) How many marbles will Denise need for her 6th pattern?

Q6 Jason is making triangle patterns with marbles. Here are his first few patterns:

pattern 1   pattern 2   pattern 3   pattern 4

(a) Draw his next triangle.

(b) Describe how the pattern is building up.

(c) How many marbles will Jason need for his 6th triangle pattern?

Q7 Denise is making different square patterns with marbles. These are her first 4 patterns:

pattern 1   pattern 2   pattern 3

(a) Draw her next square.

(b) This list shows the number of marbles she uses for each square: 1, 4, 9, 16, ...
Describe how the pattern is building up.

(c) How many marbles will Denise need for her 6th square?

Chapter 6

Multiples, factors and primes

You should be able to use multiples, factors and primes.

You should already know your tables really well. In this chapter we meet **multiples**, **factors** and **primes**. These are special words that you will need to know and use in multiplication and division.

Multiples

The multiples of 4 are 4, 8, 12, 16, 20, 24.... You should recognise this as the 4 times table. A multiple is any number in the times table.

1 Write out the first 5 multiples of (a) 5 (b) 7 (c) 12.

EXAMPLE

ANSWER

(a)   5, 10, 15, 20, 25....

(b)   7, 14, 21, 28, 35....

(c)   12, 24, 36, 48, 60....

These are just the first five numbers of the times tables. For example, the last one is 1×12, 2×12, 3×12, 4×12 and 5×12.

Factors

The factors of 20 are: {1, 2, 4, 5, 10, 20}. All these numbers 'go into' 20 exactly. A factor is a number that goes into another number exactly.

Here are some tips to help you find factors of a number:
- 1 is a factor of every number.
- The number itself is always a factor.

Most other factors come in pairs. For example, $1 \times 20 = 20$; $2 \times 10 = 20$; $4 \times 5 = 20$. If you find one factor, you can find another by finding its 'pair'.

2 Find all the factors of (a) 24 (b) 15 (c) 18 (d) 16

EXAMPLE

ANSWER

(a)   {1, 2, 3, 4, 6, 8, 12, 24}. The 'pairs' are 1×24, 2×12, 3×8 and 4×6.

(b)   {1, 3, 5, 15}. The pairs are 1×15 and 3×5.

(c)   {1, 2, 3, 6, 9, 18}. The pairs are 1×18, 2×9 and 3×6.

(d)   {1, 2, 4, 8, 16}. The pairs are 1×16, 2×8 and 4 is its own pair because $4 \times 4 = 16$.

Primes

3, 17 and 53 are all examples of prime numbers. Notice that the only factors that these numbers have are themselves and 1. A prime number is a number with only two factors, itself and 1. For example, factors of 3 are {1, 3}. Factors of 17 are {1, 17}.

Multiples, factors and primes

Here are two important facts about prime numbers:
● There is only one even prime number - this is 2.
● 1 is not a prime number (it only has 1 factor).

The prime numbers up to 50 are: 2, 3, 5, 7, 11, 13, 17, 19, 23, 29, 31, 37, 41, 43, 47. Unfortunately there is no pattern to these numbers. You just have to learn them or learn how to work them out.

EXAMPLE **3** Give a reason why 9 is not a prime number.

ANSWER It is in the 3 times table, so it has 3 as a factor.

EXAMPLE **4** You have cards with the numbers 1, 2, 3 and 10 on them. Fit each number into the four spaces on the grid so that the number is correct for its column and row.

| 1 | 2 | 3 | 10 |

	Multiples of 2	Factors of 12
Prime numbers		
Factors of 10		

ANSWER

	Multiples of 2	Factors of 12
Prime numbers	2	3
Factors of 10	10	1

Check yourself

ANSWERS AND TUTORIAL

A1 (a) 4, 8, 12, 16, 20
(b) 6, 12, 18, 24, 30
(c) 9, 18, 27, 36, 45
(d) 11, 22, 33, 44, 55
(e) 20, 40, 60, 80, 100

T1 Remember multiples are the times tables.

A2 (a) {1, 2, 3, 6}
(b) {1, 2, 5, 10}
(c) {1, 2, 3, 5, 6, 10, 15, 30}
(d) {1, 2, 3, 6, 9, 18}
(e) {1, 2, 4, 8, 16, 32}

T2 Remember factors of a number divide into it exactly.

QUESTIONS

Q1 Write down the first 5 multiples of:
(a) 4
(b) 6
(c) 9
(d) 11
(e) 20

Q2 Work out the factors of:
(a) 6
(b) 10
(c) 30
(d) 18
(e) 32

QUESTIONS

Q3 Write down:
(a) An even prime number.
(b) All the prime numbers between 30 and 40.
(c) All the prime numbers that are less than 20.

Q4

 3 **5** **20** **17** **18**

From the cards above find a number that is:
(a) A prime number bigger than 10.
(b) A multiple of 6.
(c) A factor of 10.
(d) A multiple of 4 and a multiple of 5 (one card).
(e) A multiple of 3 and a prime number.

Q5 You have cards with the numbers 1, 2, 5 and 15 written on them. Fit them into the four spaces on the grid so that the number is correct for its column and row.

| **15** | **1** |
| **5** | **2** |

	Factors of 15	Prime numbers
Multiples of 5		
Factors of 20		

Q6 The factors of 16 are {1, 2, 4, 8, 16}.
(a) How many factors does 16 have?
(b) Is your answer to (a) an odd number or an even number?
(c) What happens when you try to match the factors of 16 up in 'pairs'?

Q7 What number are these people describing?

It's a multiple of 3

It's also a multiple of 4

It's also between 10 and 20

ANSWERS AND TUTORIAL

A3 (a) 2 (b) 31, 37 (c) 2, 3, 5, 7, 11, 13, 17, 19

T3 You have to learn the prime numbers. You should only need to learn those below 20.

A4 (a) **17** (b) **18** (c) **5**

(d) **20** (e) **3**

T4 Only one number fits each description.

A5

	Factors of 15	Prime numbers
Multiples of 5	**15**	**5**
Factors of 20	**1**	**2**

T5 Some numbers fit into more than one box, but there is only one way that all 4 numbers fit into the grid.

A6 (a) 5 (b) Odd
(c) $1 \times 16 = 16$, $2 \times 8 = 16$, $4 \times 4 = 16$

T6 The rule about every factor having a pair is not true when a number is its own pair. Other numbers that have an odd number of factors like this are 4, 16, 25 and so on. You may have met these before. They are called the square numbers.

A7 12

T7 The numbers that fit the first balloon are:
3, 6, 9, 12, 15, 18, 21,...
The numbers that fit the second balloon are:
4, 8, 12, 16, 20, 24, 28,...
The numbers that fit the third balloon are:
11, 12, 13, 14, 15, 16, 17, 18, 19
12 is the only number in all three lists.

Chapter 7

LEVEL 4
ALGEBRA

Simple formulae

You should be able to use simple formulae expressed in words.

You should already know how to use a simple number machine. There are many situations in every day life where you need to use **simple formulae**. In this chapter we look at formulae and rules, expressed in words.

What is a formula?

A formula is just a rule that changes a number into another number. At the simplest level this could be 'times by 2'. This can be shown as a number machine:

In	Out
2	4
4	8
5	10
8	16

You can see that if 3 goes in, 6 comes out. The numbers that go in and the numbers that come out can be shown as a table. Check that you agree with each of these:

Formulae can be more complicated and may have more than one part to the number machine. For example: 'times by 3 and add 4':

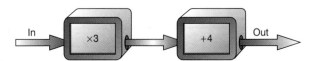

The formulae you will use include only the four basic rules of addition, subtraction, multiplication and division. Formulae may be sometimes be expressed in words.

EXAMPLE

1 The label on a chicken in my local supermarket says

> **TO COOK:**
> Allow 20 minutes cooking time for each pound plus an additional 30 minutes. This bird weighs **5 pounds**.

How long would it take to cook a 5 pound chicken?

ANSWER

The sum is $5 \times 20 + 30 = 100 + 30$

$= 130$ minutes.

This could be written as 2 hours and 10 minutes.

Check yourself

QUESTIONS

Q1 Work out the outputs from each of these number machines:

(a)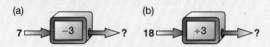

(b)

Q2 Work out the outputs from these number machines:

(a)

(b)

Q3 The following label was stuck inside an American cookery book:

> **To change from °C to °F:**
> Step 1 – Divide by 5.
> Step 2 – Multiply by 9.
> Step 3 – Add 32

(a) What temperature is 45 °C equal to in °F?
(b) Water boils at 100 °C. What is this temperature in °F?. Show how you worked out your answer.

Q4 In the local garden centre, the price of a plant is £4.00 plus £2 for every leaf. What is the cost of the plants shown?

(a)   (b)   (c)

ANSWERS AND TUTORIAL

A1 (a) 4   (b) 6

T1 Sums are $7 - 3$ and $18 \div 3$

A2 (a) 2   (b) 25

T2 You need to work out the middle step for a double number machine.

A3 (a) $45 \div 5 = 9$,
$9 \times 9 = 81$,
$81 + 32 = 113$.
So the answer is 113 °F.

(b) $100 \div 5 = 20$,
$20 \times 9 = 180$,
$180 + 32 = 212$.
So the answer is 212 °F.

T3 You might have known the last answer from Science which is why you must show your working.

A4 (a) £14   (b) £8   (c) £10

T4 The sums are $4 + 2 \times 5$, $4 + 2 \times 2$ and $4 + 2 \times 3$.

Chapter 8

LEVEL 4
ALGEBRA

Co-ordinates

You should be able to use co-ordinates in the first quadrant.

This is a new topic at this level, but you might have already used grids to draw shapes. Also, games like 'Battleships' use something like co-ordinates. In this chapter we look at ways to describe the position of a point on a grid. This is called using co-ordinates in the first quadrant.

Finding a point on a grid

When you need to find a point on a grid, there are two important rules to help you. You must always start at the **origin**. You then move across first, and up second.

The origin is the point at the bottom left hand corner of the grid. It is usually marked with an O. It has the co-ordinates (0, 0).

Point A on the grid is 3 across and 2 up from the point marked O which is the origin. We write this as (3, 2). This is called a co-ordinate. The first number is the across number and the second number is the up number.

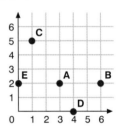

On the same grid, point B is at (6, 2). Point C is at (1, 5), point D is at (4, 0) and point E is at (0, 2).

EXAMPLE **1** (a) What are the co-ordinates of the points A, B and C?

(b) Another point D is placed on the grid so that ABCD is a square. What are the co-ordinates of D?

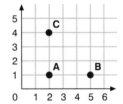

ANSWER (a) A is (2, 1); B is (5, 1); C is (2, 4)

(b) The point D must be at (5, 4)

EXAMPLE **2** Andrea draws a rectangle with corners at A(0, 2); B(6, 2); C(6, 4); and D(0, 4).

(a) What is the area of Andrea's rectangle?

(b) John multiplies all of Andrea's co-ordinates by 2. For example, his point A is at (0, 2) × 2 = (0, 4). What other co-ordinates does John get? Draw his points on a grid.

(c) What is the area of John's rectangle?

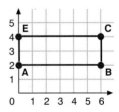

(d) Fred also multiplies Andrea's
co-ordinates by a number.
Two points of Fred's rectangle are
draw on the grid. What are
the other two co-ordinates?

(e) What is the area of Fred's rectangle ?

ANSWER

(a) 12 squares

(b) (12, 4); (12, 8) and (0, 8).
See the grid on right.

(c) 48 squares

(d) (3, 2) and (0, 2)

(e) 3 squares

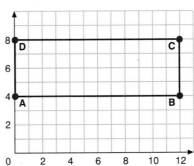

Check yourself

QUESTIONS

Q1 Give the co-ordinates
of the points A, B, C,
D, E and F from the
grid:

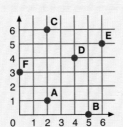

Q2 On a copy of the grid used above, mark on the
co-ordinates:
G (6, 3); H (3, 0); J (2, 5); K (0, 5); and L (5, 5).

Q3 From grid
give the
co-ordinates
of the points
A, B and C.

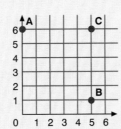

ANSWERS AND TUTORIAL

A1 A = (2, 1); B = (5, 0); C = (2, 6); D = (4, 4);
E = (6, 5); F = (0, 3)

T1 Try to get in the habit of writing co-ordinates
properly. Don't write them as 2-5 or 2/5. If you are
getting any the wrong way round, try again to
learn the rule. There is only one way to write down
a co-ordinate.

A2

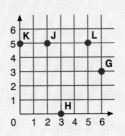

A3 (a) A is (0, 6); B is (5, 1); C is (5, 6)

27

ANSWERS AND TUTORIAL

A4 (a) P is (3, 1);Q is (5, 2); R is (3, 6)
(b) S is at (1, 5)

T4 This is not that easy to see but if you draw the points you will see that they do make a rectangle.

A5 (a) (0, 3)
(b) (5, 2)
(c) (5, 3)

T5 These are not easy to see, but if you join up all the black counters with a line you will be able to see where the other counter needs to go. Do the same for the white and grey counters.

A6 (a) A is (1, 1); B is (2, 2); C is (3, 3); D is (4, 4); E is (5, 5)
(b) All the numbers in each co-ordinate are the same.
(c) No, because the numbers are not the same.

T6 This involves a bit of pattern spotting which you learned about on pages 17–20. You can also plot points to see if they are on the same straight line.

QUESTIONS

Q4 (a) From the grid, give the co-ordinates of the points P, Q and R.

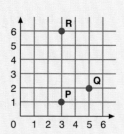

(b) Another point S is placed on the grid to make a rectangle PQRS. What are the co-ordinates of S ?

Q5 The grid below shows some black, white and grey counters. Four counters must be in a line. They do not have to be next to each other.
(a) Where should the next black counter be placed to give a line of 4 black counters?

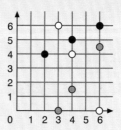

(b) Where should the next white counter be placed to give a line of 4 white counters?
(c) Where should the next grey counter be placed to give a line of 4 grey counters?

Q6 (a) From this grid, write down the co-ordinates of the points A, B, C, D and E.

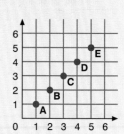

(b) What do you notice about the numbers in the co-ordinates?
(c) Could the point (8, 9) be on the same line as A, B, C, D and E?

TEST QUESTIONS

Answers with examiner's comments on page 237.

1. Carl has an old recipe for egg custard with raisins. The custard has to be cooked at 320 degrees Fahrenheit. Carl has a rule to change the temperature to degrees Celsius.

    Use Carl's rule to change 320 degrees Fahrenheit to degrees Celsius. Show each step in your calculation.

    > **Rule:**
    >
    > To change the temperature to degrees **Celsius**, **subtract 32** from the temperature in degrees **Fahrenheit**, then **multiply** the answer by **5**, then **divide** by **9**.

    (1996 Paper 1)

2. A class is planning a trip to a funfair. The pupils have found out the prices at these two funfairs:

    The teacher says that there will be time for **8 rides.**

Milltown Funfair	**Seaview Funfair**
Entry: £2.20	Entry: £4.50
plus	plus
Rides: 60p each	Rides: 20p each

    (a) How much money do you need to get into Milltown funfair and have 8 rides?
    (b) How much money do you need to get into Seaview funfair and have 8 rides?
        Ben says that he has only got £5 to get in and pay for the rides.
    (c) How many rides would Ben get at each funfair?

    (1994 Paper 1)

3. Janet joins three points on a grid to make a triangle. The co-ordinates of the points are:

    (0, 0), (1, 1), (2, 0)

    The area of Janet's triangle is 1 cm².

    Dylan **multiplies** each of Janet's co-ordinates by 2.

    (a) What is the **area** of **Dylan's** triangle?
    (b) **Multiply** each of Janet's co-ordinates **by 3.**
        Plot the **3 points** with the **new co-ordinates** on a grid. Join them up to make a new triangle.
    (c) What is the **area** of your triangle?
    (d) Nazir multiplies each of Janet's co-ordinates by **another** number. He plots two of the points (0, 0) and (10, 0) and joins them up. Plot Nazir's third point.
    (e) What **number** did Nazir **multiply** Janet's co-ordinates by?

    (1996 Paper 2)

4. Gareth is using this number machine. It multiplies all numbers by 2, then adds 1.

    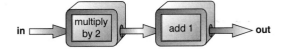

    He puts some other numbers into the number machine. Fill in the missing numbers.

Start		End
3	→	7
10	→	
5	→	
2	→	

    (1992 Paper 1)

5. You can use rods to make squares.

1 square   3 squares   5 squares

(a) Look at this number pattern.
    Find the missing number.
(b) Explain how you worked out this number.
(c) There is a rule for finding the number of rods needed to make **any** number of squares. What is this rule?

number of squares	number of rods
1	4
3	12
5	20
7	☐

number of squares (s) ⟶ | rule ? | ⟶ number of rods (r)

(1992 Paper 1)

6. A school has tables like this: ⬓   5 chairs fit round one table.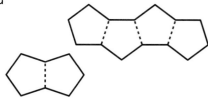

Mrs Turner puts tables together like this:

(a) Fill in the missing numbers.
(b) Describe the pattern for the number of chairs.

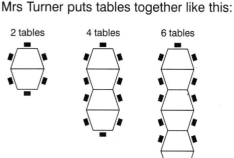

2 tables   4 tables   6 tables

Number of tables	2	4	6	8	10	12	14
Number of chairs	6	10	14	18			

(1993 Paper 3)

7. A class were making shapes with 5-sided tiles. Tracey said

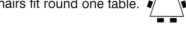

To find the perimeter of a shape like this you times the number of tiles by 3 and then you add 2.

(a) **Show** that Tracey's method is correct for the shape with 2 tiles.
(b) Use Tracey's method to work out the perimeter of a shape with 10 tiles. Do **not** draw the shape.

(1992 Paper 3)

8. Mandy and Gareth are playing a game. Mandy has to make a line of four ✕ like this to win.

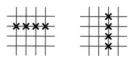

(a) Put one ✕ on the grid to make a line for Mandy.
(b) Write the co-ordinates for the four ✕ in Mandy's line.
(c) Look at the numbers in the co-ordinates.
    What do you notice?

(1993 paper 1)

Chapter 9

2-D and 3-D Shapes

You should be able to recognise a 3-D shape from a 2-D drawing and identify linking edges and corners. You should be able to draw common 3-D shapes on a 2-D grid.

You should already recognise and be able to name shapes such as the square, rectangle, cube, cuboid and pyramid.

You have probably made simple 3-D shapes out of card. To make any 3-D shape you need to draw a net for the shape first. You can sometimes draw the net on a grid to make it more accurate. Tabs are necessary to make the actual shape.

For most 3-D shapes you can count the number of edges, corners and faces.

1 This net can be folded to make a cube. How many edges, corners and faces does the cube have?

EXAMPLE

ANSWER

The cube has 12 edges, 8 corners and 6 faces.

2 Draw a net for a pyramid on a grid.

EXAMPLE

ANSWER

3 Draw the front, side and top elevations for this T shape.

EXAMPLE

These views are sometimes known as the elevations of the shape.

ANSWER

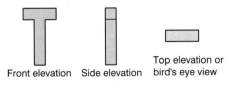

Front elevation   Side elevation   Top elevation or bird's eye view

31

Check yourself

ANSWERS AND TUTORIAL

A1 (a) Yes   (c) No
     (b) No   (d) Yes

T1 (b) There would be a hole in this cube.
     (c) There are too many edges joined together; this would be impossible to fold.

A2

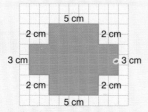

T2 Use 1 cm grid paper to draw this net accurately.

A3

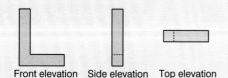

Front elevation   Side elevation   Top elevation

T3 Put in all the edges that you can see.

A4 **The dice has 6 edges, 4 corners and 4 faces.**

T4 Remember to count the edge and the face at the back that is not seen.

A5

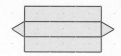

T5 The chocolate box is made out of 3 rectangles and 2 equilateral triangles. The sides of the triangles must be the same length as the width of the rectangle. Tabs are not necessary.

QUESTIONS

Q1 Could you use these nets to make a cube?

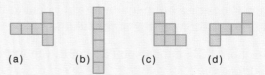

(a)   (b)   (c)   (d)

Q2 Draw an accurate net for this open box on a grid:

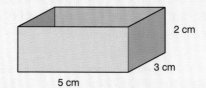

2 cm

3 cm

5 cm

Q3 Draw front, side and top elevations for this L shape:

Q4 Find the number of edges, corners and faces for this 4-sided dice:

Q5 Draw a net for this chocolate box on a dotty grid:

Chapter 10

You should recognise rotational symmetry and line symmetry. You should be able to reflect shapes in a mirror line.

You should already know how to recognise symmetry. We can see symmetry all around us: in flowers, in buildings, in our own bodies. Symmetry shows us that shapes have equal proportions. You need to know that there are two types of symmetry for 2-D shapes. These are:

- **line symmetry**, sometimes called **reflective symmetry**.
- **rotational symmetry**.

Line symmetry

A shape has line symmetry if we can draw a line of symmetry on the shape. This line of symmetry divides the shape into equal parts. You can test to see if there is a line of symmetry on a shape by using tracing paper or a mirror: a line of symmetry is sometimes called a mirror line. Shapes can have more than one line of symmetry.

1 How many lines of symmetry does this road sign have?

One line of symmetry. Lines of symmetry are usually dotted. Check by tracing the shape and folding the tracing paper on the line of symmetry or by placing a mirror on the line of symmetry.

EXAMPLE

ANSWER

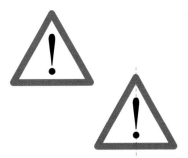

2 Reflect this shape using the dotted diagonal line as a mirror line:

You may find it easier to turn the page so that the mirror line is horizontal.

EXAMPLE

ANSWER

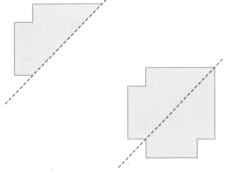

Rotational symmetry

A shape has rotational symmetry if we can turn it around so that it fits exactly onto itself in different positions. The order of rotational symmetry is the number of times a rotated shape fits exactly onto itself, before it returns to its original position. Remember that you can use tracing paper to help you find the order of rotational symmetry.

Beware! Shapes that do not have rotational symmetry are of order 1.

EXAMPLE

3 Find the order of rotational symmetry for these shapes:

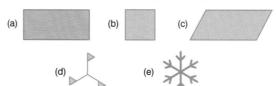

ANSWER

(a)   order 2   (c)   order 2   (e)   order 6
(b)   order 4   (d)   order 3

Congruent shapes

Congruent shapes are exactly the same size and shape but they can be in different positions. To check to see if shapes are congruent, trace one of the shapes and see if it fits exactly on top of the others. Remember that you may have to turn your tracing paper over.

EXAMPLE

4 How many of these letters are congruent?

ANSWER

All these letters are congruent.

Check yourself

ANSWERS AND TUTORIAL

A1

T1   Use a mirror to check.

A2   (a)   order 6   (c)   order 6
        (b)   order 4   (d)   order 5

T2   Use tracing paper if you are not sure.

A3   (a) and (c), (b) and (e), (d) and (f).

T3   First, trace the shapes that you think are the same, then check that you are right.

QUESTIONS

Q1   **Draw in all the lines of symmetry for these shapes:**

Q2   **Find the order of rotational symmetry for these shapes:**

(a)   (b)   (c)    (d)

Q3   **Find pairs of congruent shapes:**

(a)   (b)   (c)   (d)   (e)   (f)

Chapter 11

Measuring instruments and scales

You should be able to choose appropriate measuring instruments and units and measure accurately from a variety of scales.

You should already know the metric units: metres, grams and litres.

In most practical situations, you need to use a ruler for measuring length, a set of scales or a balance for weighing, a thermometer for taking temperatures and so on. The scale on measuring instruments is usually graduated in small divisions. Be careful that you work out how many units there are for each division.

1 What is the mass of the bag of cement?

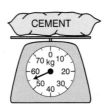

Each division is 5 kg. The bag of cement weighs 55 kg.

EXAMPLE

ANSWER

2 Give the temperature on the thermometer:

Between 0 and 10 there are 5 divisions. So each division is 2°. The temperature shown is 20 + (4 × 2) = 28°C.

EXAMPLE

ANSWER

Check yourself

QUESTIONS

Q1 Measure the lengths of these lines:

(a) ————————————————————

(b) ——————————

(c) ————

Q2 How much liquid is in the measuring jug?

Q3 How much time is left on the parking meter?

ANSWERS AND TUTORIAL

A1 (a) 6.8 cm   (b) 3.3 cm   (c) 0.9 cm

T1 (a) Or 68 mm. The units are important.
(b) The line is in between 3.3 cm and 3.4 cm so both of these answers would be accepted.
(c) Or 9 mm. Look at the line to check your answer. It looks about 1 cm long.

A2 350 ml.

T2 There are 2 divisions between 0 and 100, so each division is 50. Remember to put in the units.

A3 45 minutes.

T3 There are 4 divisions between 0 and 60, so each division is 15 (60 ÷ 4 = 15).

Chapter 12

Perimeter, area and volume

You should be able to find perimeters of simple shapes, find areas by counting squares and volumes by counting cubes.

You should already know the idea of length, area and volume.

Perimeter

To find the perimeter of a shape, you find the total distance all the way around the outside.

Remember the units are mm, cm and m.

EXAMPLE

1 Find the perimeter of the hexagon:

1 cm

1 cm   1 cm

ANSWER

The perimeter of the shape is 6 cm. Remember not to count the lines inside the shape.

EXAMPLE

2 Find the perimeter of the H shape:

2 cm   2 cm

6 cm

ANSWER

Start at the top left corner of the shape and add up the lengths around the outside.
Perimeter = 2 + 2 + 2 + 2 + 2 + 6 + 2 + 2 + 2 + 2 + 2 + 6
= 32 cm

Area

To find the area of a 2-D shape, count the number of whole squares inside the shape. Remember the units of area are cm^2 or m^2. (These are called 'squared' units).

EXAMPLE

3 Find the area of this rectangle:

3 cm

2 cm

ANSWER

There are 6 squares inside the rectangle, so the area is 6 cm^2.

EXAMPLE

4 Find the area of these shapes:

(a)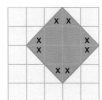

(b)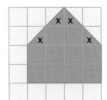

For examples like these, it is a good idea to mark the half squares with a cross first.

(a)   Inside this shape, there are 4 whole squares and 8 half squares.
So, the total area is $4 + 4 = 8$ cm².

(b)   Inside this shape, there are 10 whole squares and 4 half squares.
So, the total area is $10 + 2 = 12$ cm².

Volume

To find the volume of a 3-D shape. count the number of cubes inside
the shape. Remember the units of volume are cm³ or m³. (These are
called 'cubed' units)

5   Find the volume of this T shape:

1 cm3

Count the cubes. The volume of the shape is 9 cm³.

6   Find the volume of this cuboid:

On the top layer there are
12 cubes, so in 2 layers there
are 24 cubes. Each cube is 1 cm³,
so the volume of the cuboid is 24 cm³.

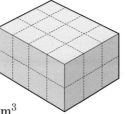

Check yourself

QUESTIONS

ANSWERS AND TUTORIAL

Q1   **Find the perimeter and area of these shapes:**

A1   **(a) Perimeter is 16 cm. Area is 12 cm².
(b) Perimeter is 20 cm. Area is 15 cm².**

T1   (a)   Just count the squares to find the area.
(b)   When finding the perimeter, mark the first
side you count with a tick. You can check the
area by counting the unshaded squares. In
diagram (b), there are 10 unshaded squares.
Add this number to your answer and you
should get the area of the whole shape:
$15 + 10 = 25$ cm².

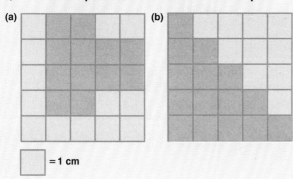

(a)   (b)

☐ = 1 cm

ANSWERS AND TUTORIAL

A2 There are a possible number of answers. Your answer could be a rotation of either of these two answers:

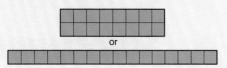

or

T2 All you need to do is to find a pair of numbers which multiply to give 16 (1×16 and 2×8).

A3 The perimeter is 12 cm.

T3 First, draw a diagram or a sketch of the larger diamond shape. Don't just multiply 9×4!

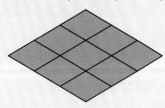

A4 18 m².

T4 Each square has an area of 1 m². There are 16 whole squares and 4 half squares. So, the total area is 16 + 2 = 18 m².

A5 15 m³.

T5 Count the cubes on each layer:
5 + 4 + 3 + 2 + 1 = 15

QUESTIONS

Q2 The area of this square is 16 cm²:

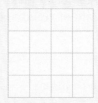

Can you draw a rectangle which has the same area?

Q3 This diamond tile has a perimeter of 4 cm. Find the perimeter of a larger diamond shape that is made by putting 9 of these tiles together.

Q4 Find the area of this carpet:

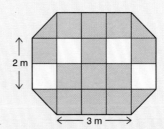

2 m

3 m

Q5 What is the volume of the shape below?

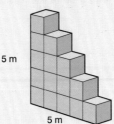

5 m

5 m

1. Maria made these shapes from straws.

Tim has some triangles and some glue.
All his triangles are like this.

Tim wants to make the same shapes as Maria.

(a) How many **triangles** will he need for each shape?
(b) How many **edges** will each shape have?

(1993 Paper 2)

2. Alana has 3 tiles.

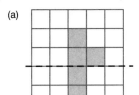 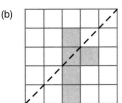

Alana joins her **3 tiles** together to make a shape.
Whole edges of the tiles must meet.
She draws her shape on triangle dotty paper.

(a) Draw **two different** shapes made from Alana's 3 tiles.
(b) The dots on the triangle dotty paper are 1 cm apart.
    What is the **perimeter** of Alana's shape?
(c) Draw a shape made from Alana's 3 tiles which has
    a **smaller** perimeter than Alana's shape.

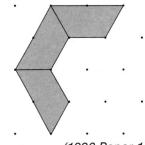

(1996 Paper 1)

3. (a) Shade in **1 more square** to make a shape which has the dashed line as a line of symmetry.
   (b) Shade in **2 more squares** to make a shape which has the dashed line as a line of symmetry.

(a)

(b)

(1996 Paper 2)

4. Nina is making Rangoli patterns. To make a pattern she draws some lines on a grid and then
reflects them in a mirror line.

Reflect each group of lines in its mirror line to make a pattern.

(a)

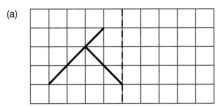

(b)

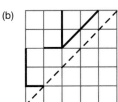

(1995 Paper 1)

5. Put a ✓ by the shapes that **have** rotational symmetry and a ✗ by the shapes that **have no** rotational symmetry.

(a)  (b) 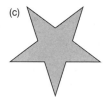 (c) 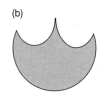 (d) (e)

(1992 Paper 3)

6. These patterns come from old Turkish coins. Find the order of rotational symmetry for each pattern.

a) 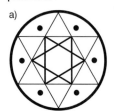 b) 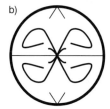 c) 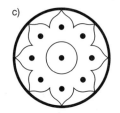 d)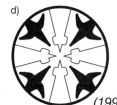

(1993 Paper 3)

7. Each side of this hexagon is 1 cm long.

(a) The **shaded** shape is made from 7 hexagon tiles. What is its **perimeter?**
(b) Make a shape made with 7 tiles which has a **smaller** perimeter.
(c) Explain what made its perimeter **less than** the perimeter of the first shape.
(d) Make a shape made with 7 tiles which has the **biggest possible** perimeter.
(e) Explain what made your shape have the biggest possible perimeter.

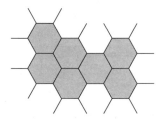

(1994 Paper 2)

8.

Kath puts 1 **small** square tile on a grid.
Den makes a **bigger** square with 4 small square tiles.
Scott makes a **bigger** square with 9 small square tiles.

(a) Show how to make a square with **more than** 9 of these small square tiles.
(b) How many tiles are there in your square?
(c) Huw wants to make some more squares with the tiles.

Write 3 other numbers of tiles that he can use to make squares.

(1996 Paper 2)

Chapter 13

Collecting data and frequency diagrams

You should be able to collect discrete data and record it in a table. You should be able to group data and represent this in a frequency diagram. You should be able to interpret such diagrams.

You should already know how to read information from tables. You should also know how to draw a simple bar chart.

We need to collect data from a wide variety of sources. When collecting data, it is usual to first design a survey sheet or write a questionnaire. You can then enter the data onto a **frequency table** using a **tally**. Once the frequency table is complete, you can draw suitable diagrams to make the data easier to understand. These **frequency diagrams** are usually drawn as **bar charts**.

Computer databases are a quick and convenient way for collecting a lot of data. Your school is likely to have a database of its pupils.

Simple data collection

Data that involves 'counting' is called discrete data. If you collect data from a small group (or sample), you can construct a frequency table using a tally.

1 The 24 pupils in Class 9Q were given 10 mental arithmetic questions. This data shows their marks out of 10:

EXAMPLE

8 7 5 10 4 8 7 6 7 7 10 5 8 9 8 9 8 8 5 8 8 7 8 9

(a) Use a tally to draw up a frequency table for the data.

(b) Draw a bar chart to illustrate the data.

(c) What mark did most pupils obtain?

ANSWER

(a)

Mark	Tally	Frequency
4	|	1
5	|||	3
6	|	1
7	⊞	5
8	⊞ ||||	9
9	|||	3
10	||	2
	TOTAL	24

Notice that for every 5 counted you use a 'gate' ⊞

(b)
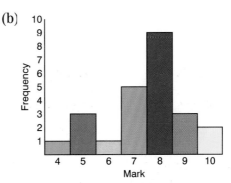

Remember to label the axes. Notice that the marks are placed under the middle of each bar.

(c) Most pupils obtained a mark of 8.

Collecting data and frequency diagrams

2 James in Form 9P designed a survey sheet to find the favourite colour of his class. His completed survey sheet looked like this:

How could James improve his survey sheet?

Colour	Frequency
Red	✓✓✓✓✓✓
Blue	✓✓✓
Green	✓✓✓✓✓
Yellow	✓✓
Black	✓
Purple	✓✓
Brown	✓✓✓
Others	✓✓✓✓✓

James could use a tally to make counting easier. He could also use the frequency column to find the total for each colour. He could then add the frequencies to check that he had included everyone.

Grouped data collection

If there is a lot of data to collect and it is spread out over a wide range of numbers, then it is more convenient to put the data into a grouped frequency table. There should be less than 10 groups and each one should be of equal width. The groups are called class intervals.

3 Mrs Whitehead recorded her pupils' Science SATS marks:

45 57 35 34 37 38 40 29 42 56 28 19 34 56 35 28
20 39 35 40 45 24 17 36 37 42 27 46 55 38 50 22

She wanted to illustrate how well the class had done, so she decided to draw a bar chart. She did this by first constructing a grouped frequency table by putting the marks into class intervals of 10 marks width.

(a) Draw up a grouped frequency table to show how she did this.

(b) Draw a bar chart to illustrate the data.

(c) A Level 5 was awarded to anyone who scored over 40. How many pupils obtained a Level 5?

(a)

Class interval	Tally	Frequency
1–10		0
11–20	|||	3
21–30	ⵌ		6
31–40	ⵌ ⵌ |||	13
41–50	ⵌ		6
51–60	||||	4
	TOTAL	32

(b)

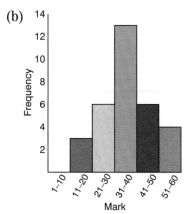

(c) 10 pupils obtained a Level 5 (6+4).

Collecting data and frequency diagrams

4 Jonathan was doing a survey on the cinema for a school project. To help him, he asked a sample of friends how many times they had visited the cinema in the past month. His bar chart looked like this:

(a) How many friends took part in the sample?

(b) How many visited the cinema more than 5 times?

(c) How many visited the cinema exactly once?

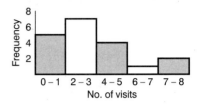

ANSWER

(a) Add together the heights of each bar:

$5 + 7 + 4 + 1 + 2 = 19$

(b) Add together the heights of the last two bars:

$1 + 2 = 3$

(c) You cannot tell this from the bar chart. The first bar shows the number of Jonathan's friends who didn't go to the cinema at all **added** to the number who visited the cinema once.

Check yourself

QUESTIONS

Q1 Mr Rhodes accessed the school database to find the number of absences last week for the pupils in class 9R. His data is given in a frequency table below:

Day	Mon	Tue	Wed	Thur	Fri
Absences	2	4	10	1	3

(a) Draw a bar chart for his data.
(b) How many pupils are there in class 9R?
(c) Can you think of a reason why so many pupils were absent on Wednesday?

ANSWERS AND TUTORIAL

A1 (a)

(b) You cannot tell from his data.
(c) Pupils could have been out on a school trip or it might have been a religious holiday.

T1 (a) Remember to label the axes.
(b) The chart only shows absences.

ANSWERS AND TUTORIAL

A2 (a) **Coffee**   (b) **130**
    (c) **It was possibly a cold or rainy day.**

T2 (a) The one with the highest line.
    (b) Add together the heights of all the lines:
        35 + 45 + 15 + 25 + 10 = 130
        Read the frequency axis carefully. Use your
        ruler to draw lines across to the axis.
    (c) This is because of the amount of hot drinks
        sold.

A3 (a)

Amount	Tally	Frequency
0p–49p	ⅢⅢ ⅢⅢ ‖	12
50p–99p	ⅢⅢ ‖‖‖‖	9
£1.00–£1.49	‖	2
£1.50–£1.99	‖‖‖‖	4
£2.00–£2.49	‖‖‖	3
	TOTAL	**30**

(b)
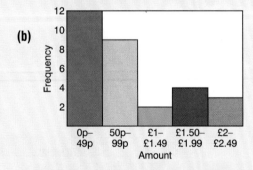

A4

No of letters	Tally	Frequency
1	ⅢⅢ ‖‖‖	8
2	ⅢⅢ ‖‖‖	8
3	ⅢⅢ ‖	6
4	ⅢⅢ ⅢⅢ	10
5	ⅢⅢ	5
6	‖	2
7	ⅢⅢ	5
8	ⅢⅢ	5

There are 49 words in the extract.

T4 Always use a tally column. By adding the numbers
    in the frequency column, you can see there are 49
    words in the extract.

QUESTIONS

Q2 The vertical line diagram (bar chart with bars
    replaced by lines) shows the number of drinks
    served in a school's canteen on Tuesday:

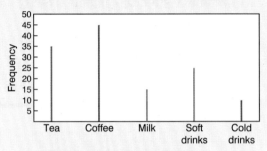

    (a) **Which drink sold the most?**
    (b) **How many drinks were sold altogether?**
    (c) **What was the weather like on Tuesday?**

Q3 Jenny wanted to find out how much pupils at her
    school spent on sweets.

    She asked 30 pupils how much they had spent
    on sweets the previous day. This is her data:

    23p; 56p; £1.20; 50p; 0p; 48p; 90p; £1.45; 60p;
    32p; £2.30; 38p; 0p; £2.10; 75p; 18p; 65p;
    £1.60; 40p; 18p; 28p; £1.50; £1.52; 65p; 0p;
    22p; 50p; £2.35; £1.82; 85p.

    (a) **Draw up a grouped frequency table for her
        data, using class intervals
        0p-49p, 50p-99p, £1.00-£1.49... and so on.**
    (b) **Draw a bar chart to illustrate her data.**

Q4 This extract is taken from Shakespeare's
    'A Midsummer Night's Dream'. Count the
    number of letters in each word and draw
    up a frequency table.
    How many words are there in the extract?

            Thou speak'st aright;
        I am that merry wanderer of the night.
        I jest to Oberon and make him smile
        When I a fat and bean-fed horse beguile,
        Neighing in likeness of a filly foal:
        And sometimes lurk I in a gossip's bowl,
        In very likeness of a roasted crab.

Mode and median

You should understand and be able to used the mode and median of a set of data.

You should already understand the term frequency and you should know how to list numbers in numerical order.

The word **average** is heard a lot on TV and seen a lot in newspapers. For example, we often hear about a person's average height or weight, the average wage of the British people, a batsman's average number of runs in a Test series, the average rainfall in Manchester. An average value is the best representative value for a set of data.

In mathematics, you need to know three common averages: the **mode**, the **median** and the **mean**. In this chapter, we revise how to calculate the modal average or mode and look at the median.

The mode

For a set of data, the mode is the value that has the highest frequency. This means it is the value that occurs the most often in the data.

The mode is a useful average because it gives the most common value. For example, Number 1 in the charts is the most common single sold in the UK in a particular week.

1 City United scored the following number of goals in their first 10 matches of the season:

0, 1, 3, 0, 2, 1, 0, 1, 3, 1

Find their modal score.

EXAMPLE

The score of 1 occurs the greatest number of times (4 times), so this is the score with the highest frequency. Therefore, the modal score is 1.

ANSWER

2 Denise kept a record of how many minutes the school bus was late over a four week period. This is her data:

2, 10, 5, 15, 3, 0, 0, 2, 8, 4, 5, 0, 0, 8, 20, 0, 5, 0, 10, 3

EXAMPLE

(a) Find the modal average for these times.

(b) Do you think this average value will help Denise to explain why she is often late for school?

Mode and median

ANSWER

(a) O occurs 6 times and this is the time with the highest frequency. The modal time is 0 minutes.

(b) No. It is obvious from her data that the bus is late quite often but the modal average makes it seem as if the bus is always on time.

The median

The median is the middle value in a set of data, once the values have been put into numerical order. The median is a useful average because it does not take into account the very high or very low values which can sometimes distort the data.

EXAMPLE **3** A newspaper article discussing average wages quotes the annual salaries of a group of people:

Civil servant	Bank clerk	Fireman	Shop manager	Teacher	Footballer	Lorry driver	Lawyer	Nurse
£24 000	£14 000	£16 500	£19 500	£21 000	£80 000	£13 500	£32 000	£14 500

(a) Find the median salary.

(b) Why is the median a good average to use?

ANSWER (a) List the salaries in order:

£13 500, £14 000, £14 500, £16 500, £19 500, £21 000, £24 000, £32 000, £80 000

There are 9 values and the middle one is the 5th value. The median salary is therefore £19 500.

(b) It does not take into account the high salary of the footballer which is not consistent with the rest of the data.

EXAMPLE **4** During December, a school's Geography Department kept a record of the temperature at midday for a 15 day period. The values, all in °C, were:

2, 4, 0, –1, –2, –1, –1, 1, 0, 0, 1, 2, 2, 4, 3.

Find the median temperature.

ANSWER List the values in order, remembering to put the minus temperatures first:

–2, –1, –1, –1, 0, 0, 0, 1, 1, 2, 2, 2, 3, 4, 4

There are 15 values and the middle one is the 8th value. You can calculate that it is the 8th value by $(15 + 1) \div 2 = 8$. The 8th value is 1, so the median temperature is 1 °C.

Check yourself

Q1 Find the mode and median for the following sets of numbers:
(a) 2, 7, 5, 2, 1, 3, 2
(b) 9, 18, 32, 16, 9, 7, 29, 10, 14
(c) 4, 5, 4, 4, 7, 8, 9, 5
(d) 42, 50, 46, 54, 38, 44, 52, 48, 40, 56

Q2 Sam wanted to find the average height of all the boys in his football team. After measuring all their heights to the nearest centimetre, he recorded the following data:

159, 155, 153, 158, 162, 160, 172, 161, 163, 165, 168

Find the median height of the team.

Q3 'LikeAglove' shoe shop kept a frequency table of the sizes of 'Sporty' shoes they sold on a particular day:
(a) Find the modal shoe size.
(b) Find the median shoe size.

Size	No. sold
3	1
4	3
5	3
6	4
7	8
8	5
9	1

A1 (a) mode = 2 median = 2
(b) mode = 9 median = 14
(c) mode = 4 median = 5
(d) no mode median = 47

T1 Put all the lists in order first.
(c) There are 8 values and the middle 2 are both 5, so the median is 5.
(d) There is no mode – the values all appear once only. For the median, there are 10 values and the middle two values are 46 and 48. The median, 47, is half way between these two.

A2 161 cm

T2 To find the median height, remember to first put the boys' heights in numerical order.

A3 (a) 7 (b) 7

T3 (a) The mode is the most common shoe size, the one with the highest frequency of sales. The mode is therefore size 7, as 8 pairs were sold, more than any other size.
(b) The median is the middle value of all the 25 pairs of shoes sold. You can either list the 13th value or notice from the table that the 13th pair of shoes sold is a size 7. It is not 6 – the middle of the sizes.

Chapter 15

Line graphs

You should be able to construct simple line graphs.

You should already know how to read information from graphs and you should understand decimal notation.

Line graphs are statistical diagrams which show how data changes between consecutive values, eg how temperature changes at various times of the day. They can be used to show 'trends' or patterns over a time period, eg the global warming of the Earth.

Line graphs, as the name suggests, connect data points by straight lines.

EXAMPLE

1 Mark recorded the outside temperature every two hours and drew a line graph to show his data.

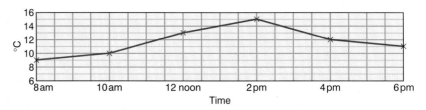

(a) What was the temperature at 2 pm?

(b) Find the increase in temperature between 10 am and 1 pm.

(c) Which two hour period had the greatest increase in temperature? How can you tell this from the graph?

ANSWER

(a) 15 °C

(b) At 10 am it was 10°C and at 1 pm it was 14 °C. The increase is 4 °C.

(c) The greatest increase in temperature was between 10 am and midday. The line on the graph between these two times has the steepest upward slope.

EXAMPLE

2 Lizzie is in hospital with a fever. Her medical chart shows her temperature on a line graph over a three day period:

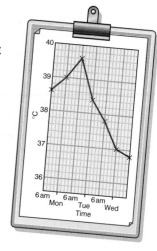

(a) What was Lizzie's temperature at 6 pm on Tuesday?

(b) What was her highest temperature?

(c) Normal body temperature is 37 °C. When did Lizzie have a normal body temperature?

(d) Why does the temperature axis not start at 0 °C?

(a) 38.4 °C. On the temperature axis there are 5 divisions for every 1, so each division on the axis is 0.2 °C.

(b) 39.6 °C.

(c) 6 pm on Wednesday. Readings were taken every 12 hours.

(d) A lot of space would be wasted and the line graph would be difficult to read because the scale would be much smaller.

Check yourself

QUESTIONS

Q1 A holiday brochure for Greece has a line graph to show the average daily high and low temperatures for different months.

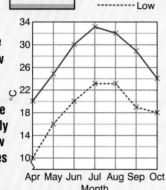

——— High
------- Low

(a) What are the average daily high and low temperatures in May?

(b) What is the difference between the high and low temperatures in September?

(c) In which month is the difference between the two temperatures the least?

Q2 The sales of the book 'A Mathematician's Diary' by Dr Easisome is given in the table.

Year	1970	1975	1980	1985	1990	1995
Sales	2100	2400	2800	3000	2900	2700

(a) Draw a line graph to show the sales of the book.

(b) Can we predict how many books will be sold in the year 2000?

ANSWERS AND TUTORIAL

A1 (a) High 25 °C Low 16 °C
(b) 10 °C
(c) October

T1 Each division on the temperature axis is 2°, so 1° is half a square.
(a) Highest and lowest points on the graph.
(b) High: 29 °C Low 19 °C
The difference is 10 °C.
(c) This is the least distance between the 2 lines. The least difference is 6 °C in October.

A2 (a)

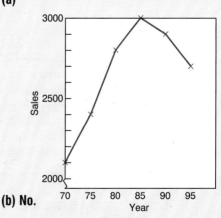

(b) No.

T2 (a) Notice the frequency axis does not start at 0. The scale would be incredibly small if it did!
(b) You can only guess.

Chapter 16

LEVEL 4
HANDLING DATA

Probability

You should understand and use simple words associated with probability, such as 'fair', 'certain 'and 'likely'.

You should already understand simple ideas about chance. We use the idea of chance every day: What will the weather be like tomorrow? What's the chance the SATs will be easy?

Probability is about measuring the chance of something happening. When we talk about probability in every-day life, we use words like: possible, likely, 50-50, fair, impossible. You need to know how to use the following in probability questions: impossible, very unlikely, unlikely, equally likely, likely, very likely and certain. We talk about the probability of an 'event'.

This probability line shows where each of the words come on a scale from least chance to greatest chance:

| Impossible | Very unlikely | Unlikely | Evens | Likely | Very likely | Certain |

EXAMPLE **1** When you roll a dice, what is the chance of getting a 6?

ANSWER There are 6 different numbers on a dice you could end up with any one of them. We say, therefore, that the chance is not very good. We say the probability of the event is unlikely.

Check yourself

ANSWERS AND TUTORIAL

A1 (a) unlikely (b) equally likely
(c) very unlikely (d) impossible
(e) very likely (f) certain (g) likely

T1 (a) There a 4 different suits to choose from.
(b) There are 3 even and 3 odd numbers.
(c) There are nearly 14 million different ways of choosing the 6 numbers.
(d) The world record is 3 mins 44.39 secs.
(e) Most cars on British roads are made in Europe.
(f) You are doing some now!
(g) Most of the letters are consonants.

QUESTIONS

Q1 For the events (a) to (g), choose one of the following: impossible, very unlikely, unlikely, equally likely, likely, very likely, certain.

(a) **Picking a heart from a well shuffled pack of cards.**
(b) **Rolling a dice and getting an even score.**
(c) **Winning the jackpot in the National Lottery.**
(d) **Running a 1500m race in 3 minutes.**
(e) **The next car you see having been made in Europe.**
(f) **Doing some revision for your SATs.**
(g) **Picking a consonant from a bag of 'Scrabble' letters.**

T E S T   Q U E S T I O N S

Answers with examiner's comments on page 238.

1. These bar charts show how two families spent money in food.

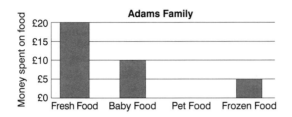

    Describe **one** difference between the families.

    (1993 Paper 3)

2. The frequency diagram shows the amount of rain that fell in a month.

    Kath said: 'There were 30 days in the month'. Explain how you know she was right.

    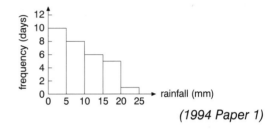

    (1994 Paper 1)

3. Lisa works in a shoe shop. She recorded the size of each pair of trainers that she sold during a week. This is what she wrote down.

    (a) Use a tallying method to make a table showing how many pairs of trainers of each size were sold during the whole week.

    (b) Which size of trainer did Lisa sell most of?

    (c) Lisa said: ' Most of the trainers sold were bigger than size 6'.

	Size of trainers sold					
Monday	7	7	5	6		
Tuesday	6	4	4	8		
Wednesday	5	8	6	7	5	
Thursday	7	4	5			
Friday	7	4	9	5	7	8
Saturday	6	5	7	6	9	4	7

    How can you tell from your table that Lisa is wrong?

    (1995 Paper 1)

4. A machine in a Youth Club sells snacks.
    Crisps: 20p; Chocolate bars: 35p; Drinks: 40p;
    Rolls: 75p; Sandwiches: £1.00

    Len writes down the amounts of money which different people spend one evening during each hour that the club is open:

    (a) Len says: '40p is the mode of the amounts of the money spent'. Explain why Len is right.

Amounts of money spent during each hour		
5pm to 6pm	6pm to 7pm	7pm to 8pm
40p	75p	£1.75
60p	55p	£1.40
55p	60p	£1.60
20p	40p	75p
40p	£1.15	£1.40
60p	40p	£1.10
55p	75p	60p
40p	40p	£1.50

(b) Len groups the amounts and makes a tally chart. Fill in Len's chart.

Then fill in the column for the total number of people who spent each amount.

(c) Len says: 'Now 50p to 99p is the mode.' Is Len right? Explain your answer.

Amount of money spent	Time			Total number of people who spent each amount
	5pm to 6pm	6pm to 7pm	7pm to 8pm	
Under 50p				
50p to 99p				
£1.00 to £1.49				
Over £1.49				

(d) Look at where the tally marks are on the chart. What do you notice about the amounts of money people spent at different times in the evening?

Give a reason which could explain the difference you notice.

(1996 Paper 2)

5. Ross drops a tray with these objects on it:

calculator

raw egg

sock

thin glass

They fall onto a wooden floor. How likely are they to break?

Put them in order with the most likely first.

(1993 Paper 2)

6. A stall at a concert sells a total of 100 balloons. These are the colours sold:

I walk through the crowds at the concert.

(a) Which colour balloon am I most likely to see first? Explain why.

(b) Which colour balloon am I least likely to see first? Explain why.

red	25
green	60
blue	3
yellow	12
Total	100

(1992 Paper 3)

Chapter 17

Long multiplication and long division

You should be able to multiply or divide a three-digit number by a two-digit number without using a calculator. This is usually called 'long multiplication' and 'long division'.

You should already know how to do 'short division' and 'short multiplication', where a 2 or 3 digit number is multiplied or divided by a single digit number.

In this chapter we look at how to multiply or divide a three-digit number by a two-digit number without using a calculator. This is usually called **long multiplication** and **long division**.

Long multiplication

You will have to do sums like this is on Paper 1 of your National Tests, a non-calculator paper. There are several ways to do long multiplication. Three of them are shown in the examples in this section. Some others are mentioned in the tutorial in the *Check yourself* section. You need to be sure of at least one of the methods described.

---

1 Small tins of beans weigh 146 grams. How much do 23 tins weigh?

EXAMPLE

ANSWER

The sum is 23 × 146. We will do this sum by the **Italian method**. This is the 'traditional' method that your parents probably remember:

Step 1	Step 2	Step 3	Step 4	Step 5
1 4 6	1 4 6	1 4 6	1 4 6	1 4 6
× 2 3	× 2 3	× 2 0	× 2	× 2 3
	4 3 8			4 3 8
		0	2 9 2 0	2 9 2 0
				3 3 5 8

Step 1: Write down the sum remembering to line up the units on the right hand side.

Step 2: Ignore the tens digit in the bottom number and multiply 146 by the units digit 3. (This is short multiplication.)

Step 3: Ignore the units digits and multiply by the 10s digit which is really 20. Do this by putting the zero in the second line of the answer.

Step 4: Multiply 146 by the 2 (short multiplication again).

Step 5: Add both answers to get the final total.

The answer is **3358**.

Long multiplication and long division

2 Seventeen buses are booked to take pupils on a school trip. Each bus holds 46 people. How many pupils will the 17 buses carry in total?

The sum is 17 × 46. We will do this one by the **box method**:

$17 = 10 + 7$

Step 1		
$46 = 40 + 6$		
×	40	6
10		
7		

Step 2		
×	40	6
10	400	60
7	280	42

Step 3

```
    4 0 0
      6 0
    2 8 0
  +   4 2
  ---------
    7 8 2
```

Step 1: Draw a box 2 squares by 2 squares (because it is 2 digit by 2 digit sum). Split the numbers into their tens and units along the top and down the side.

Step 2: Multiply the numbers at the top and the numbers at the side and put each answer in each box.

Step 3: Take the numbers from the boxes and write them down, lining up the units on the right. Then, add them together.

The answer is **782**.

3 Thirty-five students each pay £157.00 for a weeks trip to France. How much do they pay altogether?

The sum is 35 × 157. We will do this by the **Chinese multiplication** or **Napier's bones** method:

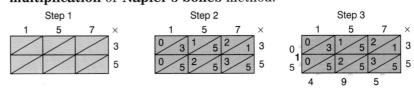

Step 1: Draw a box 3 squares by 2 squares (this is three digit by 2 digit sum). Draw diagonals across each section. Write the digits of each number across the top and down the right hand side.

Step 2: Multiply each pair of digits together and write the answer in the two spaces created by the diagonal. Note that the tens digit (even if it is zero) goes in the top left space while the units go into the bottom right space.

Step 3: Add up the numbers along each diagonal 'path', starting at the bottom right. Note the 'carry' digit of 1. Reading the numbers from left to right gives the final answer.

The answer is **5495**.

Long division

There is really only one way to do this without a calculator. It is similar to short division, you need to use **carries**. You can also use a method which involves subtraction.

4   Divide 612 by 18.

The sum could be set out like this:

Step 1	**Step 2**	**Step 3**
	3	3 4
18) 6 1 2	18) 6 ^{6}1 2	18) 6 ^{6}1 ^{7}2

Step 1: 18 into 6 does not go, so carry the 6 to the 1 to make 61.

Step 2: 18 into 61 goes 3 times, with remainder 7. Write the 3 over the 1 and carry the 7 to the 2 to make 72. (You do not need to know your 18 times table. Just work out how the table builds up: 18, 18 + 18 = 36, 36 + 18 = 54, and so on.)

Step 3: 18 into 72 goes 4 times exactly. Write the 4 over the 2. 54 + 18 = 72.

The answer is **34**.

This sum can also be set out like this:

```
        3  4
18 ) 6  1  2
     5  4
        7  2
        7  2
        0  0
```

This is probably the way your parents remember long division.

5   962 football fans need to travel to an away game in 37-seater coaches. How many coaches will they need?

We can use a method based on subtractions. 37×10 is 370 which is not as big as 962, so take it away. Take away 370 again. Take away 185 which is 5×37 (half of 370). There is 37 left so take away 1 lot of 37. We have taken away 10 lots twice, 5 lots and 1 lot. This is a total of 26 lots of 37.

```
                        9  6  2
1  0  ×  3  7  =    3  7  0  −
                        5  9  2
1  0  ×  3  7  =    3  7  0  −
                        2  2  2
      5  ×  3  7  =    1  8  5  −
                        2  2  2
      1  ×  3  7  =       3  7  −
  +                      3  7
  2  6                   0  0
```

The answer is **26**.

Check yourself

QUESTIONS

Q1 Work out these long multiplications. Use any method you are happy with.

(a) $\begin{array}{r} 48 \\ \times\ 24 \end{array}$ (b) $\begin{array}{r} 256 \\ \times\ 52 \end{array}$ (c) $\begin{array}{r} 362 \\ \times\ 36 \end{array}$ (d) $\begin{array}{r} 178 \\ \times\ 48 \end{array}$

Q2 Work out these long divisions:

(a) $16\overline{)928}$ (b) $28\overline{)924}$

(c) $23\overline{)782}$ (d) $31\overline{)961}$

Use any method you are happy with.

Q3 A milkman has to put 432 milk bottles into crates that hold 24 bottles. How many crates does he need?

Q4 Stamps cost 19p each.
(a) How many can you buy for £5.00?
(b) How much change will you get?

ANSWERS AND TUTORIAL

A1 (a) **1152**   (c) **13032**
(b) **13312**   (d) **8544**

T1 (d) As well as the three methods in the examples, you can also use a method that depends on splitting the sum down into tens and units:

$$10 \times 178 = 1780$$
$$10 \times 178 = 1780$$
$$10 \times 178 = 1780$$
$$10 \times 178 = 1780$$
$$5 \times 178 = 890$$
$$1 \times 178 = 178$$
$$1 \times 178 = 178$$
$$1 \times 178 = 178$$
$$\overline{48 \times 178 = 8544}$$

A2 (a) **58**   (b) **33**   (c) **34**   (d) **31**

T2 You can also use the **standard method**, as shown by the following examples:

(a)
$$\begin{array}{r} 5\ 8 \\ 16\overline{)9\ 2\ 8} \\ 8\ 0 \\ \hline 1\ 2\ 8 \\ 1\ 2\ 8 \\ \hline 0\ 0\ 0 \end{array}$$

(b)
$$\begin{array}{r} 3\ 3 \\ 28\overline{)9\ 2\ 4} \\ 8\ 4 \\ \hline 8\ 4 \\ 8\ 4 \\ \hline 0\ 0 \end{array}$$

A3 **18 crates.**

T3 The sum is $432 \div 24$.

A4 **26 stamps and 6p change.**

T4
$$\begin{array}{r} 2\ 6\ \ \text{r}\,6 \\ 19\overline{)5\ \ 0^{12}0} \end{array}$$

Chapter 18

Decimals

You should be able to multiply and divide whole numbers and decimals by 10, 100 and 1000. You should be able to add, subtract, multiply and divide using decimal numbers expressed to 2 decimal places.

You should already know how to multiply and divide whole numbers by 10 and 100 and how to put decimals in order of size. You should also be able to add and subtract whole numbers.

In this chapter we look at the four rule with decimals. You see how to add and subtract decimals up to 2 decimal places, and multiply and divide a decimal by a single digit whole number.

Multiplying and dividing decimals by 10 and 100

When we divided and multiplied by 10 and 100 at level 4 (see page 5), we added or knocked off one or two zeros. This does not always work, particularly with whole numbers and decimals. For example, this is what happens when we multiply decimals:

$$34.7 \times 10 = 347 \qquad 59.61 \times 100 = 5961$$
$$56.23 \times 10 = 562.3 \qquad 1.205 \times 10 = 12.05$$

The digits are moving one or two places to the left:

$$34.7 \times 10 \qquad\qquad 59.61 \times 100$$

```
        U                              U
    3  4 . 7  × 10              5  9 . 6  1  × 100
    3  4  7 .                   5  9  6  1 .
```

When you divide decimals by 10 or 100 the same thing happens but in reverse: the digits move one or two places to the right. For example:

$$34.7 \div 10 = 3.47 \qquad 59.6 \div 100 = 0.596$$
$$562 \div 100 = 5.62 \qquad 607 \div 10 = 60.7$$

```
      U                            U
  3  4 . 7   ÷ 10            5  6  2 .        ÷100
     3 . 4  7                   5 . 6  2
```

Four rules with decimals

Adding and subtracting decimals is just like adding and subtracting whole numbers. Before you had to line up the units. You still have to do this, but the unit is not always the digit on the right. The units are the numbers in front of the decimal point. At level 5, you will be expected to do multiplication and division where one of the numbers involved is a single digit number. In all four types of sum, we need to remember the rule 'Line up the decimal point.'.

Decimals

EXAMPLE

ANSWER

1 Work out 39.73 + 4.2.

The sum should be written as:

You should fill any 'gaps' with zeros. The sum is done in the usual way and the decimal point is lined up.

$$
\begin{array}{r}
39.73 \\
+\ 4.20 \\
\hline
43.93
\end{array}
$$

EXAMPLE

ANSWER

2 Work out 5.7 − 3.49.

Write the sum as:

$$
\begin{array}{r}
5.70 \\
-\ 3.49 \\
\hline
2.21
\end{array}
$$

EXAMPLE

ANSWER

3 Work out 34.56 × 7.

Write the sum as:

Do the sum like a short multiplication and then put the decimal point directly below where it started.

$$
\begin{array}{r}
34.56 \\
\times\quad\ 7 \\
\hline
241.92
\end{array}
$$

EXAMPLE

ANSWER

4 Work out 34.51 ÷ 7.

Write the sum as:

Do a short division and put the point directly above where it started.

$$
\begin{array}{r}
4.93 \\
7\overline{)34.51}
\end{array}
$$

EXAMPLE

5 Jason has these cards:

He makes the number 463 with three of the cards:

4 6 3

(a) What other card should he choose to make a number ten times bigger than 463?

(b) What other card should he choose to make a number ten times smaller than 463?

ANSWER

(a) He should choose zero to make:

4 6 3 0

(b) He should choose the decimal point to make:

4 6 . 3

6 Jenny wrote some sums in her book. After her teacher marked them as correct Jenny spilt ink on the sums. Can you find the missing number or sign in each sum?

1.	●	× 10	=	23	✓
2.	2.3	●100	=	230	✓
3.	23 ÷	●	=	2.3	✓
4.	23 ●	100	=	0.23	✓

In (1) the missing number must be 2.3
In (2) the missing sign must be ×
In (3) the missing number must be 10
In (4) the missing sign must be ÷

7 A lottery syndicate of 9 people won a prize of £147.33. If it is shared equally, how much does each person win?

They get £16.37 each:

$$\begin{array}{r} 16.37 \\ 9\overline{)147.33} \end{array}$$

Check yourself

QUESTIONS

Q1 Do the following decimal sums:
   (a) 2.6 + 5.7
   (b) 5.3 − 2.8
   (c) 7 × 3.4
   (d) 4.8 ÷ 3

Q2 Do the following decimal sums:
   (a) 3.47 + 6.85
   (b) 6.53 − 3.86
   (c) 8 × 2.36
   (d) 20.16 ÷ 8

ANSWERS AND TUTORIAL

A1 (a) $\begin{array}{r} 2.6 \\ +\ 5.7 \\ \hline 8.3 \end{array}$ (b) $\begin{array}{r} 5.3 \\ -\ 2.8 \\ \hline 2.5 \end{array}$

(c) $\begin{array}{r} 3.4 \\ \times\ 7 \\ \hline 23.8 \end{array}$ (d) $\begin{array}{r} 1.6 \\ 3\overline{)4.8} \end{array}$

T1 Line up the decimal points.

A2 (a) $\begin{array}{r} 3.47 \\ +6.85 \\ \hline 10.32 \end{array}$ (b) $\begin{array}{r} 6.53 \\ -\ 3.86 \\ \hline 2.67 \end{array}$

(c) $\begin{array}{r} 2.36 \\ \times\ 8 \\ \hline 18.88 \end{array}$ (d) $\begin{array}{r} 2.52 \\ 8\overline{)20.16} \end{array}$

T2 Line up the decimal points

ANSWERS AND TUTORIAL

A3 (a) 7 5 8 0

(b) 7 4 8

(c) 7 5 . 8

T3 Make sure you notice the difference between 10 **less** and 10 times **smaller**.

A4 The total cost is £39.37:

$$\begin{array}{r} 18.45 \\ 5.60 \\ + 15.32 \\ \hline 39.37 \end{array}$$

A5 There are 2.88 kg of potatoes left:

$$\begin{array}{r} 5.63 \\ - 2.75 \\ \hline 2.88 \end{array}$$

A6 The cost will be 550.8p (or £5.51 to the nearest penny):

$$\begin{array}{r} 61.2 \\ \times \quad 9 \\ \hline 550.8 \end{array}$$

A7 Each monthly instalment is £13.69:

$$\begin{array}{r} 13.69 \\ 9{\overline{)123.21}} \end{array}$$

A8 (a) 4.6 × 10 = 46

(b) 4.6 × 100 = 460

(c) 4.6 ÷ 10 = 0.46

(d) 4.6 ÷ 100 = 0.046

QUESTIONS

Q3 Ahmed has the following cards:

4 5 6 7 8

. 0

He makes the number 758 with three of them:

7 5 8

(a) Choose a card to make a number 10 times **bigger** than 758.
(b) Change a card to make a number 10 **less** than 758.
(c) Choose another card to make a number that is 10 times **smaller** than 758.

Q4 Paul buys a shirt for £18.45, a tie for £5.60 and a pair of cufflinks for £15.32. How much does he pay altogether?

Q5 A sack of potatoes weighs 5.63 kilograms (kg). 2.75 kg of potatoes are taken out. What is the weight of the potatoes left in the sack?

Q6 Unleaded petrol costs 61.2p per litre. How much does 9 litres cost?

Q7 Water rates for a small house are £123.21. This is paid by 9 equal monthly payments. How much is each payment?

Q8 Fill in the missing numbers or signs from the sums below:

(a) 4.6 × ☐ = 46

(b) 4.6 × 100 = ☐

(c) 4.6 ☐ 10 = 0.46

(d) 4.6 ÷ ☐ = 0.046

Chapter 19

Negative numbers

You should be able to arrange in order, add and subtract negative numbers.

You should already know that numbers below zero are negative numbers and that we show them by putting a minus sign in front. You should know that –7 is smaller than –1.

In this chapter we look at how to add and subtract negative numbers. This is a number line:

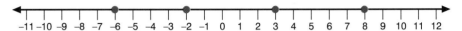

As the numbers go to the right they get bigger. As the numbers go to the left they get smaller. In the number line, 8 is bigger than 3, –2 is bigger than –6, –6 is smaller than 3. You can show this by using the signs > (bigger than) and < (smaller than).

1 Put these numbers in order: –4, 8, –6, 2, –1, with the smallest first.

EXAMPLE

Put the numbers on a number line:

ANSWER

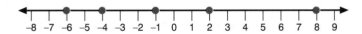

In order, with the smallest first, the numbers are –6, –4, –1, 2 and 8.

2 Put the signs > (bigger than) and < (smaller than) between these pairs of numbers to make a true statement:

EXAMPLE

(a) –4 2   (b) –8 –10   (c) 2 –8

First, draw a number line:

ANSWER

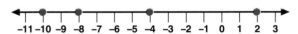

(a) –4 < 2   (b) –8 > –10   (c) 2 > –8

Adding and subtracting negative numbers

When you add and subtract negative numbers there are two rules:

- Always start counting at zero.
- Positive (+) numbers count to the right and negative (-) numbers count to the left.

EXAMPLE

ANSWER

3 Work out $+7 - 3 - 5$.

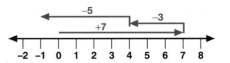

So, $+7 - 3 - 5 = -1$.

EXAMPLE

ANSWER

4 Work out $-8 - 4 + 6$.

So, $-8 - 4 + 6 = -6$.

Check yourself

ANSWERS AND TUTORIAL

A1 (a) In order: –6, –3, 5
(b) In order: –6, –3, –2, –1
(c) In order: –4, –1, 3, 7

T1 Put each set of numbers on a number line.

A2 (a) $-5 > -6$
(b) $-12 < 6$
(c) $7 > -8$

T2 Put each set of numbers on a number line.

A3 (a) +3   (g) –5
(b) +2   (h) –5
(c) +6   (i) +7
(d) –1   (j) –8
(e) –9   (k) –6
(f) –5   (l) –8

T3 Remember start at zero and count to the right for plus numbers and to the left for minus numbers. Questions (i) to (l) have the same values with one plus and one minus. These cancel each other out.

QUESTIONS

Q1 Arrange these numbers in order of size, smallest first:
(a) –3, 5, –6
(b) –3, –6, –1, –2
(c) –4, 7, 3, –1

Q2 Put the sign < or > between these numbers to make a true statement:
(a) –5   –6
(b) –12   6
(c) 7   –8

Q3 Work out the following:
(a) $-5 + 8$ (g) $-5 - 1 + 7 - 6$
(b) $6 - 4$ (h) $-3 + 4 - 5 + 6 - 7$
(c) $+3 - 5 + 8$ (i) $-3 + 7 + 3$
(d) $-5 + 8 - 6 + 2$ (j) $-4 + 4 - 8$
(e) $-3 - 3 - 3$ (k) $-1 - 6 + 1$
(f) $-7 + 6 - 4$ (l) $+7 - 8 - 7$

QUESTIONS

ANSWERS AND TUTORIAL

Q4 Complete the following number patterns:

+3 + –2 = +1
+2 + –2 = 0
+1 + –2 = –1
0 + –2 = –2
☐ + –2 = –3
☐ + –2 = ☐
☐ + –2 = ☐

A4 In the fifth row, –1 is missing. In the sixth row, –2 and –4 are missing. In the bottom row, –3 and –5 are missing.

T4 Both the first and last columns are decreasing by one each time.

Q5 You may use a calculator for this question. The diagram shows a mountain and cave system:

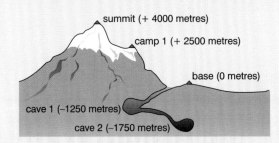

summit (+ 4000 metres)
camp 1 (+ 2500 metres)
base (0 metres)
cave 1 (–1250 metres)
cave 2 (–1750 metres)

(a) How high above cave 1 is the summit?
(b) How far below the summit is camp 1?
(c) How far is cave 1 above cave 2?
(d) How far below camp 1 is cave 2?

A5 (a) 5250 metres
(b) 1500 metres
(c) 500 metres
(d) 4250 metres

T5 You have to work from the base at zero metres.

Q6 Read the numbers from these scales:

(a)
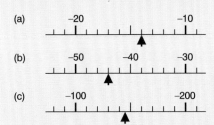
–20   –10

(b)
–50   –40   –30

(c)
–100   –200

A6 (a) –14 (b) –44 (c) –145

T6 You must be careful about what each division on the scale is worth and which way the scale reads. In (a) each division is 1 unit and the scale reads from right to left. In (b) each division is 2 units and the scale reads from right to left. In (c) each division is 10 units and the scale reads from left to right.

Q7 You may use a calculator for this question. Just before Christmas I had £56.22 in my bank account. I wrote cheques for presents totalling £75.89. My Aunt Jane then gave me a cheque for £20 which I paid in to the bank. How much did I have in my account after Christmas?

A7 £56.22 – £75.89 = –£19.67.
–£19.67 + £20.00 = £0.33.
So, I have 33p in the bank after Christmas.

T7 If you use a calculator then make sure you type the sum in correctly. If you get a little minus sign in your display this means you have put it in the wrong way.

Chapter 20

Fractional and percentage parts

You should be able to calculate fractional or percentage parts of quantities and measurements, using a calculator where appropriate.

You should already be able to recognise proportions of a whole number and use simple fractions and percentages. You should also know that 10% is one-tenth and you should be able to express 25% and 50% as fractions.

In level 4 (see page 11), we looked at some of the more common equivalent fractions and percentages. In this chapter we look at ways to work out fractions and percentages of various quantities. At this level you will use only the simpler values and your answers will always be a simple number or decimal.

Remember that 10% is the same as one-tenth. 10% is the easiest percentage to work out, particularly if you are using pounds (£). One tenth is the same as dividing by 10, which we have already seen means moving the digits one place to the right.

EXAMPLE **1** Find 10% of £23.50.

ANSWER £23.50 ÷ 10 = £2.35.

You could also use a calculator to do 10% × £23.50. Your calculator may have a % button. Try it to see if it gives the correct answer. If it doesn't then you can do 10 × 23.50 ÷ 100, or 10 ÷ 100 × £23.50.

Most of the other percentages that you will be asked to find can be worked out by first finding 10%. One special percentage that you should know is that $\frac{1}{3} = 33\frac{1}{3}\%$.

EXAMPLE **2** Increase 300 by 20%.

ANSWER 10% of 300 is 30. 20% is 2 lots of 10%. 20% of 300 is 2 x 30 = 60.

300 increased by 20% is 300 + 60 = 360.

EXAMPLE **3** Find 45% of 340.

ANSWER 45% of 340 can be done as 45 × 340 ÷ 100 = 153

EXAMPLE **4** Find $\frac{4}{5}$ of 120.

Fractions of quantities can be found in two ways. Firstly, find $\frac{1}{5}$ of 120, which you can do by dividing 120 by 5. $120 \div 5 = 24$.

$\frac{4}{5}$ is $4 \times \frac{1}{5}$, and 4×24 is 96. So, $\frac{4}{5}$ of 120 is 96.

The second way to do this problem is to multiply by 4 and then divide by 5:

$4 \times 120 = 480$, $480 \div 5 = 96$.

ANSWER

5 Find $\frac{3}{4}$ of 150

EXAMPLE

ANSWER

First, find $\frac{1}{4}$ of 150:

$150 \div 4 = 37.5$. $\frac{3}{4}$ is $3 \times \frac{1}{4}$, so $3 \times 37.5 = 112.5$

You can also multiply by 3 and divide by 4:

$3 \times 150 = 450$, $450 \div 4 = 112.5$

Check yourself

QUESTIONS

Q1 Find 10% of:
(a)	£320	(f)	£32.50
(b)	£410	(g)	£12.70
(c)	£60	(h)	70p
(d)	£32	(i)	150 elephants.
(e)	£7	(j)	25 packets of sweets.

Q2 Find 20% of:
(a)	£320	(f)	£41.50
(b)	£410	(g)	£16.40
(c)	£60	(h)	60p
(d)	£32	(i)	250 elephants.
(e)	£9	(j)	45 packets of sweets.

ANSWERS AND TUTORIAL

A1
(a)	£32	(f)	£3.25
(b)	£41	(g)	£1.27
(c)	£6	(h)	7p
(d)	£3.20	(i)	15 elephants.
(e)	£0.70 or 70p	(j)	$2\frac{1}{2}$, or 2.5 packets of sweets.

T1 Remember 10% is the same as dividing by 10.

A2
(a)	£64	(f)	£8.30
(b)	£82	(g)	£3.28
(c)	£12	(h)	12p
(d)	£6.40	(i)	50 elephants.
(e)	£1.80	(j)	9 packets of sweets.

T2 To find 20%, find 10% and then double it.

ANSWERS AND TUTORIAL

A3 (a) £120   (d) £90   (g) £277.50
(b) £16   (e) £1   (h) £13.44
(c) £40   (f) £15   (i) £4.55

T3 30% is 3 times 10% etc. 25%, 50% and 75% are $\frac{1}{4}$, $\frac{1}{2}$ and $\frac{3}{4}$, respectively. 1% is the same as dividing by 100.

A4 (a) 200   (b) 120   (c) 30   (d) 40

T4 To find $\frac{2}{3}$, first find $\frac{1}{3}$ by dividing by 3 and then double your answer.

A5 (a) 75   (b) 24   (c) 30   (d) 15

T5 To find $\frac{3}{4}$, first find $\frac{1}{4}$ by dividing by 4 and then times your answer by 3.

A6 (a) 14   (b) 20   (c) 28   (d) 15

T6 Find the single fraction first.

A7 20 square feet.

T7 $\frac{1}{7}$ is 10 square feet.

A8 (a) 500 g.   (b) 40 washes.

T8 (a) 25% is $\frac{1}{4}$ which is an extra 100g
(b) $\frac{1}{4}$ of 32 is 8.

QUESTIONS

Q3 Find:
(a) 30% of £400   (f) 5% of £300
(b) 40% of £40   (g) 75% of £370
(c) 50% of £80   (h) 24% of £56
(d) 25% of £360   (i) 65% of £7
(e) 1% of £100
(You will need a calculator for (g) (h) and (i).)

Q4 Find $\frac{2}{3}$ of:
(a) 300   (c) 45
(b) 180   (d) 60

Q5 Find $\frac{3}{4}$ of:
(a) 100   (c) 40
(b) 32   (d) 20

Q6 Find:
(a) $\frac{2}{3}$ of 21   (c) $\frac{4}{5}$ of 35
(b) $\frac{2}{3}$ of 30   (d) $\frac{3}{8}$ of 40

Q7 A kitchen wall is to have a window put into it. The area of the wall is 70 square feet. Because it is an outside wall, the window cannot cover more than $\frac{2}{7}$ of the area of the wall. What is the biggest area that the window could have?

Q8 A bottle of shampoo contains 25% extra:
(a) A regular bottle contains 400 g. How much does the new bottle contain?
(b) Mark uses a regular bottle to wash his hair 32 times. How many washes will he get out of the new bottle?

T E S T   Q U E S T I O N S

Answers with examiner's comments on page 239.

1. Gwen makes kites to sell. She sells the kites for £4.75 each.

(a) Gwen sells 26 kites. How much does she get for the 26 kites?

(b) Gwen has a box of 250 staples. She uses 16 staples to make each kite.
How many complete kites can she make using the 250 staples?

(1996 paper 1)

2. A **standard** size box of salt has a volume of $300\,cm^3$.

(a) What is the volume of a **special offer** box of salt, which is 20% bigger?

(b) The standard size box contains enough salt to fill up 10 salt pots.
How many salt pots can be filled up from the special offer box of salt?

(1996 paper 2)

3. Gary and Sue share a pizza:
Gary is on a diet. He only eats $\frac{3}{8}$ of the pizza.

A whole pizza is 840 calories.
How many calories does Gary have?

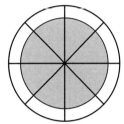

(1993 paper 1)

4. Nasreen is working out the size of the corridor.
She counts her paces:

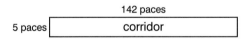

142 paces

5 paces | corridor

She measures **one** pace. It is 73 cm.

(a) Work out the length of the corridor in centimetres.

(b) Change the length and the width into metres.

(1992 paper 3)

5. Gary wants to print a rectangle on a T-shirt.
The price for printing a rectangle in one colour is:

£1 for up to $4000\,mm^2$
£2 for $4000\,mm^2$ and over

These are the measurements of Gary's rectangle:

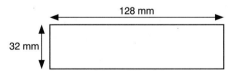

128 mm

32 mm

Gary thought that the price would be £1.
Work out the actual area of Gary's rectangle
to check if he was right.

(1994 paper 1)

6. In a competition, all boats have sails with an area of 15 m². The competition has this rule:

> Advertisements must cover **less** than 20% of the sail.

The advertisement on this sail covers exactly 20% of the sail:
Work out the area of the advertisement.
Show your working.

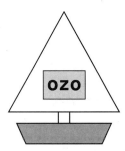

(1994 paper 2)

7. (a) Alan had a special rectangle. Alan cut off $\frac{1}{3}$ of the rectangle.

He had a square left. Alan put back the piece he had cut off.

He said "I've added on $\frac{1}{3}$ of the square.".

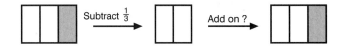

He was wrong. Explain why.
What fraction of the **square** did he add on?

(b) Look at shape 1 and shape 2:

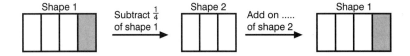

What fraction of **shape 2** is added on to get back to shape 1?

(c) Look at the numbers on the bottom of the fractions in (a) and (b). Suppose you subtract $\frac{1}{8}$ of the shape you started with. You want to get back to the shape you started with. What fraction **of the new shape** would you add on?

(1994 paper 1)

8. Lee has these cards

He made the number 32.4 with four of his cards.
Use some of Lee's cards to show the number **10 times** as big as 32.4.
Use some of Lee's cards to show the number **100 times** as big as 32.4.

(1994 paper 2)

Chapter 21

Number patterns, square numbers and opposite operations

You should be able to check your answers by working backwards.

You should already be able to recognise a number pattern and to describe how it is building up. In this chapter we do some more work on number patterns and look at a special series of numbers.

Inverse operations

Working backwards in maths means 'undoing' mathematical operations. To 'undo' maths we need to do the opposite of the operation that we did first. The mathematical name for opposite is **inverse**. At this level, you need to know that:

- The inverse operation for multiplication (times) is division.
- The inverse operation for division is multiplication.
- The inverse operation for addition is subtraction.
- The inverse operation for subtraction is addition.

Square numbers

You need to know one special set of numbers: the square numbers. This is the pattern made by the first 4 square numbers:

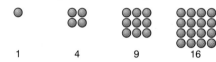

1   4   9   16

The next pattern would contain 25 dots.

Another way of working out square numbers is to times numbers by themselves. For example,

$1 \times 1 = 1$	$3 \times 3 = 9$	$5 \times 5 = 25$
$2 \times 2 = 4$	$4 \times 4 = 16$	$6 \times 6 = 36.$

Because square numbers are so special, they have their own mathematical sign and most calculators have a special button that works them out. The 'square' sign is a small two written slightly above and to the right of the number, as in: $3^2 = 9$.

x^2

EXAMPLE

1 (a) Describe how this pattern is building up:

1, 4, 9, 16, 25

(b) Find the next two terms in the number pattern.

ANSWER

(a) The terms start at 1 and go up by 3, then by 5, then by 7 and so on.

(b) The next terms are 36 and 49.

You can find these by adding 11 to 25 and by adding 13 to 36.

EXAMPLE

2 Write down the next two lines of this number pattern:

$$1 = 1 = 1 \times 1 = 1^2$$
$$1 + 3 = 4 = 2 \times 2 = 2^2$$
$$1 + 3 + 5 = 9 = 3 \times 3 = 3^2$$

ANSWER

$$1 + 3 + 5 + 7 = 16 = 4 \times 4 = 4^2$$
$$1 + 3 + 5 + 7 + 9 = 25 = 5 \times 5 = 5^2$$

Each line starts by adding up odd numbers. This gives the square numbers which can be written either as a number times itself, or as the number followed by the special square sign.

Square roots $\sqrt{}$

To undo square we do square root. The square root of 9 is 3. The square root of 81 is 9. The square root also has its own button on most calculators. You will need to find out how your calculator works to do a square root.
On most scientific calculators you type in: 　**1** **2** **1** **√**

or on D.A.L. calculators you type in: 　**√** **1** **2** **1** **=**

In both, the display gives the answer 11.

EXAMPLE

3 Find the square root of: 　(a) 81 　(b) 169 　(c) 75

ANSWER

You won't need a calculator for the first one if you know your tables, but it will be useful for the last two.

(a) 9 　　(b) 13 　　(c) 8.66

The last answer is not exact. It is 'rounded off' (see page 72).

Number machines and inverses

Sometimes, you are told what comes out of a number machine and you then have to find out what went into that machine: to do this, you need to do the inverse operation.

EXAMPLE

4 Find the numbers that went into each of these machines:

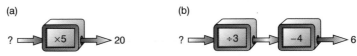

ANSWER

(a) The number 4 went in because $5 \times 4 = 20$, but you would do this by reversing the number machine and doing $20 \div 5 = 4$.

(b) The number 30 went in because if we reverse this machine we get:

5 Use the rule: 'Start with a number and multiply by 2 and then add 1' to find which numbers are missing from this table.

The 5 in the first column goes to 11 in the second column. The 21 goes back to 10, the 12 goes to 25 and the 15 goes back to 7.

Start	End
1	3
5	☐
☐	21
12	☐
☐	15

EXAMPLE

ANSWER

Check yourself

QUESTIONS

Q1 What is the opposite operation to:
(a) + 7   (c) × 5
(b) − 6   (d) ÷ 9

Q2 Find the numbers that went into these machines:

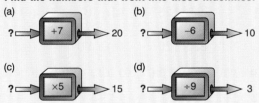

Q3 What numbers went into these machines:

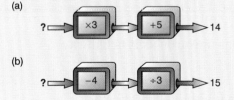

Q4 Answer this question without a calculator:
(a) Find the square of: (i) 3; (ii) 9; (iii) 10
(b) Find the square root of: (i) 36; (ii) 64; (iii) 1

ANSWERS AND TUTORIAL

A1 (a) − 7   (c) ÷ 5
(b) + 6   (d) × 9

T1 The operation changes, but the number stays the same.

A2 (a) 13   (b) 16   (c) 3   (d) 27

T2 Reverse the machines:

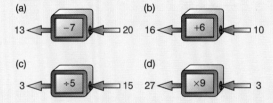

A3 (a) 3   (b) 49

T3 Reverse the machines:

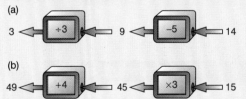

A4 (a) (i) 9; (ii) 81; (iii) 100
(b) (i) 6; (ii) 8; (iii) 1

T4 To square, times a number by itself. Square root is the opposite.

Chapter 22

LEVEL 5
ALGEBRA

Approximating and rounding off

> You should be able to check your solutions by approximating.

You should already know how to multiply and divide by 10.

In everyday life we 'round off' or 'approximate' numbers. Rounding off is also useful in maths. It is useful to have a rough idea of what an answer should be before you do a sum.

Rounding off

At this level you need to round off to the nearest whole number, or to the nearest 10, 100 or 1000.

EXAMPLE 1 Round these calculator displays to the nearest whole number:

(a) 3.89   (b) 6.23   (c) 15.4   (d) 0.763

ANSWER
(a) 4   (b) 6   (c) 15   (d) 1

If the decimal part is 0.5 or more, then you go up to the next whole number. If it is below 0.5, go down to the whole number.

EXAMPLE 2 Round these numbers off to the nearest 10:

(a) 17   (b) 34   (c) 123   (d) 85   (e) 22.9

ANSWER
(a) 20   (b) 30   (c) 120   (d) 90   (e) 20

If a number is 'halfway', as in part (d), the rule is to go upwards.

EXAMPLE 3 Round these numbers off to the nearest 100:

(a) 172   (b) 345   (c) 123   (d) 85   (e) 250

ANSWER
(a) 200   (b) 300   (c) 100   (d) 100   (e) 300

The number in (e) goes upwards as it is halfway.

EXAMPLE 4 Round these numbers off to the nearest 1000:

(a) 1340   (b) 3405   (c) 2780   (d) 8500   (e) 250

ANSWER
(a) 1000   (b) 3000   (c) 3000   (d) 9000   (e) 0

The number in (d) goes upwards as it is halfway. In part (e), 250 is nearer to zero than 1000.

Multiplying multiples of ten and a hundred

Multiples are the times tables, so multiples of 10 are 20, 30, and so on, and multiples of 100 are 200, 300, and so on. If you want to work out 40×30 you do $4 \times 3 = 12$ and then, as there are two zeros in the sum, put two zeros on to the end of your answer:

$$3\,0 \times 4\,0 = 1\,2\,0\,0$$
$$3 \times 4$$

5 Write down the answers to:

(a) 20×30 (b) 40×500 (c) 70×3000

EXAMPLE

(a) 600   (b) 20 000   (c) 210 000

ANSWER

In (b), $4 \times 5 = 20$. You still have to put the three zeros on.

Dividing multiples of 10 and 100

Most of the divisions you do will be straightforward. For example, if you want to do $1200 \div 60$, you do $12 \div 6 = 2$. Then, because there were two zeros in the first number and one zero in the second number, and 2 zeros minus 1 zero equals 1 zero, you write down one zero at the end. (You can also 'cross off' the zeros:

$$1\,2\,0\,\cancel{0} \div 6\,\cancel{0} = 2\,0$$
$$1\,2 \div 6$$

6 Write down the answers to:

(a) $600 \div 20$ (b) $800 \div 40$ (c) $900 \div 30$

EXAMPLE

(a) 30   (b) 20   (c) 30

ANSWER

Estimating answers to sums

To estimate an answer, you round off and then do the sum in your head. If you use a calculator you will not get any marks.

7 Find an approximate answer to these sums:

EXAMPLE

(a) 19.6×5.3 (b) $\dfrac{99.6 - 42.1}{12.1}$ (c) $\dfrac{11.8 \times 56.3}{5.8}$

ANSWER

(a) The answer is about 100, because $19.6 \approx 20$, $5.3 \approx 5$ and $20 \times 5 = 100$ ($\approx$ means 'is approximately').

(b) $\dfrac{99.6 - 42.1}{12.1} \approx 6$ because $99.6 \approx 100$, $42.1 \approx 40$ and $12.1 \approx 10$. 100 take away 40 is 60 and 60 divided by 10 is 6.

(c) $\dfrac{11.8 \times 56.3}{5.8} \approx 100$ because $11.8 \approx 10$, $56.3 \approx 60$ and $5.8 \approx 6$. 10 multiplied by 60 is 600, and 600 divided by 6 is 100.

**Approximating and
rounding off**

Check yourself

ANSWERS AND TUTORIAL

A1 (a) 2   (b) 17   (c) 10

A2 (a) 40   (d) 80   (g) 50
     (b) 50   (e) 110   (h) 500
     (c) 70   (f) 100

T2 Even though (f) and (h) are hundreds, the answers
     are still to the nearest 10.

A3 (a) 200   (c) 300
     (b) 600   (d) 500

A4 (a) 3000   (c) 1000
     (b) 2000   (d) 5000

A5 (a) 2400   (c) 35000
     (b) 7000   (d) 180000

A6 (a) 20   (c) 5
     (b) 10   (d) 30

A7 (a) $50 \times 60 = 3000$
     (b) $10 \times 70 = 700$
     (c) $5 \times 70 = 350$
     (d) $300 \times 600 = 180000$

A8 $60 + 40 = 100, 30 - 20 = 10$
     and $100 \div 10 = 10$.

QUESTIONS

Q1 Round off these calculator displays to the
     nearest whole number:

     (a) 2.134   (b) 16.78   (c) 10.06

Q2 Round off these numbers to the nearest 10:
     (a) 44   (e) 109
     (b) 52   (f) 99
     (c) 69   (g) 51
     (d) 75   (h) 501

Q3 Round of these numbers to the nearest 100:
     (a) 170   (c) 308
     (b) 620   (d) 450

Q4 Round off these numbers to the nearest 1000:
     (a) 2700   (c) 1450
     (b) 2034   (d) 4500

Q5 Write down the answers to these sums:
     (a) 40×60 (c) 50×700
     (b) 10×700 (d) 300×600

Q6 Write down the answers to these sums:
     (a) $400 \div 20$ (c) $500 \div 100$
     (b) $700 \div 70$ (d) $1800 \div 60$

Q7 Estimate answers to these sums:
     (a) 47×62
     (b) 11.4×69
     (c) 5.1×73
     (d) 285×613

Q8 Estimate the answer to this sum:

$$\frac{55.7 + 41.6}{27.3 - 19.1}$$

Chapter 23

Simple Formulae

> You should be able to write down a formula or rule using mathematical symbols.

You should know how to use simple formulae expressed in words.

In this chapter you will see how to write down a formula or rule using mathematical symbols. This means you will use letters for numbers – this is what most people think of as Algebra.

We have already seen that a formula is just a rule that changes a number into another number. Take the simple rule 'add 2'. We can show this as a number machine:

If 3 goes in, then $3 + 2 = 5$ comes out.
If 7 goes in, then $7 + 2 = 9$ comes out.

We can say that if a number goes in, then the number plus 2 comes out. We can save time by saying, 'If n goes in, then $n + 2$ comes out,'. We use the letter n to stand for any number.

The number machine would be:

You can have number machines for the other three basic mathematical rules: subtraction, multiplication and division:

Multiplication can also be written as 5n and division can be written as $\frac{n}{4}$. We assume there is a multiplication sign between letters and numbers, even though no sign is written in. A line, like you see in a fraction, means divide.

Formulae can be more complicated and there can be more than one part to the number machine. For example: 'times by 3 and add 4.'.

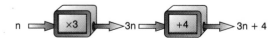

The formulae you have to use at this level use only the four basic rules of addition, subtraction, multiplication and division. You might also use the operation of squaring. This is written as n^2.

1 Write down the algebraic formula that comes out of each of these number machines:

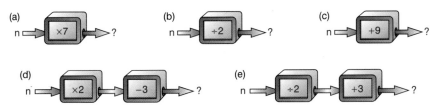

(a)   7n

(c)   n + 9

(e) $\dfrac{n}{2} + 3$

(b) $\dfrac{n}{2}$

(d)   2n – 3

There are other ways to write some of these:

(a)   could be 7 × n, or n × 7. It could not be n7.

(b)   could be n ÷ 2.

(d)   could be 2 × n – 3, or n x 2 - 3.

(e)   could be n ÷ 2 + 3.

2 Find the missing functions from these machines:

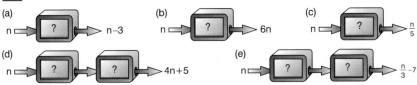

(a)   –3

(c)   ÷ 5

(e)   ÷ 3 and – 7

(b)   × 6

(d)   × 4 and + 5

Letters for numbers

We can describe everyday situations using algebra. For example: my brother is two years younger than me. If I am x years old, how old is my brother? Whatever age I am, my brother is 2 years less. So, if I am x years old, my brother is $x – 2$ years old. If I am 14, he is 14 – 2, which is 12.

3 A class are baking biscuits. Ann bakes B biscuits. Barry bakes 3 more biscuits than Ann. Carol bakes twice as many biscuits as Ann. Derek bakes 4 less biscuits than Carol.

Write down in the table how many biscuits each person bakes. Then, write down the total number of biscuits baked.

Person	Biscuits
Ann	B
Barry	B + 3
Carol	
Derek	
Total	

Carol bakes 2B biscuits. Derek bakes 2B – 4 biscuits. Altogether they bake: B + B + 3 + 2B + 2B - 4 = 6B – 1 biscuits.

Check yourself

QUESTIONS

Q1 Write down the formula from each of these number machines:

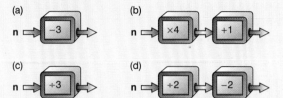

(a)

n → −3 →

(b)

n → ×4 → +1 →

(c)

n → ÷3 →

(d)

n → ÷2 → −2 →

Q2 Find the rule missing from these machines:

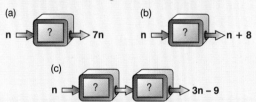

(a)

n → ? → 7n

(b)

n → ? → n + 8

(c)

n → ? → ? → 3n − 9

Q3 Mrs Jones has written the following terms on the board and asked the class to add them up:

$$2n + 3$$
$$4n − 5$$
$$+ \quad n$$
$$\underline{\quad n + 7 \quad}$$

(a) These are the answers for 3 pupils.
Alf: 13n, Bert: 8n − 15, Charles: 8n + 5.
Who is correct?

(b) Add the following together:
3n − 6 + 7 − n + 2n + 4.

Q4 This square has a side of n centimetres:

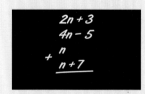

(a) Explain why the perimeter of the square is 4n cm.

(b) Two similar squares are put together in a line:

Rod thinks that the perimeter of this shape is 8n. Explain why he is wrong.

(c) What is the perimeter of the two squares?

ANSWERS AND TUTORIAL

A1 (a) n − 3   (b) 4n + 1, or 4 × n + 1

(c) n ÷ 3 or $\dfrac{n}{3}$ (d) $\dfrac{n}{2} - 2$

T1 In (b), you could put n × 4 but not n4.

A2 (a) × 7
(b) + 8
(c) × 3 and − 9.

T2 The answer to (c) has to be in this order.

A3 (a) **Charles is correct.**

T3 2n + 4n + n + n = 8n
3 − 5 + 7 = + 5
You cannot mix up letters and numbers.

(b) **4n + 5**

T3 Do the letters separately from the numbers:
3n − n + 2n = 4n; −6 + 7 + 4 = 5

A4 (a) Because n + n + n + n = 4n
(b) Because two sides meet and are not on the perimeter.
(c) n + n + n + n + n + n = 6n

T4 Think of a number sum:
3 + 3 + 3 + 3 = 4 × 3 = 12.
If it works with numbers, it works with letters.

Chapter 24

Using formulae and rules: co-ordinates in all four quadrants

You should be able to use simple rules or formulae involving one or two operations.

You should already know how to use a simple number machine. On page 24, we saw how to work out the numbers that come out of a number machine. You also know how to write the operation done by a number machine as a rule using algebra. In this section, we use rules with algebra to solve problems.

First, we need to look at co-ordinates using negative numbers. There are two rules when using co-ordinates: 'start at the origin (0,0).' and 'move across first and up second.'.

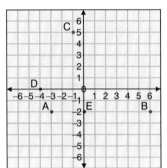

These rules hold true, but for a negative number, we move to the left or downwards. Point A on the grid is 3 to the left and 2 down from the origin (0,0). We write this as: (–3, –2). Point B is at (6, –2), point C is at (–1, 5), point D is at (–4, 0) and point E is at (0, –2).

EXAMPLE

1 (a) What are the co-ordinates of the points A, B and C in the grid on the right:

(b) Another point, D, is placed on the grid so that ABCD is a square. What are the co-ordinates of D?

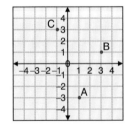

ANSWER

(a) A is (1, –3), B is (3, 1), C is (–1, 3)

(b) The point D must be at (–3, –1)

Multiplying and dividing negative numbers

To use number machines fully, you also need to be able to multiply and divide negative numbers. To do this, treat the negative numbers as ordinary numbers, and then put a minus sign in front. For example, 3×-2 is the same as 3×2, which is 6, with a minus sign, –6.

Division is very much the same. $-16 \div 2$ means divide –16 by 2. Again this is just the normal sum $16 \div 2$, with a minus in front. The answer to this is 8, so the answer to the first sum is –8.

Look at the table:

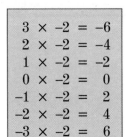

$$3 \times -2 = -6$$
$$2 \times -2 = -4$$
$$1 \times -2 = -2$$
$$0 \times -2 = 0$$
$$-1 \times -2 = 2$$
$$-2 \times -2 = 4$$
$$-3 \times -2 = 6$$

It is a curious fact that if you multiply two negative numbers together, you get a positive (plus) number. Also, if $3 \times -2 = -6$, then $-6 \div -2 = 3$. In other words, if you divide two negative numbers, you get a positive number.

LEVEL **5**
ALGEBRA

**Using formulae and
rules: co-ordinates in
all four quadrants**

2 Write down the answers to these sums:

(a) 3×-4 (c) -6×-6 (e) $20 \div -4$
(b) 5×-7 (d) $12 \div -3$ (f) $24 \div -8$

(a) -12 (c) 36 (e) -5
(b) -35 (d) -4 (f) -3

3 (a) Use this number machine to complete the table:

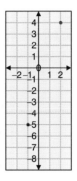

In	Out
2	4
1	
0	
-1	-5
-2	

(b) The co-ordinates (2, 4) and (–1, –5) are plotted on
the grid. Use the other three sets of co-ordinates
in the table to plot three more points on the grid.
What do you notice about the five points?

(a) The pairs of numbers are (2, 4); (1, 1); (0, –2); (–1, –5); (–2, –8).

(b) If you join the points together, you get a straight line.

Mappings

A 'mapping' is a rule that changes one number to a different number.
Mappings are sometimes shown as diagrams. For example, below are
mapping diagrams for y = 2x , y = x – 2 and y = 2x – 2:

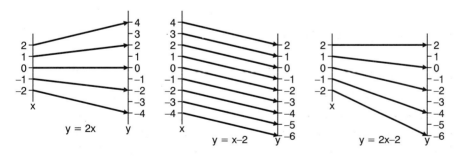

4 Draw mapping diagrams for these number machines using only
whole numbers:

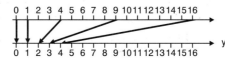

LEVEL **5**
ALGEBRA

**Using formulae and
rules: co-ordinates in
all four quadrants**

Check yourself

ANSWERS AND TUTORIAL

QUESTIONS

A1   A = (–5, 5); B = (–4, 3); C = (1, 4);
D = (4, –2); E = (–3, –3); F = (–5, –2).

Q1   Give the
co-ordinates of
points A, B, C,
D, E and F on
the grid:

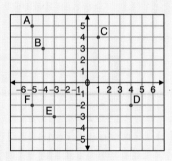

A2

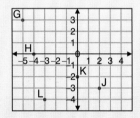

Q2   On a copy of the grid in Q1, mark on
the co-ordinates: G (–5, 3); H (–4, 0);
J (2, –3); K (0, –2); L (–3, –4).

A3   (a)   A = (–2, 4); B = (3, 4); C = (1, –2).
(b)   D = (–4, –2).

T3   It might help to draw the parallelogram.

Q3   (a)   From the grid
below, give the
co-ordinates of
points A, B and C.
(b)   Another point, D,
is placed on the
grid to make a
parallelogram
ABCD. What are the co-ordinates of D?

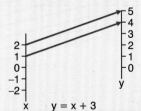

A4   The other co-ordinates are (0, 3); (–1, 2) and
(–2, 1). They make a straight line:

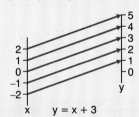 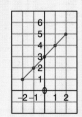

Q4   The mapping diagram below shows y = x + 3.
The lines for x = 2 and x = 1 are drawn.

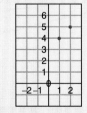

(a)   Complete the mapping diagram for x = 0,
–1 and –2.
(b)   The two lines drawn give co-ordinates (2, 5)
and (1, 4). These have been plotted on the
grid. Plot the points given by the other three
lines. What do you notice about the points?

1. Here is a rule for joining numbers: 'Multiply the number by 3, then take away 1.'

   (a) Fill in the missing numbers in the table:

1	joins to	
3	joins to	
5	joins to	
7	joins to	
9	joins to	
11	joins to	

   (b) The line in the circle shows that 4 joins to 11: Draw a line to show what 8 joins to and draw a line to show what 12 joins to.

   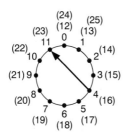

   (1993 Paper 1)

2.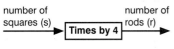

number of dots D	number of lines L
2	1
3	2
4	3
5	4

   number of dots → **subtract 1** → number of lines

   The diagram shows how you can work out the number of lines when you know the number of dots. Write a rule for this using D and L.

   (1993 Paper 3)

3. You can use rods to make squares:

   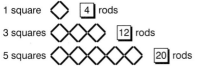

   1 square ◇ [4] rods

   3 squares ◇◇◇ [12] rods

   5 squares ◇◇◇◇◇ [20] rods

   number of squares (s) → **Times by 4** → number of rods (r)

   There is a rule shown on the right for finding the number of rods needed to make **any** number of squares. Write this rule using algebra. (Use the letters **s** and **r**.)

   (1992 Paper 1)

4. Rosemary drew these rectangles using a computer:
   Rectangle A has **width 3** and **length 5**:
   The computer repeated these instructions to draw the other rectangles:
   new **width** = previous **width** × 2.
   new **length** = previous **length** + previous **width**.
   Complete this table:

   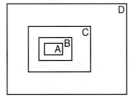

	width	length
rectangle A	3	5
rectangle B		
rectangle C		
rectangle D		

   (1994 paper 1)

5. These pupils were asked to say some square numbers in order.

   Val 4   Liz 9   Huw 16   Paul 25

   Put their numbers into this function machine:

   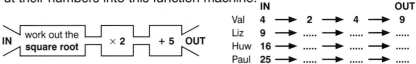

   IN → work out the **square root** → × 2 → + 5 → OUT

	IN			OUT
Val	4 →	2 →	4 →	9
Liz	9 →	..... →	..... →	.....
Huw	16 →	..... →	..... →	.....
Paul	25 →	..... →	..... →	.....

   (a) Fill in the spaces to find the numbers which come out.
   (b) **Two** numbers in the OUT column are **prime numbers**. What are they?

   (1994 Paper 2)

6. Jo is planting a small orchard. She plants **cherry** trees, **plum** trees, **apple** trees and **pear** trees.
n stands for the number of **cherry** trees Jo plants.

(a) Jo plants the **same** number of **plum** trees as **cherry** trees.
How many **plum** trees does she plant?

(b) Jo plants **twice** as many **apple** trees as **cherry** trees.
How many **apple** trees does she plant?

(c) Jo plants **7 more pear** trees than **cherry** trees. How many **pear** trees does she plant?

(d) How many trees does Jo plant **altogether**? Write your answer as simply as possible.

(1995 Paper 2)

7. A teacher has 5 bags of marbles and 3 extra marbles.
Each bag has n marbles inside:
She asks: *'How many marbles are there altogether?'*.
The pupils say:

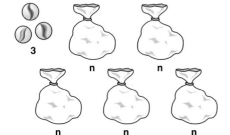

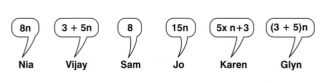

8n	3 + 5n	8	15n	5x n+3	(3 + 5)n
Nia	Vijay	Sam	Jo	Karen	Glyn

(a) Name one pupil who is **right**.

(b) Name another pupil who is **right**.

(c) Choose one of the correct answers for (a) or (b) and explain why it shows the right number of marbles.

(1994 Paper 1)

8. Four people play a game with counters. Each person starts with one or more bags of counters. Each bag has **m** counters in it.
The table shows what happened during the game:

	Start	During game	End of game
Lisa	3 bags	lost 5 counters	3m – 5
Ben	2 bags	won 3 counters	2m + 3
Cath	1 bag	lost 2 counters	
Fiona	4 bags	won 6 counters, and lost 2 counters	

Write an expression in the table to show what **Cath** and **Fiona** had at the end of the game. Write each expression as **simply as possible**.

(1996 Paper 1)

Chapter 25

Angles

You should be able to measure angles to the nearest degree and know the language associated with angle.

You should already know that an angle is a measure of turn and is measured in degrees. You should know that a complete turn is 360°, a half turn is 180° and a right angle is 90°. These diagrams show the right angle and also some important words which describe angles:

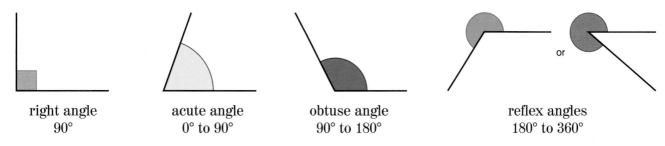

right angle	acute angle	obtuse angle	reflex angles
90°	0° to 90°	90° to 180°	180° to 360°

Measuring and drawing angles

You use a **protractor** to measure or draw angles. Use the diagrams above to help you get started. A protractor has an inside and outside scale so that you can measure an angle from both sides. You should be able to measure or draw angles to within 1°, so you need to be very careful. Remember to use a sharp pencil for drawing and marking.

1 Measure these angles:

(a)

(b)

(a)

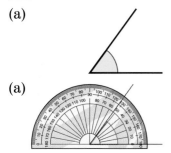

(b)

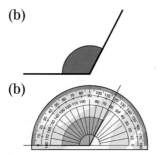

The angle is acute so it must be less than 90°. Line up your protractor as shown in the diagram. You need to line up the base line on the protractor, the line that starts from 0°, with the horizontal line that makes the angle. Use the inside scale.

Count round anticlockwise in 10° until you meet the other line of the angle. Now count the units. The angle is 53°.

The angle is obtuse, so it must be greater than 90°. Line up your protractor as shown. The base line on the protractor must start from 0°, so use the outside scale. Count round clockwise in 10° until you meet the other line of the angle. Now count the units. The angle is 118°.

Calculating angles

You can calculate the size of an angle on a diagram without having to measure it if you know the following facts:

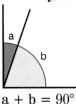

$a + b = 90°$
a and b are
complementary angles

$a + b = 180°$
a and b are
supplementary angles

$a + b = 360°$
a and b are
conjugate angles

EXAMPLE

2 Calculate the size of the angle marked x on each diagram:

(a)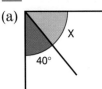

(b)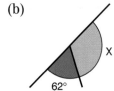

(c)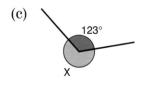

ANSWER

(a) The 2 angles add up to 90°, so $x = 90° - 40° = 50°$

(b) The 2 angles add up to 180°, so $x = 180° - 62° = 118°$

(c) The 2 angles add up to 360°, so $x = 360° - 123° = 237°$

Check yourself

ANSWERS AND TUTORIAL

QUESTIONS

A1 **(a)** 74   **(b)** 137

T1 You might have to extend the lines before you can measure the angles.
  (a) The base line on the protractor needs to be vertical. It is an acute angle.
  (b) It might help if you turn the page round until one of the lines is horizontal. This is an obtuse angle.

A2 (a)   (b)

T2 Try drawing angles from a horizontal line about 5 cm long.

Q1 Measure these angles to the nearest degree:
  (a)
  (b)

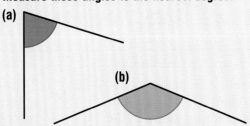

Q2 Draw these angles using a protractor:
  (a) 39°   (b) 172°

Chapter 26

Symmetry of 2-D shapes

You should be able to recognise all the symmetries of 2-D shapes.

You should already know how to find the number of lines of symmetry and the order of rotational symmetry for a 2-D shape.

Polygons

A polygon is a 2-D shape with any number of straight sides. A regular polygon has equal sides and equal angles. Most of the polygons you will come across have special names: these are given in the table below – make sure you learn them.

Number of sides	3	4	5	6	7	8	9	10
Name	triangle	quadrilateral	pentagon	hexagon	heptagon	octagon	nonagon	decagon

Line symmetry for 2-D shapes

Some 2-D shapes have line symmetry. This means you can cut them exactly in half using straight lines. If you can use only one line, we say the shape has 1 line of symmetry; if you can use two lines, we say the shape has 2 lines of symmetry, and so on. You can check that the following shapes show line symmetry by using tracing paper or a mirror:

 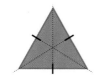

isosceles triangle   equilateral triangle   rectangle   square   regular hexagon
1 line of symmetry   3 lines of symmetry   2 lines of symmetry   4 lines of symmetry   6 lines of symmetry

1 Draw the lines of symmetry on these 2-D shapes:

(a)

(b)

(c)

    a kite

a diamond
(or rhombus)

an egg shape
(or ellipse)

(a)

(b)

(c)

1 line of symmetry   2 lines of symmetry   2 lines of symmetry

Symmetry of 2-D shapes

Rotational symmetry for 2-D shapes

If a shape has rotational symmetry, it can be turned, or rotated and will look the same from different angles. You can check the following shapes using tracing paper:

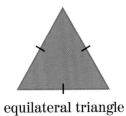

equilateral triangle
order 3

rectangle
order 2

square
order 4

parallelogram
order 2

regular hexagon
order 6

EXAMPLE 2 Find the order of rotational symmetry for these hexagons:

(a)

(b)

(c)

ANSWER (a) Order 2 (b) Order 3 (c) Order 1 (no rotational symmetry).

Check yourself

ANSWERS AND TUTORIAL

A1 (a 2
(b) 1
(c) 2

T1 Look back at the diagrams if you are not sure.

A2 (a) 2
(b) 6
(c) 4

T2 Look back at the diagrams if you are not sure.

A3 It has 8 lines of symmetry and its order of rotational symmetry is also 8.

QUESTIONS

Q1 Without looking at any diagrams, write down the number of lines of symmetry for:
(a) a rectangle.
(b) an isosceles triangle.
(c) a diamond.

Q2 Without looking at any diagrams, write down the order of rotational symmetry for:
(a) a parallelogram.
(b) a regular hexagon.
(c) a square.

Q3 Draw a regular octagon accurately. How many lines of symmetry does it have? What is its order of rotational symmetry?

Chapter 27

Metric and Imperial units

You should know the rough metric equivalents of imperial units in common use and be able to convert between one metric unit and another.

You should already know that the standard units of the metric system are the metre (m), the gram (g) and the litre (l). You should also know how to multiply and divide by powers of 10. You should be familiar with the Imperial units still in common use.

Metric units

Make sure you know the following:

LENGTH	MASS	CAPACITY (VOLUME)
10 mm = 1 cm	1000 mg = 1 g	1000 ml = 1 l
100 cm = 1 m	1000 g = 1 kg	100 cl = 1 l
1000 m = 1 km	1000 kg = 1 tonne	1000 cm^3 = 1 l

A metre rule   A kilogram of sugar   A litre of lemonade

When you deal with units it is useful to remember this important rule:

'To change from a larger unit to a smaller unit – multiply':   LARGE ⟶ small ⟶ ×

To change from a smaller unit to a larger unit – divide':   small ⟶ LARGE ⟶ ÷

1 Express each quantity in terms of the unit given in brackets:

EXAMPLE

(a) 3.2 m (cm)   (c) $1\frac{1}{2}l$ (cl)   (e) 3.2 tonnes (kg)
(b) 2500 g (kg)   (d) 78 mm (cm)   (f) 850 ml (l)

(a) 3.2 × 100 = 320 cm   (d) 78 ÷ 10 = 7.8 cm
(b) 2500 ÷ 1000 = 2.5 kg   (e) 3.2 × 1000 = 3200 kg
(c) 1.5 × 100 = 150 cl (f) 850 ÷ 1000 = 0.85 l

ANSWER

2 Mr Hardy's passport states his height as 1.83 m.
What is his height in centimetres?

EXAMPLE

Larger to smaller unit – multiply.
1.83 × 100 = 183 cm.

ANSWER

3 Mrs Hall is making a Christmas cake.

Her recipe requires the following ingredients: $\frac{1}{4}$ kg plain flour, $\frac{1}{4}$ kg butter, 400 g sultanas, 350 g raisins, 300 g currants, 250 g brown sugar and 60 g candied peel. Find the total mass of ingredients required in kilograms.

First change all masses to grams (changing them all to kilograms would give you difficult fractions to work with), then add them together. ($\frac{1}{4}$ kg = 250 g)

$250 + 250 + 400 + 350 + 300 + 250 + 60 = 1860$ g.

Smaller to larger unit – divide. $1860 \div 1000 = 1.86$ kg.

Imperial units

It is worth learning the following conversion tables:

LENGTH	MASS	CAPACITY (VOLUME)
12 inches (ins) = 1 foot (ft) 3 feet = 1 yard (yd) 1760 yards = 1 mile (m)	16 ounces (oz) = 1 pound (lb) 14 pounds = 1 stone (st) 2240 pounds = 1 ton	8 pints (pt) = 1 gallon (g)

4 The world's heaviest man was alleged to be Jon Minnoch who weighed in at about 980 lb. How many stones did he weigh?

Smaller to larger unit – divide. $980 \div 14 = 70$ stones.

Imperial units and their metric equivalents

Approximate metric equivalents for the Imperial units still in use:

LENGTH	MASS	CAPACITY (VOLUME)
1 in is about 2.5 cm 1 ft is about 30 cm 1 yd is about 90 cm 1 mile is about 1.6 km (or 5 miles is about 8 km)	1 oz is about 30 g 1 lb is about 450 g 1 st is about 6.5 kg 1 ton is about 1 tonne	1 pint is about 0.5 l 1 gallon is about 4.5 l

Remember: to change imperial to metric units, multiply.

5 Monsieur Braun is on holiday in England and he sees a road sign on the M1 stating it is 120 miles to Birmingham. Approximately, how many kilometres is this?

$120 \times 1.6 = 192$. So, the distance is approximately 192 km.

**Metric and
Imperial units**

6 Mr Hargreaves buys a 'firkin' of beer for his firm's Christmas Party. The beer is to be served in $\frac{1}{2}l$ glasses. How many glasses of beer can be served? (A 'firkin' is a barrel of beer containing 9 gallons).

EXAMPLE

Change 9 gallons into litres. This is $9 \times 4.5 = 40.5\ l$. To find the number of glasses, find $40.5 \div \frac{1}{2}$. $40.5 \div 0.5 = 81$.
So, approximately 81 glasses of beer can be served.

ANSWER

Check yourself

QUESTIONS

Remember: you can use your calculator.

Q1 Express each quantity in terms of the unit given in brackets:
- (a) 8.32 km (m)
- (b) 152 cm (m)
- (c) 4385 g (kg)
- (d) 800 mg (g)
- (e) $4.7\,l$ (cl)
- (f) 420 cm³ (l)

Q2 A lorry carrying 85 sacks of potatoes to a local supermarket comes to a bridge displaying this sign:

> **MAXIMUM
> WEIGHT
> 10 TONNES**

The driver knows that the mass of the lorry is $4\frac{1}{2}$ tonnes and that the mass of each sack is 50 kg. Can the lorry cross the bridge safely?

Q3 Using the conversions tables given earlier (pages 87 and 88), find the approximate metric equivalents for the following: (the units required are in brackets).

| 500 gallons crude oil | 2 lb flour | To the Beach 1/2 mile → |

(metres)   (litres)   (grams)   (metres)

ANSWERS AND TUTORIAL

A1
- (a) 8320 m
- (b) 1.52 m
- (c) 4.385 kg
- (d) 0.8 g
- (e) 470 cl
- (f) 0.42 l

T1
- (a) $8.32 \times 1000 = 8320\,\text{m}$
- (b) $152 \div 100 = 1.52\,\text{m}$
- (c) $4385 \div 1000 = 4.385\,\text{kg}$
- (d) $800 \div 1000 = 0.8\,\text{g}$
- (e) $4.7 \times 100 = 470\,\text{c}l$
- (f) $420 \div 1000 = 0.42\,l$

(a) and (e): larger to smaller units, so multiply.

(b), (c), (d) and f): smaller to larger units, so divide.

A2 Yes.

T2 The mass of the sacks is
$85 \times 50 = 4250\,\text{kg} = 4.25\,\text{tonnes}$.
The total mass is $4.5 + 4.25 = 8.75$ tonnes.
8.75 is less than ($<$)10, so it is safe to cross.

A3
- (a) 1.8 m
- (b) 2250 l
- (c) 900 g
- (d) 800 m

T3
- (a) 1 foot = 30 cm, 6 feet = 180 cm = 1.8 m.
- (b) $500 \times 4.5 = 2250\,l$.
- (c) $2 \times 450 = 900\,\text{g}$.
- (d) l mile = 1.6 km = 1600 m
  $\frac{1}{2}$ mile = 800 m.

Chapter 28

LEVEL **5**
SHAPE, SPACE
AND MEASURES

Estimation

You should be able to make a sensible estimate of a range of measures in relation to everyday situations.

You should already know the metric system of units for length, mass and capacity. You should be able to name some everyday items which are about 1 metre, 1 kilogram and 1 litre.

EXAMPLE **1** Which units would you use to estimate the following:

(a) the length of a school playing field?
(b) the mass of a train?
(c) the distance from London to Moscow?
(d) the volume of water in Lake Windermere?
(e) the thickness of an exercise book?
(f) the mass of a sheet of paper?

ANSWER

(a) metres	(c) kilometres	(e) millimetres
(b) tonnes	(d) litres	(f) grams

EXAMPLE **2** The coach is 10 m long. Make sensible estimates for the length of the lorry, motor bike and taxi.

ANSWER Lorry: about 20 m; motor bike: about 2 m, taxi: 3–4 m.

Check yourself

ANSWERS AND TUTORIAL

A1 Your answers should be close to these:
(a) about 2 mm. (d) about 200 cm.
(b) about 30 g. (e) about 2–3 kg
(c) about 300 *l*.

T1 Remember you can check these afterwards.

A2 About 5 g.

T2 2.5 kg = 2.5 × 1000 g = 2500 g.
2500 ÷ 500 = 5 g.

QUESTIONS

Q1 Make sensible estimates for the following:
(a) the thickness of a glass (in mm).
(b) the mass of a packet of crisps (in g).
(c) the capacity of a full bath of water (in *l*).
(d) the height of your front door (in cm).
(e) the mass of a large dictionary (in kg).

Q2 A ream of photocopying paper (500 sheets) has a mass of about 2.5 kg. Use this information to estimate the mass of a single sheet of paper.

1. This is a rough sketch of the net for a prism:

Draw face A of the prism. Your drawing must be full size and accurate.

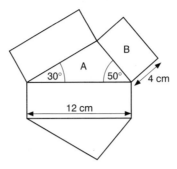

(1993 Paper 2)

2. Julie wants to make a boat out of card. She first makes a rough sketch of the boat. It is made out of a triangle and a trapezium:

(a) Make an accurate full size drawing of the triangle for the sail.
(b) Make an accurate full size drawing of the trapezium for the boat.

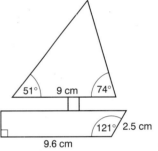

(1995 Paper 1)

3. Robert and Gwen must put 63 tins of food into a lift. Each tin weighs 840 g.

(a) Work out the total mass of the 63 tins in grams.
(b) In the lift there is a sign:
It shows the greatest load that the lift can carry safely. Is it safe to carry the 63 tins together in the lift?

> **Greatest load 50kg**

(c) Robert and Gwen must put the tins into a cupboard. All the tins are the same size. Gwen has measured the height of a tin. It is 14 cm. Robert has measured the height of the cupboard. It is 1.24 m. How many layers of tins can they keep in the cupboard?

(1995 Paper 2)

4. This is a sign in a lift:

> **This lift can carry up to 1000 pounds**

Six people want to use the lift.
They weigh: 65 kg, 85 kg, 114 kg, 72 kg, 93 kg, 79 kg.
One kilogram is just over two pounds.
Can they all go in the lift at the same time? Show how you worked this out.

(1992 Paper 1)

5. Carl has an old recipe for
egg custard with raisins:

He starts to change the amounts
into metric measures. Fill in the gaps
to show the **approximate amounts**
and the **units** which Carl should use.

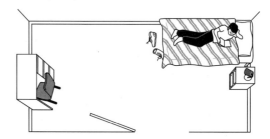

Egg custard with Raisins
$\frac{1}{4}$ **pound** of raisins

1 pint of milk
3 eggs
Put the raisins in an **8 inch** bowl.
Mix the eggs and milk and pour over the raisins.
Bake in the oven at 320° Fahrenheit
for about an hour.

About **100 grams** of raisins
About **0.5** _____ of milk
3 eggs
Put the raisins in a _____ **centimetre** bowl.

(1996 Paper 1)

6. This is a drawing of a boy in his room:

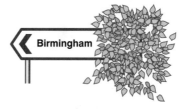

(a) Estimate the length of the real bed.
(b) Estimate the length of the real room.
Use your answer to part (a) to help you.

(1993 Paper 2)

7. Each measurement below can be given in different units. Fill in the units which would be
used. Choose your units from this list: **feet, kilometres, metres, miles**.

(a) The height of the girl is 1.53 ....
or 5 ....

(b) The distance from Cardiff to
Birmingham is 196 .... or 122 ....

(1993 Paper 1)

8. Find the number of lines of symmetry and the order of rotational symmetry
for each 2D-shape:

a)

b)

c)

d)

e)

(1992 Paper 2)

Chapter 29

Mean and range

You should understand and use the mean of a set of discrete data. You should be able to compare two distributions using the range and one of the averages.

You should already know how to collect data and you should understand the term 'average'. You should also know how to interpret frequency tables and diagrams.

The mean

The 'average' contents of a box of drawing pins is 144. The 'average' annual rainfall in Borrowdale is 43.9 cm (the wettest place in England!). When we calculate these averages, it is the 'mean average' (or just the word mean) that has been found. Remember in mathematics there are three types of average: mean, mode and median (see pages 45 to 47).

The mean is a useful average because it takes all values into account. To find the mean of a set of data, you add up all the values and divide by the number of values in the list:

$$\text{mean (the symbol for the mean is } \bar{x}) = \frac{\text{all the values added together}}{\text{the total number of values}}$$

Townley Grammar School for Girls

1 A sponsored cycle race was held to help raise money for a school minibus. 10 pupils gave in the following amounts of money: £6, £10, £8, £12, £14, £20, £5, £10, £15, £16. Find the mean amount that the pupils raised.

The total amount raised is £116.
The mean is £116 ÷ 10, which is £11.60.

EXAMPLE

ANSWER

2 After watching the TV news about life in China, Mandy wanted to find out the average number of children per family in her class at school. She asked 20 of her friends how many children were in their family, including themselves. She then made a frequency table for her data:

Number of children	Frequency
1	6
2	7
3	5
4	2

EXAMPLE

From the table she decided that she could calculate the mean average for the number of children in each family. Show how she could do this. Why could Mandy's answer not show an accurate estimate of the average family size for all families in Britain?

Mean and range

Number of children	Frequency	Total number of children in all 20 families
1	6	1 × 6
2	7	2 × 7
3	5	3 × 5
4	2	4 × 2

The table shows that 6 families had 1 child, 7 families had 2 children, and so on. We can add a column to the table to work out the total for all 20 families:

If you add together:
6 + 14 + 15 + 8 = 43.
The mean is 43 ÷ 20 = 2.15 children per family. Notice that it is usual to leave your answer as a decimal.

It would not be a good estimate because Mandy chose only 20 families: this is too small a sample to be able to represent the whole country (it did not include any families with no children, for example).

The range

For a set of data, it is sometimes necessary to show how the data is 'spread out' over all the values. To do this, we find the 'range' for the data. The range is the highest value minus the lowest value. Knowing the range is useful when we need to compare two sets of data.

EXAMPLE

3 Steve and Joanne kept a record in their school work diaries of all their maths' test marks. The table shows their results at the end of the year:

Steve's marks	42%	53%	68%	59%	64%	48%	70%	40%
Joanne's marks	55%	52%	66%	50%	55%	51%	53%	50%

(a) Find the mean and range of their marks.

(b) Comment on these results.

(a) Steve's mean mark = 444 ÷ 8 = 55.5%. Steve's range of marks is 70 – 40 = 30%. Joanne's mean mark is 432 ÷ 8 = 54%. Joanne's range of marks is 66 – 50 = 16%.

(b) Steve's average mark was higher, but Joanne had a smaller range of mark. This shows that she was more consistent.

EXAMPLE

4 Mrs Corbett and Mr Baxter both do their shopping at 'SuperShop' once a week. The amounts they spent over a 5 week period are given in the table:

	Week 1	Week 2	Week 3	Week 4	Week 5
Mrs Corbett	£95.70	£102.30	£93.00	£98.10	£101.60
Mr Baxter	£86.90	£84.00	£87.80	£79.40	£80.50

(a) Find the mean and range of the amounts they spent.

(b) What can you deduce from these values?

(a) Mrs Corbett's mean amount spent is £490.70 ÷ 5 = £98.14. Her range is £102.30 – £93 = £9.30. Mr Baxter's mean amount spent is £418.60 ÷ 5 = £83.72. His range is £87.80 – £79.40 = £8.40.

(b) On average Mrs Corbett spends more - the Corbett family might be larger than the Baxter family. The ranges are very close, showing both of them are very consistent in their shopping habits.

ANSWER

Check yourself

QUESTIONS

Remember that you can use your calculator.

Q1 Find the mean and range of each set of numbers:
(a) 12, 14, 18, 17, 14, 11, 16, 10.
(b) 135, 143, 150, 149, 158, 162.
(c) 3.2, 5.4, 2.5, 4.6, 3.8.

Q2 Over the year, the average monthly temperatures for Narvic in Norway are:
–6 °C, –5 °C, –3 °C, 2 °C, 6 °C, 10 °C, 14 °C, 13 °C, 9 °C, 4 °C, 0 °C, –2 °C.
Find the mean and range of these temperatures.

Q3 The bar graph shows the amount of time Claire and Sarah spent on homework during the week.

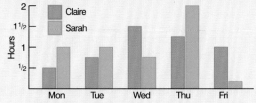

(a) Find the average amount of time each one spent on homework during the week.
(b) Find the range of times for each of them.
(c) Using these values, comment on what you notice.

ANSWERS AND TUTORIAL

A1 (a) 14 and 8. (c) 3.9 and 2.9.
(b) 149.5 and 27.

T1 (a) The mean is 112 ÷ 8 = 14.
The range is 18 – 10 = 8.
(b) The mean is 897 ÷ 6 = 149.5.
The range is 162 – 135 = 27.
(c) The mean is 19.5 ÷ 5 = 3.9.
The range is 5.4 – 2.5 = 2.9.

A2 3.5 °C and 20 °C.

T2 The mean is 42 ÷ 12 = 3.5. Be careful how you add together the minus numbers and remember to count 0. The range is 20 °C (14 – (–6) = 20).

A3 (a) Claire: 1 hour; Sarah: 1 hour.
(b) Claire: 1 hour; Sarah: $1\frac{3}{4}$ hours
(c) Their means are the same. This shows they spent the same amount of time on their homework over the week. Sarah's range is wider than Claire's which shows she is more variable on the time she spends.

T3 (a) Claire's mean is
$$\frac{\frac{1}{2} + \frac{3}{4} + 1\frac{1}{2} + 1\frac{1}{4} + 1}{5} = 1 \text{ hour.}$$
Sarah's mean is
$$\frac{1 + 1 + \frac{3}{4} + 2 + \frac{1}{4}}{5} = 1 \text{ hour.}$$
(b) Claire's range is $1\frac{1}{2} - \frac{1}{2} = 1$ hour.
Sarah's range is $2 - \frac{1}{4} = 1\frac{3}{4}$ hours.

Chapter 30

Pie charts

You should be able to interpret graphs and diagrams, including pie charts and make sense of them.

You should already know how to interpret frequency tables and diagrams.

Data is easily displayed on bar charts and frequency diagrams and can be readily interpreted. If there are not too many **categories** for the data, then it is often useful to display the data on a **pie chart** or **circular diagram.** Pie charts are very useful for displaying data because they are very easy to understand at a glance. This is why they are often used in advertising and in the business world.

EXAMPLE

1 Mr Hebson was doing surveys with his Year 9 class in their maths lesson. Each pupil had to do a survey of their own choice and then draw a pie chart to display their data.

Val decided to show how she has spent her day at school:

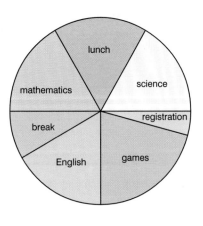

(a) Which lesson was the longest? How can you tell?

(b) If Val spent six hours at school:

(i) How long was the maths lesson?

(ii) If maths and English lessons lasted for the same time, how long was break?

ANSWER

(a) Games.

The slice or **sector** labelled games is the largest.

(b) (i) 1 hour.

The sectors for maths, lunch and science are all the same size and take up half of the diagram – this represents 3 hours. So, maths is 1 hour.

(ii) $\frac{1}{2}$ hour.

The sectors for English and break take up $\frac{1}{4}$ of the diagram which represents $1\frac{1}{2}$ hours. English is 1 hour, so this leaves $\frac{1}{2}$ hour for break.

2 In the same survey, David decided to find out what method of transport the pupils in the class had used to get to school that morning:

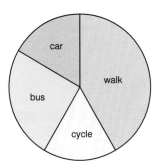

(a) What does the diagram tell you about those pupils who cycled or came by car?

(b) If 9 pupils came on the bus, how many pupils were in the class?

(c) Can you tell how many walked?

(a) The same number of pupils cycled or came by car, since the sectors are the same size.

(b) 36. The bus sector is $\frac{1}{4}$ of the chart which represents 9 pupils, so total number of pupils is 4 x 9 = 36.

(c) Not easily, since it is difficult to find the fraction of the diagram for those who walked. It is more than $\frac{1}{4}$ which is 9 pupils, and less than $\frac{1}{2}$ which is 18 pupils. You could estimate that about 15 pupils walked to school.

Check yourself

QUESTIONS

Q1 The pie chart shows the age distribution of Britain:

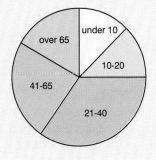

(a) Estimate the size of the fraction for:
   (i) the under 10 age group.
   (ii) the 21-40 age group.
(b) Can you find the population of Britain from the diagram?
(c) The population of Britain is nearly 60 million. Estimate the number of people who are over 65.

ANSWERS AND TUTORIAL

A1 (a) (i) About $\frac{1}{8}$. (ii) About $\frac{1}{3}$.
    (b) No. (c) About 10 million.

T1 (a) (i) About 8 of these sectors would fit in the chart.
       (ii) About 3 of these sectors would fit in the chart.
       These are only estimates: you will be allowed answers that are close to these fractions.
    (b) The pie chart only shows the proportions of the population.
    (c) $60 \div 6 = 10$. The sector is about $\frac{1}{6}$ of the diagram.

ANSWERS AND TUTORIAL

A2 (a) **About 20%**
    (b) (i) **£60.**
         (ii) **12%.**

T2 (a) An answer between 16% and 24% is
         acceptable.
    (b) (i) 1% of £400 is £4.
              15% is £4 × 15 = £60.
         (ii) Use part (i) to help: 1% of £400 is £4, so, £48
              is 12%.

QUESTIONS

Q2 The pie chart shows how Mr and Mrs Hadwin
    spend their money during a typical week of the
    year:

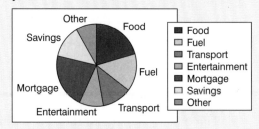

(a) **Estimate the percentage amount they
     spend on food.**
(b) **One week, Mr and Mrs Hadwin have £400
     to spend.**
(i) **If they spend 15% on fuel, how much
     money is this?**
(ii) **If they spend £48 on transport, what
     percentage of the total is this?**

A3 (a) **360° ÷ 24 = 15°.**
    (b)

Activity	Angle of sector	No. of hours
Sleeping	135°	9
School	105°	7
Meals	30°	2
Watching TV	45°	3
Travelling	15°	1
Youth Club	30°	2

T3 (a) 1 complete turn = 360°. 1 day = 24 hours.
         1 hour = 360° ÷ 24 = 15°.
    (b) The angles were made easy to measure.
         Check the total is 360°. Divide the angles
         by 15 to get the number of hours.

Q3 Mitchell drew a pie chart to show how he
    spent the day:

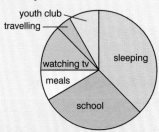

He calculated that each hour of the day is
represented by 15° on the pie chart.
(a) **Show how he
     calculated
     that 1 hour
     equals 15°.**
(b) **By measuring
     the angle for
     each sector,
     complete the
     frequency
     table:**

Activity	Angle of sector	No. of hours
Sleeping		
School		
Meals		
Watching TV		
Travelling		
Youth Club		

Chapter 31

You should understand and use the probability scale from 0 to 1.
You should be able to find and justify probabilities using either
experimental evidence or theoretical probabilities.

You should already know the terms unlikely, likely, fair and certain.
The probability of an event happening can be anywhere between
impossible and certain, as this probability scale shows:

In maths, probability is calculated either by using theory, by doing
experiments or by collecting data. The probability that an event will
happen is usually written as a fraction, but it can also be given as a
decimal or a percentage. An event that is impossible has a probability
of 0 and an event that is certain has a probability of 1. All other
probabilities lie between 0 and 1.

1 Draw an arrow on a scale to show the probability of getting a
'head' when a coin is thrown.

EXAMPLE

There are two possibilities: 'heads'
or 'tails'. This is a 1 in 2 chance or $\frac{1}{2}$.

ANSWER

2 Draw an arrow on a scale to show the probability of
getting a '6' when a dice is thrown.

EXAMPLE

There are six possible scores:
1, 2, 3, 4, 5, 6.
This is a 1 in 6 chance or $\frac{1}{6}$.

ANSWER

Check yourself

QUESTIONS

Q1 Draw arrows on a probability scale to show the
probabilities for the following events:
(a) Picking a club from a well shuffled pack of
cards.
(b) Choosing a letter at random from the word
'ABSTEMIOUS' that is a vowel.
(c) Winning a game of chess, playing against
a very skilled player.
(d) You getting maths homework next week.

ANSWERS AND TUTORIAL

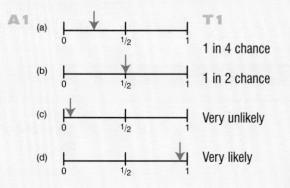

A1
(a)

T1
1 in 4 chance

(b)
1 in 2 chance

(c)
Very unlikely

(d)
Very likely

Chapter 32

Calculating probabilities

You should know that different outcomes may result from repeating the same experiment.

You should already know how to use the probability scale from 0 and 1. You will need to learn how to calculate or estimate probability by using experimental data or statistical data. Probabilities can be calculated by using different methods.

Method 1: equally likely outcomes

An **event** is a particular 'happening' for which we want to find the probability. Every event has a set of 'outcomes': different possibilities that could happen. When throwing a coin, for example, there are 2 outcomes: 'heads' or 'tails'. When throwing a dice there are 6 outcomes: 1, 2, 3, 4, 5 or 6. All the outcomes have the same chance of happening. We say that they are 'equally likely outcomes'. So, the probability of getting a 'head' is a 1 in 2 chance or $\frac{1}{2}$ and the probability of getting a 6 is a 1 in 6 chance or $\frac{1}{6}$. We can write these probabilities as: P('head') = $\frac{1}{2}$ and P(6) = $\frac{1}{6}$.

So, an important definition is:

$$\textbf{P(event)} = \frac{\textbf{number of favourable outcomes}}{\textbf{total number of outcomes possible}}$$

This formula for calculating a probability gives a **probability fraction** for an event. This fraction can also be written as a decimal or a percentage. Remember that a probability must lie between 0 and 1.

EXAMPLE

1 Find the probability of choosing a picture card from a well shuffled pack of cards.

ANSWER

There are 12 favourable outcomes: (4 Kings + 4 Queens + 4 Jacks). There are 52 equally likely outcomes possible: (the number of cards in a pack).

P(picture card) = $\frac{12}{52}$ = $\frac{3}{13}$

Method 2: experimental data

To estimate the probability for some events, sometimes it is necessary to carry out an experiment first, to show all the outcomes that can arise.

EXAMPLE

2 To estimate the probability that a drawing pin lands 'point up' or 'point down' when dropped, Alison dropped 50 drawing pins onto a table.

Point up	Point down
22	28

Estimate the probability that a drawing pin lands 'point up'. If Alison repeats the experiment will she get the same results?

There are 22 favourable outcomes out of 50 possible outcomes.

P(drawing pin lands point up) $= \frac{22}{50} = \frac{11}{25}$.

It is unlikely that she will get exactly the same results, but her probability fraction should be about the same.

Method 3: statistical data

To estimate the probability for some events, it is sometimes necessary to carry out a survey or look at historical data first.

ANSWER

3 Louise wanted to estimate the percentage of the people in England who are left-handed. She carried out a survey on 40 pupils in her year at school and drew a pie chart to show her data:

Use Louise's chart to estimate the percentage of people who are left-handed. How could Louise obtain a more realistic percentage?

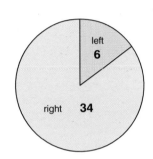

EXAMPLE

P(left-handed)$= \frac{6}{40} = \frac{3}{20}$.

ANSWER

So, an estimate for the number of left-handed people is 15%. To obtain a more realistic percentage, she would have to survey a complete age range of people and ask more people.

Check yourself

QUESTIONS

Q1 A card is chosen from a well shuffled pack. Find:
(a) P(choosing an ace).
(b) P(choosing a heart).
(c) P(choosing a King or a Queen).

ANSWERS AND TUTORIAL

A1 (a) $\frac{1}{13}$ (b) $\frac{1}{4}$ (c) $\frac{2}{13}$

T1 The total number of equally likely outcomes is 52.
(a) $\frac{4}{52} = \frac{1}{13}$ (b) $\frac{13}{52} = \frac{1}{4}$ (c) $\frac{8}{52} = \frac{2}{13}$

Always remember to cancel fractions.

ANSWERS AND TUTORIAL

A2 (a) $\frac{1}{4}$ (b) $\frac{5}{8}$ (c) $\frac{1}{2}$

T2 The total number of equally likely outcomes is 8.

(a) $\frac{2}{8} = \frac{1}{4}$ (there are two '3's).

(b) $\frac{5}{8}$ (do not include the '2's).

(c) $\frac{4}{8} = \frac{1}{2}$ (there are 4 even numbers).

A3 $\frac{2}{7}$

T3 The total number of equally likely outcomes is 49. The number of favourable outcomes is 14 (3, 13, 23, 30, 31, 32, 33, 34, 35, 36, 37, 38, 39, 43). P(at least one 3 on 1st ball) $= \frac{14}{49} = \frac{2}{7}$.

A4 (a) **30%**   (b) **60%**   (c) **80%**

T4 The total number of equally likely outcomes is 100.

(a) P(blue) $= \frac{30}{100} = 30\%$.

(b) P(green or red) $= \frac{60}{100} = 60\%$.

(c) P(not green) $= \frac{80}{100} = 80\%$.

If it's not green then it must be red, blue or yellow.

A5 (a) $\frac{21}{30}$ (b) $\frac{1}{10}$ (c) $\frac{4}{5}$

T5 The total number of equally likely outcomes is 60.

(a) P(car or van) $= \frac{42}{60} = \frac{21}{30}$

(b) P(lorry or bus) $= \frac{6}{60} = \frac{1}{10}$

(c) P(not a motorbike) $= \frac{48}{60} = \frac{4}{5}$. (60 − 12 = 48).

QUESTIONS

Q2 This 8-sided spinner is used in a game: Find:

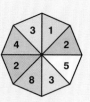

(a) P(a score of 3).
(b) P(a score greater than 2).
(c) P(an even score).

Q3 In the National Lottery there are 49 balls numbered 1 to 49. What is the probability that the first ball that comes out has at least one 3 on it?

Q4 A box contains coloured counters for the game 'Tiddlywinks'. If there are 40 red, 30 blue, 20 green and 10 yellow counters, and one is taken out at random, find the percentage probability of getting:
(a) a blue counter.
(b) a green or red counter.
(c) a counter that is not green.

Q5 James is ill at home and, to keep himself occupied, decides to do a survey on the type of vehicles that pass his house as he looks through his bedroom window. After one hour he had collected the following data:

Vehicle	Car	Van	Lorry	Bus	Motorbike
Frequency	35	7	4	2	12

Estimate the probability that the next vehicle to pass James' house is:
(a) a car or van.
(b) a large vehicle.
(c) a vehicle with more than 2 wheels.

TEST QUESTIONS

Answers with examiner's comments on page 240.

1. The school basketball team has an important match next week. The captain can choose Karen or Jo to be in the team. This term Karen and Jo have both played in 6 matches.

   The following list shows their scores: *Karen: 12 10 12 14 12 12.*
   Jo: 10 2 4 30 2 24.

   > Karen's mean or average score is 12.
   > Karen's range (her highest score – her lowest score) is 4.
   >
   > Jo's mean or average score is 12.
   > Jo's range is 28.

   Use the mean and range of Karen's scores and Jo's scores to choose whom you would pick to play in the next match. It doesn't matter which player you choose but you must use the mean **as well as** the range to **explain** which player is better.

   (1992 Paper 3)

2. Rita and Yoko counted the number of chips they got from two school dinner servers. This is what they found out:

   > **Number of chips**
   > **Server 1** *32, 33, 34, 35, 33, 31, 34, 33, 35, 30*
   > **Server 2** *39, 26, 25, 26, 39, 27, 40, 39, 39, 40*

   They worked out the **mean** for each server:

   They decided server 2 was better because the mean was bigger.

Mean	
Server 1	*33*
Server 2	*34*

   Then they worked out the **range** for each server:

   The **ranges** made them change their minds.
   They decided server 1 was better.
   Say why the **low range** for server 1 was good.

Range	
Server 1	*5*
Server 2	*15*

   (1993 Paper 2)

3. At a sports centre, people take part in one of five different sports. This table shows the percentage of people who played badminton, football and squash on Friday:

   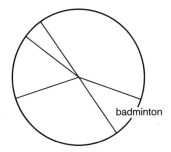

FRIDAY	
Badminton	10%
Football	40%
Squash	5%
Swimming	?
Tennis	?

   (a) Label the correct two sections of the pie chart **football** and **squash**.
       Badminton has been labelled for you.
   (b) On Friday **more** people went swimming than played tennis.
       Use the chart to estimate the percentage of people who went swimming.
   (c) Use the chart to estimate the number of people who played tennis.
       Make sure you have accounted for all the people.

   (1995 Paper 1)

4. There are 24 pupils in Jim's class.
He did a survey of how the pupils
in his class travelled to school:

Jim's class (24 pupils)

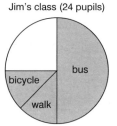

(a) 4 pupils travelled to school by train.
Show this on Jim's pie chart
as accurately as you can.
Label this part **train**. Label the remaining part **car**.

(b) There are 36 pupils in Sara's class.
She did the same survey and
drew a pie chart to show her results:
15 pupils travelled by **bus** and 6 pupils **walked**.
On Sara's pie chart write how many pupils
travelled by **train**, **car** and **bicycle**.

Sara's class (36 pupils)

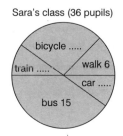

(c) Jim says: '15 pupils in Sara's class travelled by **bus**.
Only 12 pupils in my class travelled by **bus**.
Sara's pie chart shows fewer people travelling
by bus than mine does. So Sara's chart must be
wrong.' Explain why Jim is **wrong**.

(1996 Paper 1)

5. Sue puts 5 white beads and 1 black bead in a bag:
Sue takes a bead without looking.

Ed puts 8 white beads and 1 black bead in a bag:
Ed takes a bead without looking.

(a) The arrow shows the probability that Sue gets a **black** bead from her bag:

Put an arrow on the line to show the probability that Ed gets a **black** bead from his
bag. Put Ed's name above the arrow. How did you decide which side of Sue's arrow
to put Ed's arrow?

(b) Bob puts 2 white beads and 1 black bead in a bag:
Bob thinks he has a 50% chance of taking a
black bead without looking. He is wrong. Explain why.
What is the chance that Bob gets a black bead?

(c) Put an arrow on the line in part (a) to show the
probability that Bob gets a **black** bead from his bag.
Put Bob's name above the arrow.

(1994 Paper 1)

Levels 3-5

Mental arithmetic test 1: Levels 3 to 5

The Questions: Time: 5 seconds

1   Write the number three thousand and six in figures.

1	

2   What number should you subtract from twenty to get the
    answer thirteen?

2	

3   What is fifty-eight multiplied by ten?

3	

4   In a survey, one quarter of people liked tennis.
    What percentage of people liked tennis?

4	%

5   What is forty-two divided by six?

5	

6   Change one hundred and thirty millimetres into centimetres.

6	cm

7   What is four point seven multiplied by one hundred?

7		4.7

The Questions: Time: 10 seconds

8   What is double thirty-two?

8	

9   How many five pence coins make forty-five pence?

9	coins

10 What is seven hundred and fifty-eight to the nearest ten?

10	

11 On your answer sheet are two numbers. Write down the
    number which is half-way between them.

11		16	22

12 On your answer sheet is a scale.
    Estimate the number shown by the arrow.

12	

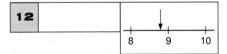

13 A television programme starts at ten minutes to seven. It lasts
    twenty-five minutes. At what time does the programme finish?

13	

14 One third of a number is twelve. What is the number?

14	

15 Gary collects ten pence coins. Altogether he has twelve
    pounds. How many ten pence coins is that?

15	coins

16 What number is nine squared?

16	

17 In a group of sixty-three children, twenty-nine are boys.
    How many are girls?

17	girls

18   What is one quarter of thirty-two?

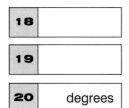

19   Subtract one hundred from six thousand and three.

20   The temperature in London was minus three degrees.
     Barcelona was twenty degrees warmer. What was the
     temperature in Barcelona?

| 20 | degrees |

21   Ten per cent of a number is thirteen. What is the number?

22   Write the number four and a half million in figures.

23   Write eight tenths as a decimal number.

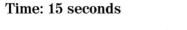

The Questions: **Time: 15 seconds**

24   The numbers on your answer sheet show how
     many children go to a Youth Club on three
     days. How many is this altogether?

| 24 | | 18   15   20 |

25   What is the cost of five cassettes at one pound
     ninety-nine pence each?

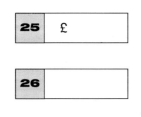

| 25 | £ |

26   The year is nineteen ninety-seven. What year
     will it be four hundred years from now?

27   A bag of oranges costs one pound forty-nine
     pence. How many bags could you buy with ten
     pounds?

| 27 | bags |

28   Look at the map on your sheet.
     The scale is one centimetre to five kilometres.
     Estimate how many kilometres it is by road
     from town A to town B.

| 28 | km |

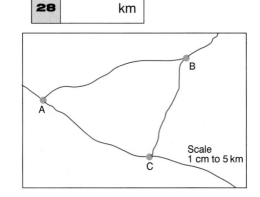

Scale
1 cm to 5 km

Chapter 33

Working with decimals

You should be able to order and approximate decimals when solving numerical problems.

You should already be able to add and subtract decimals with up to two decimal places. You should also know how to multiply a decimal with up to two decimal places by a single digit number.

This chapter looks at decimals in more detail and deals with rounding off decimals with different numbers of decimal places.

Place values in decimals

The number 234 has 2 hundreds, 3 tens and 4 units. Hundreds, tens and units are called the **column headings** or **place value** of the digits. These are all whole numbers. When we get parts of numbers we use decimals. To separate the parts from the whole number we use a decimal point. It always comes after the units digit.

Each column heading is ten times bigger than the one on the right of it or ten times smaller than the one on the left of it. This means that the column heading after the point is ten times smaller than 1 which is equal to $\frac{1}{10}$ or 0.1. The next after that is $\frac{1}{100}$ or 0.01. The next after that is $\frac{1}{1000}$ or 0.001. These are also called 'tenths', hundredths', 'thousandths'.

These are the place values for the number 362.794:

hundreds	tens	units	**decimal point**	tenths	hundredths	thousandths
3	6	2	.	7	9	4

1 Give the place value of the digit underlined in these numbers:

(a)   5.6<u>5</u>   (b)   0.71<u>4</u>   (c)   23.0<u>6</u>

(a)   6 tenths or 0.6   (b)   4 thousandths or 0.004

(c)   6 hundredths or 0.06

2 Put these decimals in order, smallest first:

2.3   2.202   2.32   2.21   2.33

2.202   2.21   2.3   2.32   2.33

Add zeros to give each number the same number of digits (same place value):

2.202   2.210   2.300   2.320   2.330

Working with decimals

Rounding off decimals

To estimate the answer to a sum that contains decimals, you need to round off the decimals. In previous levels you have rounded decimals to the nearest whole number or nearest 10. This will not work for a number like 0.326 - it would round off to zero ! Instead, round off to the first decimal place value in the number. For example, 0.326 rounds off to 0.3; 0.067 rounds off to 0.07 and 0.458 rounds off to 0.5.

EXAMPLE

3 (a) Round these numbers off to the nearest tenth:

   (i)   0.53   (ii) 0.189   (iii) 0.85

   (b) Round these numbers off to the nearest hundredth:

   (i)   0.032   (ii) 0.089   (iii) 0.055

ANSWER

(a) (i)   0.5 (1 decimal place, or 1 dp).

   (ii) 0.2 (1 dp)

   (iii) 0.9 (1 dp). Round upwards.

(b) (i)   0.03 (2 dp)

   (ii) 0.09 (2 dp)

   (iii) 0.06 (2 dp). Round upwards.

   You should always show how many decimal places you have rounded off to so that an examiner can see the level of accuracy of your working.

Mental calculations with decimals

After you have rounded off decimals, you can use them to estimate the answers to division and multiplication sums. For example, to work out 0.6×0.7, we work out $6 \times 7 = 42$ and we count the number of decimal places in the sum. There are 2 and there will be the same number in the answer, so the answer is 0.42:

$$0.6 \qquad \times \qquad 0.7 \qquad = 0.42$$
1 decimal place + 1 decimal place = 2 decimal places

EXAMPLE

4 Write down the answers to these sums:

(a) 0.5×0.7 (c) 0.5×0.03

(b) 0.04×0.08 (d) 0.5×0.6

ANSWER

(a) 0.35   (b) 0.0032   (c) 0.015   (d) 0.3

   In (b) and (c) you have to add zeros to make the decimal places up. In (d) the answer is actually 0.30 because $5 \times 6 = 30$ but it is not necessary to write down the final zero.

Calculating with decimals and whole number multiples of 10

To calculate answers to questions which use whole numbers and decimals we can use some of the techniques we learnt at level 5 for multiplying and dividing by tens and hundreds.

When you multiply a whole number by a decimal, each time you move the digits one place to the left on one number, you must move the digits one place to the right on the other. For example:

$0.8 \times 500 = 8 \times 50 = 400$
$0.06 \times 30 = 0.6 \times 3 = 1.8$

5 Work out the answers to:

EXAMPLE

(a) 0.7×40 (c) 500×0.3

(b) 0.06×400 (d) 70×0.08

ANSWER

(a) 28   (b) 24   (c) 150   (d) 5.6

When we divide, we move the digits to give a whole number. Each time we do this we add a zero on to the other number. For example:

$40 \div 0.5 = 400 \div 5 = 80.$
$300 \div 0.06 = 3000 \div 0.6 = 30000 \div 6 = 5000$

6 Work out the answers to

EXAMPLE

(a) $20 \div 0.5$ (c) $80 \div 0.02$

(b) $600 \div 0.06$ (d) $800 \div 0.4$

ANSWER

(a) $200 \div 5 = 40$

(b) $6000 \div 0.6 = 60000 \div 6 = 10000$

(c) $800 \div 0.2 = 8000 \div 2 = 4000$

(d) $8000 \div 4 = 2000$

Estimating with decimals

We can now use all of the methods described so far to estimate the answers to questions.

7 Estimate answers to:

EXAMPLE

(a) 532×0.61 (b) $789 \div 0.39$ (c) $\dfrac{32 \times 0.78}{0.25}$

ANSWER

(a) Round 532 to 500, round 0.61 to 0.6. The sum then becomes
$500 \times 0.6 = 50 \times 6 = 300$.

(b) Round 789 to 800, round 0.39 to 0.4.
The sum then becomes $800 \div 0.4 = 8000 \div 4 = 2000$.

(c) Round 32 to 30, round 0.78 to 0.8.
The top line is $30 \times 0.8 = 3 \times 8 = 24$.
Round 0.25 to 0.3. The sum then is $24 \div 0.3 = 240 \div 3 = 80$.

Check yourself

ANSWERS AND TUTORIAL

A1 (a) 4 tenths (c) 4 hundredths
(b) 6 hundredths (d) 2 thousandths

T1 You need to learn the column headings.

A2 4.002 4.02 4.022 4.202 4.21

T2 Add zero to give each decimal the same number of places.

A3 (a) 0.7 (b) 0.1 (c) 0.7 (d) 2.8

T3 Tenths is the first decimal place. Show this by putting (1 dp) after the answer.

A4 (a) 0.55 (b) 0.24 (c) 0.82 (d) 2.38

T4 Put (2 dp) after these answers.

A5 (a) 0.42 (e) 35
(b) 0.0016 (f) 40
(c) 0.009 (g) 360
(d) 0.45 (h) 6.3

T5 Count the decimal places.

A6 (a) 60 (b) 5000 (c) 2000 (d) 4000

T6 Make (a) $300 \div 5$ and so on.

A7 (a) $700 \times 0.08 = 56$
(b) $900 \div 0.3 = 3000$
(c) $50 \times 0.03 \div 0.3 = 1.5 \div 0.3 = 5$
(d) $300 \times 0.06 \div 0.9 = 18 \div 0.9 = 20$

T7 There can be other answers. They must be about the same and you must not use a calculator.

QUESTIONS

Q1 Give the place value of the digit underlined in these numbers:
(a) 2.4̲6 (c) 32.0̲4
(b) 3.5̲6̲7 (d) 0.97̲2

Q2 Put these decimals in order, smallest first:
4.02 4.21 4.002 4.202 4.022

Q3 Round these numbers off to the nearest tenth:
(a) 0.73 (c) 0.65
(b) 0.137 (d) 2.81

Q4 Round these numbers off to the nearest hundredth:
(a) 0.553 (c) 0.816
(b) 0.235 (d) 2.378

Q5 Write down the answers to these questions:
(a) 0.6×0.7 (e) 0.7×50
(b) 0.02×0.08 (f) 0.08×500
(c) 0.3×0.03 (g) 600×0.6
(d) 0.5×0.9 (h) 70×0.09

Q6 Work out the answers to:
(a) $30 \div 0.5$ (c) $60 \div 0.03$
(b) $300 \div 0.06$ (d) $200 \div 0.05$

Q7 Estimate answers to:
(a) 689×0.078 (c) $\dfrac{48 \times 0.029}{0.26}$
(b) $921 \div 0.27$ (d) $\dfrac{312 \times 0.061}{0.89}$

Chapter 34

Comparing numbers, fractions and percentages

You should be able to compare numbers and evaluate one number as a fraction or percentage of another.

You should already know how to simplify fractions (cancel fractions to their simplest terms) and you should understand what a percentage is. Fractions and percentages are very common in everyday life and you need to be able to use them confidently.

Comparing numbers

We can use a variety of methods to compare numbers. For example, we can compare 6 to 8 by writing 6:8 (the sign : means compared to). This is called a **ratio**. This ratio can be cancelled by a factor of 2 to give 3:4. The ratios 3:4 and 6:8 are the same   3:4 is the simplest form.

We can also express ratios as 1:n. To do this, we divide both by the first number in the ratio. To express 6:8 in the form 1:n we divide by 6. This gives $1:1\frac{1}{3}$ or 1:1.33.

1 Write these ratios in their simplest form:

(a)   5:10   (b)   6:9   (c)   15:35   (d)   12:27

EXAMPLE

(a)   1:2   (b)   2:3   (c)   3:7   (d)   4:9

ANSWER

2 Write these ratios in the form 1:n:

(a)   6:9   (b)   12:15   (c)   10:35   (d)   8:36

EXAMPLE

(a)   1:1.5   (b)   1:1.25   (c)   1:3.5   (d)   1:4.5

ANSWER

Expressing numbers as fractions of another number

In a class of 30 students, 18 are girls. We can express this as a fraction: there are 18 girls out of 30 students, or $\frac{18}{30}$. This can be cancelled by a factor of 6 to $\frac{3}{5}$.

3 A radio is priced at £60. £15 is taken off the price. What fraction of the original price is the reduction? Give the fraction in its lowest terms.

EXAMPLE

The fraction is $\frac{15}{60}$ which cancels by factor of 15 to $\frac{1}{4}$.

ANSWER

Comparing numbers, fractions and percentages

Expressing a number as a percentage of another

In the same class of 30 students, what percentage are girls? What percentage are boys? To change a fraction to a percentage we multiply by 100 (find out more about this on page 114). The calculation is $18 \div 30 \times 100$.

This can be done on a calculator as $18 \div 30 \times 100$ or $18 \times 100 \div 30$.

Some calculators also have a percentage button:

This does not work the same way on all calculators so make sure you know what your calculator does!

The answer is 60%. Boys must make up 40% of the class as $60 + 40 = 100$.

EXAMPLE

4 In a sale, a car is reduced by £120 from £960. What percentage reduction of the original price is this?

ANSWER

The percentage is $\dfrac{120}{960} \times 100$ which is $12\frac{1}{2}\%$

Calculating percentages of numbers

We have already looked at percentages such as 10% and 25%. In this section we look at how to calculate any percentage.

The word percentage means 'out of one hundred', so 13% of 90 means 13 hundredths of 90. This is the sum $\frac{13}{100} \times 90$.

On a calculator we do this as $13 \div 100 \times 90$. The answer is 11.7 This could be rounded off to 12.

EXAMPLE

5 (a) Find 12% of £68

(b) Find 45% of 165 books

ANSWER

(a) $12 \div 100 \times 68 = £8.16$

(b) $45 \div 100 \times 165 = 74.25 = 74$ books

Check yourself

QUESTIONS

Q1 Write these ratios in their simplest form:
(a) 2:10   (c) 5:45
(b) 8:20   (d) 15:55

Q2 Write these ratios in the form 1:n:
(a) 2:10   (c) 9:45
(b) 8:20   (d) 45:9

Q3 What fraction is:
(a) 12 of 48   (c) 8 of 30
(b) 16 of 40   (d) 9 of 30
Give the answers in their simplest form.

Q4 After having a special food a plant grows from
32 cm tall to 44 cm tall. What fraction of the
original height is the increase? Give the fraction
in its lowest terms.

Q5 (a) What percentage is 15 of 45?
(b) What percentage is 27 of 45?
(c) What percentage is 9 of 50?

Q6 After an attack by poachers there were 120
elephants left out of a herd of 150.
(a) What percentage decrease is this of the
original herd of elephants?
(b) What percentage of the original herd is left?

Q7 (a) Find 16% of £78
(b) Find 30% of 190 pupils
(c) Find 18% of £120
(d) Find 35% of 200 .
(e) Find 52% of £138
(f) Find 48% of 59 desks

ANSWERS AND TUTORIAL

A1 (a) 1:5   (b) 2:5   (c) 1:9   (d) 3:11

T1 Cancel by the highest common factor.

A2 (a) 1:5   (b) 1: 2.5   (c) 1:5   (d) 1:0.2

T2 Divide by the first number.

A3 (a) $\frac{1}{4}$ (b) $\frac{2}{5}$ (c) $\frac{4}{15}$ (d) $\frac{3}{10}$

T3 Write as fractions, then cancel.

A4 The increase is 44 − 32 = 12 cm.
The fraction is $\frac{12}{32} = \frac{3}{8}$

T4 The highest common factor (HCF) is 4

A5 (a) 33.3%   (b) 60%   (c) 18%

T5 The calculation in (a), for example,
is 15 ÷ 45 × 100.

A6 (a) 30 elephants have been killed:
30 ÷ 150 × 100 = 20%
(b) 100% − 20% = 80%

T6 In (b) take the decrease away from 100.

A7 (a) 16 × 78 ÷ 100 = £12.48
(b) 30 × 190 ÷ 100 = 57 pupils
(c) 18 × 120 ÷ 100 = £21.60
(d) 35 × 200 ÷ 100 = 70
(e) 52 × 138 ÷ 100 = £71.76
(f) 48 × 59 ÷ 100 = 28.32 = 28 desks

T7 You can divide by 100 first and then multiply. The
answer will still be the same.

Chapter 35

LEVEL 6 NUMBER

Equivalent fractions, decimals and percentages

You should understand and use the equivalences between fractions, decimals and percentages.

You should already know some of the equivalences between fractions, percentages and decimals. You should be able to cancel fractions and you should know how to divide and multiply decimals by 100.

In level 5, you learnt that fractions, decimals and percentages are basically the same. It is a matter of experience and judgement which to use when solving problems. In this chapter you learn how to convert between them.

Converting between percentages to decimals

To change a decimal to a percentage you multiply by 100. To change a percentage into a decimal you divide by 100.

EXAMPLE **1** Convert these percentages to decimals:

(a) 33% (b) 65% (c) 5%

ANSWER (a) $33 \div 100 = 0.33$ (b) $65 \div 100 = 0.65$ (c) $5 \div 100 = 0.05$

EXAMPLE **2** Convert these decimals to percentages:

(a) 0.24 (b) 0.7 (c) 0.625

ANSWER (a) $0.24 \times 100 = 24\%$ (b) $0.7 \times 100 = 70\%$

(c) $0.625 \times 100 = 62.5\%$

Converting between fractions and percentages

To change a fraction into a percentage divide the numerator (top number) by the denominator (bottom number) and multiply by 100, To change a percentage into a fraction write the percentage as a fraction with a denominator (bottom number) of 100 and then cancel down if possible.

EXAMPLE **3** Convert these fractions to percentages:

(a) $\frac{5}{8}$ (b) $\frac{1}{12}$ (c) $\frac{2}{3}$

ANSWER (a) $5 \div 8 \times 100 = 62.5\%$ (b) $1 \div 12 \times 100 = 8.33\%$ (2 dp)

(c) $2 \div 3 \times 100 = 66.7\%$ (1 dp)

(b) and (c) are rounded off to a sensible answer.

4 Convert these percentages to fractions:

(a) 45% (b) 62% (c) 80%

(a) $\frac{45}{100} = \frac{9}{20}$ (b) $\frac{62}{100} = \frac{31}{50}$ (c) $\frac{80}{100} = \frac{4}{5}$

EXAMPLE

ANSWER

Converting between fractions and decimals

To change a fraction into a decimal divide the numerator (top number) by the denominator (bottom number). To change a decimal to a fraction write the decimal, without the decimal point, as a fraction of 10 or 100 (see table) and then cancel down if you can.

number of decimal places	denominator
1	10
2	100
3	1000

5 Convert these fractions to decimals:

(a) $\frac{3}{8}$ (b) $\frac{4}{5}$ (c) $\frac{2}{7}$

(a) $3 \div 8 = 0.375$ (b) $4 \div 5 = 0.8$

(c) $2 \div 7 = 0.286$ (rounded off to 3 dp)

EXAMPLE

ANSWER

6 Convert these decimals to fractions:

(a) 0.3 (b) 0.76 (c) 0.125

(a) $\frac{3}{10}$ (b) $\frac{76}{100} = \frac{19}{25}$ (c) $\frac{125}{1000} = \frac{1}{8}$

(a) does not cancel, (b) cancels by 4 and (c) cancels by 125.

EXAMPLE

ANSWER

The best one to use

You will find it easier to spot which method to use in any question if you know your equivalences well. This will save you time as the following examples show.

7 A jacket priced at £63 is reduced by 33.3%. How much does the jacket now cost?

33.3% is the fraction $\frac{1}{3}$. As 63 divides easily by 3, use the fraction. $\frac{1}{3}$ of 63 = 21 and £63 − £21 = £42.

EXAMPLE

ANSWER

8 A line 25 centimetres long is increased by a factor of 1.2. How long is the new line?

With a calculator 25 × 1.2 is an easy sum. 0.2 is the fraction $\frac{1}{5}$ and $\frac{1}{5}$ of 25 is 5, so the answer is 30. In this case there is not much to choose between the different methods.

EXAMPLE

ANSWER

Equivalent fractions, decimals and percentages

9 To convert from miles to kilometres you multiply by $\frac{8}{5}$. How many kilometres is 32 miles?

The fraction $\frac{8}{5}$ is the decimal 1.6. It is easier to multiply by 1.6 than $\frac{8}{5}$.

$32 \times 1.6 = 51.2$ kilometres.

Check yourself

ANSWERS AND TUTORIAL

A1 (a) 0.67 (b) 0.22 (c) 0.08 (d) 0.175

T1 Move digits two places to the right.

A2 (a) 44% (b) 40% (c) 87.5% (d) 66%

T2 Move the digits two places to the left.

A3 (a) 75% (b) 20% (c) 28.6% (d) 88.9%

T3 (c) and (d) are rounded off to one dp.

A4 (a) $\frac{7}{25}$ (b) $\frac{12}{25}$ (c) $\frac{2}{5}$ (d) $\frac{2}{3}$

T4 Write over 100 then cancel down

A5 (a) 0.1 (c) 0.875
(b) 0.625 (d) 0.344 (3 dp)

A6 (a) $\frac{9}{10}$ (b) $\frac{17}{25}$ (c) $\frac{3}{8}$ (d) $\frac{13}{20}$

T6 Write over 10, 100 and so on, then cancel if you can.

A7 (a) 45% (b) 290 g

T7 45% of 100 is 45 so 45% of 200 is 90. You can also multiply 200 by 1.45

A8 (a) $\frac{1}{5}$ (b) 6 gallons

T8 $\frac{1}{5}$ of 5 gallons is 1 gallon.

A9 $\frac{9}{20}$ is 0.45. $170 \times 1.45 = 246.5$

T9 This can be rounded to 246 or 247 fish.

QUESTIONS

Q1 Convert these percentages to decimals:
(a) 67% (c) 8%
(b) 22% (d) 17.5%

Q2 Convert these decimals to percentages:
(a) 0.44 (c) 0.875
(b) 0.4 (d) 0.66

Q3 Convert these fractions to percentages:
(a) $\frac{3}{4}$ (b) $\frac{1}{5}$ (c) $\frac{2}{7}$ (d) $\frac{8}{9}$

Q4 Convert these percentages to fractions:
(a) 28% (c) 40%
(b) 48% (d) 66.7% (1dp)

Q5 Convert these fractions to decimals:
(a) $\frac{1}{10}$ (b) $\frac{5}{8}$ (c) $\frac{7}{8}$ (d) $\frac{11}{32}$

Q6 Convert these decimals to fractions:
(a) 0.9 (c) 0.375
(b) 0.68 (d) 0.65

Q7 (a) What % is equivalent to the decimal 0.45?
(b) A 200 g tin of cocoa is increased by factor of 1.45. How much does the new tin weigh?

Q8 (a) What fraction is the same as 20%?
(b) A 5 gallon can of paint is increased by 20%. How much paint is in the new tin?

Q9 A survey finds that the number of fish in a pond has increased by about $\frac{9}{20}$. If there were 170 fish in the pond, how many fish are now in the pond?

Chapter 36

Solving ratio problems

You should be able to calculate using ratios in appropriate situations.

You should already know how to write down a ratio and how to cancel down a ratio. In this chapter we look at how to use ratios to solve problems.

Cancelling ratios

So far all the ratios you have seen have involved only two numbers. But we can use ratios to compare as many numbers as we like. To find the simplest ratio we need to cancel down using the largest number that goes into all of the numbers (this is called the **highest common factor**).

EXAMPLE

1 Michael earns £100 a week. He saves £20, spends £30 on rent, £25 on food and the rest of his money on entertainment.

(a) How much does he spend on entertainment?

(b) Express savings: rent: food: entertainment as a ratio in its simplest form.

(c) Michael decides to save an extra £10 a week. He saves equal amounts on food and entertainment. What is the new ratio savings: rent: food: entertainment in its simplest form?

ANSWER

(a) $100 - (20 + 30 + 25) = 100 - 75 = 25$

(b) The ratio is 20: 30: 25: 25. This has a highest common factor of 5. The ratio cancels down to 4:6:5:5.

(c) He now spends money in the ratio 30:30:20:20. This cancels by 10 to 3:3:2:2.

Calculating with ratios

Many everyday problems use ratios. Most recipes, for example, give quantities of food to feed 4 people. If you need to feed 5 you would need ratios to increase all the quantities to allow for the extra person.

EXAMPLE

2 A recipe for pancake batter uses eggs, flour and milk in the ratio 1 egg to 3 ounces of flour to 5 fluid ounces of milk. If 3 eggs are used, how much flour and milk should be used?

ANSWER

The ratio is 1:3:5. If the first number is increased to 3, 3 times each value is

3:9:15.

So, 9 ounces of flour and 15 fluid ounces of milk are needed.

Solving ratio problems

3 £45 is to be shared between two people in the ratio 2:3. How much do they get each?

2:3 is 2 + 3 = 5 shares. 45 ÷ 5 = 9, so each share is £9.

The first person gets 2 × 9 = £18. The second person gets 3 × 9 = £27. (As a check £18 + £27 = £45.)

The key to solving ratio problems is to work out what one share is worth!

Check yourself

ANSWERS AND TUTORIAL

A1 (a) 2:3:4   (d) 1:2:4
     (b) 1:3:5   (e) 4:7:9:11
     (c) 2:5:6:7   (f) 2:3:7:10

T1 The factors are 2, 5, 3, 7, 2 and 6.

A2 (a) 5:2:1   (b) 2:1:1

T2 (a) The ratio is 15:6:3. Factor 3. In (b) The new ratio is 12:6:6. Factor 6

A3 (a) £16:£12   (b) £3: £9: £18
     (c) £55:£65

T3 Add the 'shares' and divide.

A4 1000 hardback books.

T4 2 + 5 = 7 shares. 1400 ÷ 7 = 200. 200 × 5 = 1000.

A5 560 fiction books.

T5 Start by dividing by 5 this time.

QUESTIONS

Q1 Cancel each of these ratios to its simplest form:
     (a) 4:6:8   (d) 7:14:28
     (b) 5:15:25   (e) 8:14:18:22
     (c) 6:15:18:21   (f) 12:18:42:60

Q2 In a day, Colin's computer is turned off for 15 hours, used for games for 6 hours and used for his work for 3 hours.
     (a) Write the ratio of time that Colin's computer is off : playing games : used for work.
     (b) After his boss finds out Colin has to work 3 more hours each day. He uses this time to work on his computer but still plays games for the same time. What is the new ratio for off: playing games: used for work?

Q3 (a) Share £28 in the ratio 4:3.
     (b) Share £30 in the ratio 1:3:6.
     (c) Share £120 in the ratio 11:13.

Q4 The ratio of paperback books to hardback books in my local library is 2:5. There are 1400 books altogether in the library. How many of them are hardback books?

Q5 In the same library (1400 books) the ratio of fiction books to non-fiction books is 2:3. How many fiction books are there?

T E S T   Q U E S T I O N S

Answers with examiner's comments on page 240.

1. Gary wants to print a rectangle on a T-shirt. The price for printing a shape in one colour is:

    up to 4000 mm²   £1
    4000 mm² and over   £2

    (a) These are the measurements of Gary's rectangle.
        Estimate its area. Also write the numbers you have
        used instead of 128 and 32.

    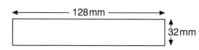

    (b) Using his estimate Gary thought that the price would be £1.
        Work out the actual area of Gary's rectangle to check if he was right.
    (c) Use your estimate to check if the area you calculated in part (b) could be correct.
        Describe how you did this.

    (1994 Paper 1)

2. Rosemary drew these squares using a computer:

    The sides of the squares are in the ratios 1:3:6:9.

    (a) The side of square Q is 12 mm. Use the ratios
        above to find the sides of squares P, R and S.
    (b) Write this ratio in its **simplest form**: side of square R : side of square S.
    (c) Write the ratio: Perimeter of square R : perimeter of square S.
    (d) Compare the ratios in parts (b) and (c). What do you notice about the ratios?

    (1993 Paper 3)

3. Steve needs to know the answer to 214 × 92. He works it out as 2354 but he thinks that he
    may have made a mistake.

    (a) Make a rough estimate of 214 × 92 and show the numbers that you use.
    (b) Compare your estimate with Steve's answer. Do you think he made a mistake
        in his calculation? Say why.
    (c) Now work out the exact answer to 214 × 92. Do not use a calculator for this.

    (1993 Paper 3)

4. Tanya says 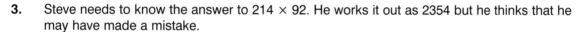 an increase from 40 to 80 is a 100% increase   Scott says   so a decrease from 80 to 40 is a 100% decrease

    Tanya is right. Scott is wrong. Say why a decrease from 80 to 40 is not a 100% decrease.

    (1993 Paper 3)

5. (a) One morning last summer Ravi carried out a survey of the birds in the school garden. He saw
        5 pigeons, 20 crows, 25 seagulls and 45 sparrows. Complete the line below to show the ratios

        pigeons : crows : seagulls : sparrows
        1 : .... : .... : ....

    (b) What percentage of all the birds Ravi saw were sparrows?
    (c) One morning this spring Ravi carried out a second survey. This time he saw the same
        number of pigeons; 25 % fewer crows; 60 % more seagulls; $\frac{2}{3}$ of the number of sparrows.
        Complete the line below to show the ratios for the second survey

        pigeons : crows : seagulls : sparrows
        1 : .... : .... : ....

    (1995 Paper 2)

6. Bill, Ravi, and Eric are three divers in a competition. Each type of dive has a dive rating. Easy dives have a **low** rating; hard dives have a **high** rating. Every dive is marked by five judges who each give a **mark out of 10**.

How to calculate the score for a dive:

i. Look at all five marks. Remove the highest and the lowest marks.

ii. Add together the middle three marks to give a total.

iii. Multiply this total by the dive rating.

(a) Bill does a dive with a dive rating of 3.34. The judges give the marks 7.0, 7.5, 8.0, 8.0, 8.5. What is Bill's score?

(b) Ravi scored 82.68 on his first dive. The dive had a dive rating of 3.18. What was the **total** of the middle three marks given by the judges?

(c) Eric is getting ready to take his final dive. He needs to score at least 102.69 to win the competition. Eric decides to do a dive with a dive rating of 3.26. Explain why Eric has made a poor decision. Show your working.

(1996 Paper 1)

7. The information on the right is about ice-cream sold in a shop. Use this information to estimate the total income for the summer of 1995.

> Last summer 14 723 ice creams were sold.
>
> Roughly the same number of ice creams is likely to be sold in the summer of 1995.
>
> The ratio of cones to tubs sold is likely to be about 1 : 1.
>
> The cost of a cone is 60 pence. The cost of a tub is 40 pence.

(a) Write down the number you will use instead of 14 723.

(b) Write down the value you will use for the cost of an ice cream.

(c) Write down your estimate of the total income for the summer of 1995.

(1995 Paper 1)

8. Emlyn is doing a project on world population. He has found some data about the population of the regions of the world in 1950 and 1990.

Regions of the world	Populations (in millions) in 1950	Populations (in millions) in 1990
Africa	222	642
Asia	1558	3402
Europe	393	498
Latin America	166	448
North America	166	276
Oceania	13	26
World	2518	5292

(a) In **1950**, what percentage of the world's population lived in **Asia**? Show each step in your working.

(b) In **1990**, for every person who lived in **North America** how many people lived in **Asia**? Show your working.

(c) For every person who lived in **Africa** in 1950 how many people lived in **Africa** in **1990**? Show your working.

(d) Emlyn thinks that from **1950** to **1990** the population of **Oceania** went up by **100%**. Is Emlyn right? Tick the correct box: ☐ Yes ☐ No ☐ Cannot tell
Explain your answer.

(1996 Paper 2)

Chapter 37

Finding the nth term

You should be able to give a rule for the next term of the nth term of a number pattern where the pattern increases by a fixed amount each time.

In Level 4 Algebra you saw how number patterns built up and how to find next terms by writing down each term. But, if you want to find the 100th term, you cannot write out a 100 terms very easily. In this chapter we look at a rule which lets you to find any term of a number pattern without writing down each term. This is called finding a **general rule**. We say that we are finding the **nth term**.

Inductive rules

When we say something like, 'The numbers go up by 3 each time.', this is an **inductive rule**. You need the previous term to find the next one.

1   A teacher writes this number pattern on the board:

(a)   Describe how this number pattern is building up.

(b)   Find the   (i) 6th term   (ii) 10th term   (iii) 100th term

EXAMPLE

$$3, 7, 11, 15, 19, ...$$

ANSWER

(a)   The pattern is going up by 4 each time.

(b)   (i) $19 + 4 = 23$ (ii) $19 + 4 + 4 + 4 + 4 + 4 = 39$
(iii) The 100th term is 95 terms more than the 5th term so it is $19 + 95 \times 4 = 399$.

Finding the answer to (b) part (iii) is quite difficult. You can find the 10th term by 'counting on' but you cannot find the 100th. It is easier to use an algebraic rule.

Algebraic rules

An algebraic rule uses only the term number. You do not need to know the previous term.

In Example 1, the algebraic rule is: nth term = $4n - 1$. This means $4 \times n - 1$. The 10th term is $4 \times 10 - 1$ which is $40 - 1$ which equals 39. The 100th term is $4 \times 100 - 1 = 400 - 1 = 399$.

How can you find this rule? The easiest way is to use the 'difference method'.

The common difference

Take away each term from the term following it to find the difference between them:

The number you get is the number you need to add on each time. You get a 4: this tells you that the algebraic rule will have 4n in it. This also means that it will have something to do with the 4 times table. Next, write down the 4 times table next to the number pattern:

4n	4	8	12	16	20	24
4n – 1	3	7	11	15	19	23

It should then be obvious what you have to add on or take away. In this case the original number pattern is 1 less than the 4 times table. So the rule is 4n – 1.

EXAMPLE **2** Find the nth terms of each of these number patterns:

(a)   7, 12, 17, 22, 27, ...   (b)   1, 4, 7, 10, 13, ...

ANSWER (a) The difference is 5 so it will have 5n in the algebraic rule and have something to do with the 5 times table. Comparing the pattern and the 5 times table:

5n	5	10	15	20	25	....
?	7	12	17	22	27	....

It is clear that the pattern is 2 more than the 5 times table. The rule to find the nth term is therefore 5n + 2.

(b) The difference is 3 so the algebraic rule will have 3n in it and will be related to the 3 times table. Comparing the pattern and the 3 times table:

3n	3	6	9	12	15	....
?	1	4	7	10	13	....

It is clear that the pattern is 2 less than the 3 times table. The rule to find the nth term is therefore 3n – 2.

EXAMPLE **3** John is making matchstick patterns. Here are his first three patterns:

pattern 1   pattern 2   pattern 3

How many matches (m) will he need for the nth pattern? Write your rule using the letters m and n.

ANSWER If we write down the number of matches as a number pattern we get:

10, 15, 20, ...

The difference is 5. (It is going up 5 more each time). Comparing the pattern to the 5 times table gives:

5n	5	10	15
?	10	15	20

The pattern is 5 more than the 5 times table. The rule is m = 5n + 5

Write this as m = 5n + 5 because this is a rule connecting the number of matches (m) and the pattern number (n) so you must use the equals sign.

Check yourself

QUESTIONS

Q1 Find the nth term of each of these number patterns:
(a) 3, 6, 9, 12, 15, ...
(b) 1, 3, 5, 7, 9, ...
(c) 2, 5, 8, 11, 14, 17, ...
(d) 2, 8, 14, 20, 26, 32, ...

Q2 For each of the series of pictures below:

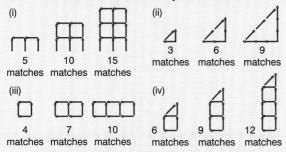

(i)
5 matches 10 matches 15 matches

(ii)
3 matches 6 matches 9 matches

(iii)
4 matches 7 matches 10 matches

(iv)
6 matches 9 matches 12 matches

(a) How many matches are needed for the nth pattern?
(b) Write down a rule connecting the number of matches needed (m) and the pattern number (n)

Q3 These are the lockers at the local sports centre:

Row E	5	10	15	20	25
Row D	4	9	14	19	24
Row C	3	8	13	18	23
Row B	2	7	12	17	22
Row A	1	6	11	16	21

(a) Explain why the locker number in the nth column of Row A is given by the rule $5n - 4$.
(b) Find a similar rule for the locker number in the nth column of each of the rows B, C, D and E.
(c) Adding up the columns of locker numbers gives 15, 40, 65, 90, 115, ... Find a rule for the nth term of this number pattern.

ANSWERS AND TUTORIAL

A1 (a) 3n   (c) 3n – 1
(b) 2n – 1   (d) 6n – 4

T1 Look for difference and compare the pattern to the times table. In (a) the pattern is the same as the times table.

A2 (a) (i) 5n   (ii) 3n
(iii) 3n + 1   (iv) 3n + 3
(b) (i) m = 5n   (ii) m = 3n
(iii) m = 3n + 1   (iv) m = 3n + 3

T2 For each example write out a table.
For example, for a (i):
Pattern: 1   2   3   4   5
Matches: 5   10   15   20   25
There are other answers, for example, (iv) could be m = 3(n + 1).

A3 (a) It goes up in 5 and 5 × 1 – 4 = 1 and so on.
(b) Row B is 5n – 3, Row C is 5n – 2, Row D is 5n – 1 and Row E is 5n.
(c) 25n – 10.

T3 This pattern goes up by 25 each time. If you add all the rules for rows A, B, C, D and E you get:
5n – 4 + 5n – 3 + 5n – 2 + 5n – 1 + 5n
This adds up to 25n – 10.

Chapter 38

Linear equations

You should be able to set up and solve linear equations with whole number coefficients.

You should already know how to use a number machine and find the inverse function. You have already met the idea of solving equations. In this chapter we look at setting up and **solving linear equations**. A linear equation is an equation that only has single letters in it (no square terms). Solving means finding the value of the letter.

The use of letters in equations

Using letters for numbers is common in maths. Most problems can be solved using common sense.

EXAMPLE

1 Find the number missing from the box to make these sums true:

(a) $\Box + 5 = 11$ (c) $\Box \div 2 + 5 = 7$

(b) $3 \times \Box + 1 = 10$ (d) $2 \times \Box - 7 = 13$

ANSWER

(a) The number in the box is 6 because $6 + 5 = 11$.

(b) The number in the box is 3 because $3 \times 3 + 1 = 10$.

(c) The number in the box is 4 because $4 \div 2 + 5 = 7$.

(d) The number in the box is 10 because $2 \times 10 - 7 = 13$.

You probably managed to do these problems quite easily. They are all examples of equation problems. They could have been written using a letter, not an empty box, as the unknown number:

(a) $y + 5 = 11$ (c) $\frac{y}{2} + 5 = 7$

(b) $3y + 1 = 10$ (d) $2y - 7 = 13$

We usually use y or x as the unknown letter but you can use any letter.

Solving equations

There are lots of ways of writing down the steps you go through in solving equations. Basically we are trying to 'undo' the equation. To undo the equation you must know how it was set up in the first place. The basic rule that governs how things are set up is **BODMAS**.

This stands for **B**rackets, **O**f (or p**O**wer), **D**ivide, **M**ultiply, **A**dd, **S**ubtract. This is the order that you must do things.

For example, $2x - 3 = 9$ is solved by taking the number x, multiplying by 2, and then subtracting 3. You can see what happens in this flow diagram:

$$x \longrightarrow \boxed{\times 2} \xrightarrow{2x} \boxed{-3} \longrightarrow 2x - 3$$

Linear equations

The three methods shown in this table all solve this equation.

1 Reverse flow diagram	2 Doing the same thing to both sides	3 Reverse operations
Set up the flow diagram, then reverse it and change all the operations in the boxes to the inverse operations. Run the number through and the answer comes out on the left.	$2x - 3 = 9$ $2x - 3 + 3 = 9 + 3$ $2x = 12$ $\dfrac{2x}{2} = \dfrac{12}{2}$ $x = 6$	$2x - 3 = 9$ $2x = 12 \ (+3)$ $x = 6 \ (\div 2)$

You will hear lots of rules like 'Change sides, change signs' and 'What you do to one side you do to the other'. There are so many ways to solve equations that we cannot show them all. In the rest of the examples we use the third method.

There is one rule that you can always follow however. Always check your answer works! If you do that then it will show you if you have made a mistake.

2 Solve these equations:

(a) $4a - 7 = 8$ (b) $\dfrac{b - 2}{4} = 7$ (c) $\dfrac{c}{2} + 5 = 3$

(a) $4a = 15 \ (+7)$
    $a = 3.75 \ (\div 4)$
    Check: $4 \times 3.75 - 7 = 15 - 7 = 8$ ✓

(b) $b - 2 = 28 \ (\times 4)$
    $b = 30 \ (+2)$
    Check: $30 - 2 = 28,$
    $\qquad 28 \div 4 = 7$ ✓

(c) $\dfrac{c}{2} = -2 \ (-5)$
    $c = -4 \ (\times 2)$
    Check: $-4 \div 2 + 5 = 3$ ✓

Equations with more than one letter term

At this level, equations with 2 letter terms are the most difficult that you will be asked to solve. The rule to follow is: 'Get rid of the smallest letter term by moving it to the other side of the equals sign'. When you do this, its sign changes (if it was plus, it becomes minus; if it was minus it becomes plus). Then you solve the equation in the normal way.

Linear equations

3 Solve the following equations:

EXAMPLE

(a) $4c - 28 = 2c + 4$ (b) $2d + 3 = 13 - 3d$

ANSWER

(a) $2c$ is the smallest letter term. To 'get rid' of it you have to move it from the right hand from the left side to the right side. This gives:
$4c - 2c - 28 = 4$
Collect the letter terms together $(4c - 2c = 2c)$
$2c - 28 = 4$
$2c = 32 \ (+28)$
$c = 16 \ (\div 2)$
Check: $4 \times 16 - 28 = 2 \times 16 + 4$
$\qquad\qquad 64 - 28 = 32 + 4$
$\qquad\qquad 36 = 36 \ \checkmark$

(b) $-3d$ is the smallest letter term. Move it from the right side to the left side. This gives:
$2d + 3d + 3 = 13$
Collect the letter terms $(2d + 3d = 5d)$
$5d + 3 = 13$
$5d = 10 \ (-3)$
$d = 2 \ (\div 5)$
Check: $2 \times 2 + 3 = 13 - 3 \times 2$
$\qquad\qquad 4 + 3 = 13 - 6$
$\qquad\qquad 7 = 7 \ \checkmark$

Check yourself

ANSWERS AND TUTORIAL

A1 (a) 19 (b) 8 (c) 40 (d) –1

T1 Check your answers!

A2 I started with 8.

T2 $8 \times 3 = 24$.
$24 - 5 = 19$.

QUESTIONS

Q1 **Find the number missing from the box to make these sums correct:**

(a) ☐ – 6 = 13   (c) ☐ ÷ 4 – 5 = 5

(b) 2 × ☐ – 1 = 15   (d) 3 × ☐ + 7 = 4

Q2

I am thinking of a number. I have multiplied it by 3 and then subtracted 5 from the answer. The final answer is 19. What number did I start with?

QUESTIONS

Q3 Solve these equations:

(a) $3a + 5 = 14$ (b) $\dfrac{b+3}{4} = 7$

(c) $\dfrac{c}{4} - 5 = 3$

Q4 Mr. Wilson needs 27 bulbs for his garden. He buys two packets of bulbs and 7 single bulbs. There are the same number of bulbs in each of the packets.

(a) Set up an equation to represent this situation.

(b) Use your equation to find the number of bulbs in each packet.

Q5 Solve these equations:

(a) $3c - 21 = c + 5$

(b) $2e - 3 = 15 - 4e$

(c) $3d + 8 = 5d - 2$

(d) $4f - 7 = 20 + f$

Q6 Four pupils hold up cards with algebraic expressions:

$3b - 4$	$4b - 5$	$3b + 2$	$b + 4$
Alex	Bob	Cath	Denise

(a) Show that $b = 1$ makes Alex and Bob's cards worth the same value.

(b) Find the value of b that makes Bob and Cath's cards worth the same value.

(c) Find the value of b that makes Bob and Denise's cards worth the same value.

(d) Two pupils have cards that can never have the same value. Which two pupils are they? Explain your answer.

ANSWERS AND TUTORIAL

A3 (a) 3   (b) 25   (c) 32

T3 Do not forget to check!

A4 (a) $2y + 7 = 27$ (b) $2y = 20 \; (-7)$
                                       $y = 10 \; (\div 2)$

T4 Check: $2 \times 10 + 7 = 27$ ✓

A5 (a) $c = 13$ (c) $d = 5$

     (b) $e = 3$ (d) $f = 9$

T5 Remember to 'get rid' of smallest letter term. In (a) subtract c; in (b) add $4e$; in (c) subtract $3d$; in (d) subtract f.

A6 (a) $3 \times 1 - 4 = 4 \times 1 - 5 = -1$

(b) $b = 7$ (c) $b = 3$

(d) **Alex and Cath: if $3b - 4 = 3b + 2$, no value of b will work.**

T6 In (b) the equation is $4b - 5 = 3b + 2$. In (c) the equation is $4b - 5 = b + 4$. In (d) try to find a number. You can't!

Chapter 39

Mappings and graphs

You should be able to express a mapping algebraically and interpret the general features of it.

You should already know how to write down an algebraic expression from a number machine, how to draw a mapping diagram and how to plot points in all four quadrants. This chapter shows how number machines, mapping diagrams, algebraic rules and graphs are all connected.

Take a simple rule such as $y = 2x + 3$.
A number machine for this would look like this:

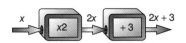

In (x)	Out (y)
–2	–1
0	3
1	5
–1	1

The table next to the number machine shows the numbers that come out of the machine (the y values) when various numbers are put into it (the x values).

These pairs of numbers can be written as a co-ordinate (x, y).
In a co-ordinate the first number is the x value and the second is the y value. For the table above the co-ordinate pairs are: (–2, –1), (0, 3), (1, 5) and (–1, 1).

We can also show this rule on a mapping diagram:

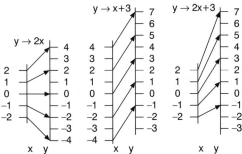

The first two diagrams break the rule down into two parts. These are the same as the boxes in the number machine above. The third diagram does the whole rule in one go. We can take the numbers at each end of the arrows and make them into co-ordinates. This will give the co-ordinate pairs (2, 7), (1, 5), (0, 3), (–1, 1) and (–2, –1).

We can plot all the co-ordinate pairs on a graph:

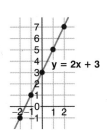

Of course you do not need to do a mapping diagram, a number machine *and* a graph every time you want to show a rule: they are *different ways* of showing the *same thing*.

1 Use the number machine with inputs of –2, –1, 0, 1 and 2 to complete the graph of y = 4x – 1.

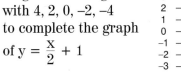

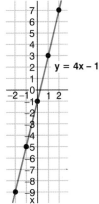

The co-ordinate pairs are (–2, –9), (–1, –5), (0, –1), (1, 3), (2, 7).

2 Use the mapping diagram starting with 4, 2, 0, –2, –4 to complete the graph of $y = \dfrac{x}{2} + 1$

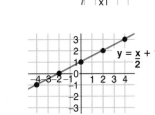

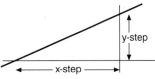

The co-ordinate pairs are (–4, -1), (–2, 0), (0, 1), (2, 2), (4, 3). The inputs were chosen as even numbers so that they would easily divide by 2.

Gradient

All graphs have a measure of steepness called the **gradient** which is found by this rule:

To find the gradient of a line, make that line the sloping part of a right angled triangle. You can find the gradient using the equation:

$$\text{gradient} = \frac{\text{y-step}}{\text{x-step}}$$

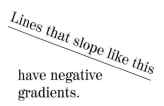

Lines that slope like this have positive gradients.

Lines that slope like this have negative gradients.

3 Find the gradient of these lines:

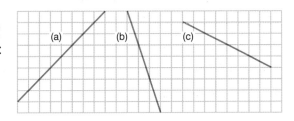

Drawing right angled triangles anywhere on the grid will give answers that cancel down to:

(a) 1   (b) –3   (c) $-\frac{1}{2}$ or –0.5
(b) and (c) are negative gradients

4 Draw lines with gradients of

(a) 2   (b) $\frac{1}{3}$ (c) –4

(a) If a line has a gradient of 2 there is a y-step of 2 for every x-step of 1. You can repeat this as much as you like.

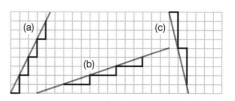

(b) If a line has a gradient of $\frac{1}{3}$ there is a y-step of 1 for every x-step of 3.

(c) If a line has a gradient of –4 there is a y-step of –4 for every x-step of 1. This is a negative gradient so the y-step goes down.

Check yourself

ANSWERS AND TUTORIAL

A1 Co-ordinate pairs are (–2, –3), (–1, 0), (0, 3), (1, 6), (2, 9).

$y = 3x + 3$

A2 Co-ordinate pairs are (–6, –3), (–3, –2), (0, –1), (3, 0), (6, 1).

$y = \frac{x}{3} - 1$

T2 Choose multiples of 3 as this avoids fractions.

A3 (a) 2 (b) –2 (c) $\frac{1}{3}$

T3 (a) and (b) have the same steepness but (b) is a negative gradient.

A4

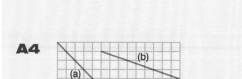

T4 (a) is 1 across 1 down. (b) is 3 across 1 down.

QUESTIONS

Q1 Use the number machine with inputs of –2, –1, 0, 1 and 2 to complete the graph of y = 3x +3.

$y = 3x + 3$

x → ×3 → 3x → +3 → 3x + 3

Q2 Complete the mapping diagram below and use it to complete the graph of $y = \frac{x}{3} - 1$

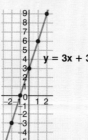

$y = \frac{x}{3} - 1$

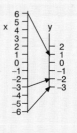

Q3 Measure the gradient of these lines:

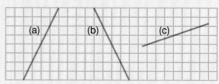

Q4 Draw lines with gradients of
(a) –1 (b) $-\frac{1}{3}$

Chapter 40

Drawing linear graphs

You should be able to express a mapping algebraically and interpret the general features of it.

You should already know how to measure a gradient and how to find co-ordinate pairs from a rule written as a mapping diagram, a number machine, or an algebraic rule. This chapter uses some of the ideas in the previous chapter to show you how to draw linear graphs. A linear graph is a straight line graph.

There are three ways to draw linear graphs:

- Plot the points.
- Do a **gradient-intercept**.
- Use the **cover-up rule**.

Typical equations for linear graphs are $y = 3x - 1$ and $2x + 5y = 10$. The graph of the first equation can be drawn by plotting the points or doing a gradient intercept. The graph of the second equation can be drawn using the cover up rule.

Plotting points

You only need two points to draw a straight line but it is better to always use three. Remember the numbers that go into the number machine or algebraic rule are the x-values. The x-value is always the first number in a co-ordinate. What comes out are the y-values, always the second number in a co-ordinate.

Sometimes you are told what x-values to use. If not you can choose them. Choose sensible values like –2, –1, 0, 1 and 2.

In a graph, the horizontal line through the origin (0, 0) is called the **x-axis** and the vertical line through the origin is called the **y-axis**.

---

1 Draw the line $y = 3x - 1$ if x is between –3 and 3 (this can be written as $-3 \leqslant x \leqslant 3$)

In this question we are given a range of values for x. Use x = –3, x = 0 and x = 3 as the three starting values and work out $y = 3x - 1$:

x = –3, y = 3 × –3 – 1 = –10.
This gives the co-ordinates (–3, –10).

x = 0, y = 3 × 0 – 1 = –1.
This gives the co-ordinates (0, –1).

x = 3, y = 3 × 3 – 1 = 8.
This gives the co-ordinates (3, 8).

You can put these results into a table:

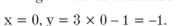

x	–3	0	3
y	–10	–1	8

This gives the graph :

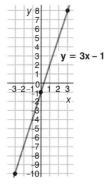

$y = 3x - 1$

Drawing linear graphs

Gradient intercept

Measure the gradients of the line in Example 1. You should find that it is 3. Look at where the line crosses the y-axis. This should be at –1. Look at the equation for this graph:

$$y = 3x - 1$$

3, the number in front of x (called the x-coefficient) is the gradient and –1, the number on its own is the intercept on the y-axis.

We can write this rule using an equation to use with all graphs:

$$y = mx + c$$

where m is the gradient and c is the intercept on the y-axis.

EXAMPLE | **2** | Draw the line $y = \dfrac{x}{3} + 2$

ANSWER

You know that the intercept, the point where the line crosses the y-axis is +2.

You also know that the line has a gradient of $\frac{1}{3}$. This means for an x-step of 3, there is a y-step of 1. Draw as many triangles as you like or do a table and join up the points.

x	–3	0	3
y	1	2	3

Finding the equation of a line from the graph

You can look at a graph and measure the gradient the line. This gives you the m value in the general equation:

$$y = mx + c$$

You can find the value of c by looking where the line crosses the y-axis.

EXAMPLE | **3** | Find the equations of these lines:

(a) 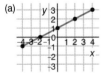   (b)   (c)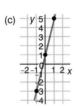

ANSWER | (a) $y = \frac{1}{2}x + 1$ (b) $y = x + 2$ (c) $y = 4x + 1$

Check the gradients and intercepts are correct.

Special lines

There are some special lines that you need to learn:

- A line that is vertical and so parallel to the y-axis. The equation for any line like this is: x = a, where a is a number.
- A line that is horizontal and so parallel to the x-axis. The equation for any line like this is: y = a, where a is a number.
- A line that starts bottom left and goes at an angle of 45° to the top right, passing through the origin (0, 0). The equation for this line is y = x.
- A line that starts bottom right and goes at an angle of 45° to the top left, passing through the origin (0, 0). The equation for this line is y = –x.

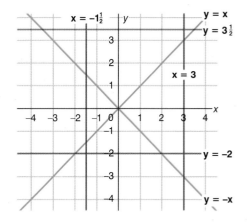

You can soon check that these rules are true by taking some points on these lines and showing that they obey the rules.

Note that the x-axis is the line y = 0 and the y-axis is the line x = 0.

The cover up rule

You can draw lines like 2x + 5y = 10 using the gradient intercept method but the equation has to be rearranged first. This is Level 8 algebra, which you would not be expected to do yet. It is easier to think about the point where this line crosses the x-axis. At this point, the value of y is zero. This means the y-term disappears so we can cover it up and solve the simple equation that is left. We can therefore find where the line crosses the x-axis:

2x + * = 10, so when y = 0, x = 5.

When the line crosses the y-axis the x-value is zero. We can use the same rule:

* + 5y = 10, so when x = 0, y = 2.

The line crosses the x-axis at 5 and the y-axis at 2. Plot these points and join them up.

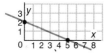

Normally we would need another point to check, but at this level we have to settle for just two.

4 Draw these lines:

(a) 3x + 4y = 12   (b) 2x – 7y = 14

(a)

(b)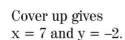

Cover up gives x = 4 and y = 3.

Cover up gives x = 7 and y = –2.

133

Check yourself

ANSWERS AND TUTORIAL

A1   (a) $y = -\frac{1}{2}x + 1$
       (b) $y = 2x$
       (c) $y = 3x + 2$

T1   In (b) the intercept is at the origin so $c = 0$.

A2   (a)   Points are $(-3, -4)$, $(0, -3)$, $(3, -2)$
       (b)   Points are $(-1, -6)$, $(0, -4)$, $(1, -2)$, $(2, 0)$

T2   There are other answers but the ones given are
sensible ones. Only three of the five points in (b)
are actually needed to draw the graph.

Graphs for Questions 2, 3 and 4:

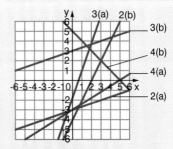

T4   (a) By cover up $x = 5$, $y = -3$
       (b) By cover up $x = 5$, $y = 5$

Graphs for Questions 5 and 6:

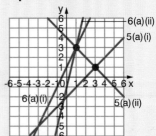

A5   Lines meet at $(3, 1)$.

A6   Lines meet at $(1, 3)$.

QUESTIONS

Q1   By measuring the gradient of each of these lines
and finding where they cross the y-axis give the
equation of each line.

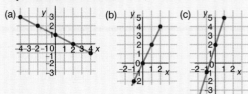

In the next
5 questions,
use a grid
like this:

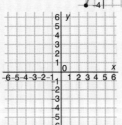

Q2   Using the plotting points method draw
the graphs of:

       (a) $y = \frac{x}{3} - 3$ (b) $y = 2x - 4$

Q3   Use the gradient intercept method to draw
these lines:

       (a) $y = 3x - 2$ (b) $y = \frac{x}{3} + 3$

Q4   Use the cover up rule to draw these lines:
       (a) $3x - 5y = 15$ (b) $x + y = 5$

Q5   (a)   Draw these two lines on the same axes:
           (i) $y = x - 2$ (ii) $x + y = 4$
       (b)   Where do the lines meet ?

Q6   (a)   Draw these two lines on the same axes
           (i) $y = 2x + 1$ (ii) $y = 4x - 1$
       (b)   Where do the lines meet?

TEST QUESTIONS

Answers with examiner's comments on page 241.

1. Lucy was investigating straight lines and their equations. She drew these lines:

   (a) $y = \frac{1}{2}x$ is in each equation. Write one fact this tells you about all the lines.
   (b) The lines cross the y axis at (0, –3), (0, 0) and (0, 4). Which part of each equation helps you to see where the line crosses the y axis?
   (c) Lucy decided to investigate more lines. She needed longer axes. Where will the line $y = \frac{1}{2}x - 20$ cross the y axis?
   (d) Draw another line on the graph which is parallel to $y = \frac{1}{2}x$. Write the equation of your line.

   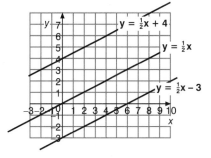

   (1994 Paper 2)

2. Four people each have a card.

    Ann   Rob   Carol   Daisy

   | 3b – 4 | 2b + 10 | b + 3 | b + 2 |

   Ann and Daisy have worked out a value for b to make their cards worth the same as each other. They wrote: 'If 3b – 4 = b + 2, then b = 3.'

   (a) Work out the value for b which will make Ann and Rob's cards worth the same as each other so that 3b – 4 = 2b + 10.
   (b) There are two people whose cards will never be worth the same as each other. Who are they? Explain your answer.

   (1994 Paper 2)

3. A teacher has 5 bags of marbles and 3 extra marbles.

   Each bag has n marbles inside. She asks: 'How many marbles are there altogether ?' The pupils say:

   | 8n | 3 + 5n | 8 | 15n | 5 × n+3 | (3 + 5)n |
   | Nia | Vijay | Sam | Jo | Karen | Glyn |

   There are 88 marbles altogether. Use one pupil's correct answer to complete the equation

   .... = 88

   Solve the equation to find n, the number of marbles in a bag.

   (1994 Paper 1)

4. This is a series of patterns with grey and black tiles.

   Pattern number 1   Pattern number 2   Pattern number 3

   (a) How many grey and black tiles will there be in pattern number 8?
   (b) How many grey and black tiles will there be in pattern number 16?
   (c) How many grey and black tiles will there be in pattern number P?
   (d) T = total number of grey tiles and black tiles in a pattern. P = pattern number.
       Use symbols to write down an equation connecting T and P.

   (1996 Paper 2)

5. A school has tables like this: 5 chairs fit round one table:

Mr Brown puts tables together like this:

The numbers of chairs he uses for up to 5 tables are shown below.

number of tables	1	2	3	4	5
number of chairs	5	7	9	11	13

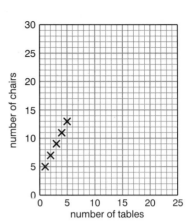

The points on the grid also show how many chairs he uses for up to 5 tables.

(a) There are 30 pupils in Mr Brown's class. How many tables should he put together so that each pupil has a chair? Use the graph to find the answer.

(b) Show on the grid how you have used the graph to find the answer.

(1993 paper 3)

6. Ice creams are sold as cones or tubs at the Beach Kiosk. A cone costs 60 pence. A tub costs 40 pence. The income (F) in pence of the Beach Kiosk can be calculated from the equation $F = 60x + 40y$ where x is the number of cones sold and y is the number of tubs sold.

(a) On 1st June 1994, $x = 65$ and $y = 80$. Work out the income. Show your working.

(b) On June 2nd 1994, $F = 4800$ and $x = 50$. Work out how many tubs were sold. Show your working.

(c) During the first week of last summer 950 ice-creams were sold. 437 of them were tubs. What percentage of the ice creams sold were tubs?

(1995 Paper 1)

7. The diagram shows the graph of the straight line $y = 3x$.

(a) Draw the graph of the straight line $y = 2x$. Label your line $y = 2x$.

(b) Write the equation of another straight line which goes through the point (0, 0).

(c) The straight line with the equation $y = x - 1$ goes through the point (4, 3). On the diagram draw the graph of the straight line $y = x - 1$. Label your line $y = x - 1$

(d) Write the equation of the straight line which goes through the point (0, –1) and is **parallel** to the straight line $y = 3x$.

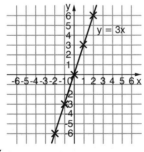

(1996 Paper 2)

8. Three people play a game with counters.
Each person starts with some bags of counters.
Each bag has m counters in it. This table shows what happened during the game.

	Start	During game	End of game
Lisa	3 bags	lost 5 counters	$3m - 5$
Ben	2 bags	won 3 counters	$2m + 3$
Maria	4 bags	won 2 counters	$4m + 2$

(a) At the end of the game, **Lisa** and **Ben** had the **same** number of counters. Write an **equation** to show this.

(b) Solve the equation to find **m**, the number of counters in each bag at the start of the game.

(1996 Paper 1)

Chapter 41

Isometric drawings

You should recognise common 2-D representations of 3-D objects.

You should know how to make 3-D models by drawing a net. You should understand front, side and top elevations for a 3-D shape. Drawing a 2-D representation of a 3-D shape can be difficult because you need to take into account the *perspective* of the drawing. This chapter shows you an easy way to draw 3-D shapes using **isometric paper** (triangular dotty paper). The shapes you will draw are **isometric projections**.

1 Draw the front, side and top elevations, and the isometric projection for the triangular prism.

EXAMPLE

ANSWER

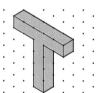

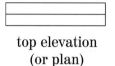

| front elevation | side elevation | top elevation (or plan) | isometric projection |

2 Draw an isometric projection for this letter 'T' when it is standing upside down.

EXAMPLE

ANSWER

Check yourself

QUESTIONS

Q1 Draw an isometric projection for this cuboid when it is standing on its face BCGF.

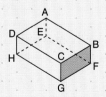

ANSWERS AND TUTORIAL

A1

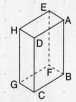

T1 Draw the face BCGF first, then the vertical edges 3 units high.

Chapter 42

Geometrical properties of shapes

You should know the properties of quadrilaterals and be able to recognise quadrilaterals from their properties. You should be able to solve problems using angle and symmetry properties of polygons and properties of intersecting and parallel lines. You should be able to explain these properties.

You should already know the language associated with angles and line and rotational symmetry for 2-D shapes. This chapter covers geometrical properties of 2-D shapes.

Describing geometric shapes

Each corner of this **quadrilateral** is called a **vertex**. The quadrilateral ABCD has 4 **vertices**. Each side is described by the 2 letters at each vertex. The quadrilateral has 4 sides: AB, BC, CD and AD. Each angle can be described in 3 different ways. For the angle at A you could:
(i)   use a small case letter – a.
(ii)   use the vertex letter with a 'hat' – $\hat{A}$.
(iii) use the 2 sides that form the angle – $D\hat{A}B$ or $B\hat{A}D$.

Properties of special quadrilaterals

You need to know the basic geometrical facts about the following quadrilaterals.

The square.

The 2 diagonals AC and BD bisect each other at right angles. The diagonals bisect the right angle at each vertex.

The rectangle.

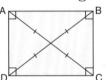

The diagonals AC and BD are equal in length (AC = BD). The diagonals bisect each other.

The parallelogram.

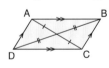

Opposite sides are equal and parallel. The diagonals AC and BD bisect each other but are not equal. Opposite angles are equal.
$\hat{A} = \hat{C}$ and $\hat{B} = \hat{D}$.

The rhombus.

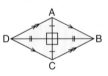

All sides are equal and opposite sides are parallel.The diagonals AC and BD bisect each other at right angles but are not equal. The diagonals bisect the angles at the vertices.

The kite.

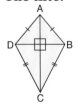

Two pairs of equal sides adjacent to each other. The diagonal AC bisects the diagonal BD at right angles.

The trapezium.

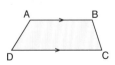

Only one pair of parallel sides.

Geometrical properties of shapes

1 In the rectangle ABCD, AB = 8 cm, BC = 6 cm and AC = 10 cm. Write down the lengths of

(a) CD

(b) BD

(c) DX

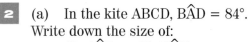

EXAMPLE

(a) 8 cm (opposite side).

(b) 10 cm (diagonals are equal).

(c) 5 cm (diagonals bisect each other).

ANSWER

2 (a) In the kite ABCD, $B\hat{A}D = 84°$.
Write down the size of:
(i) $A\hat{X}B$ (ii) $B\hat{A}X$

(b) Explain why $\hat{B} = \hat{D}$.

EXAMPLE

(a) (i) $A\hat{X}B = 90°$ (diagonals intersect at right angles).
(ii) $B\hat{A}X = 42°$ (diagonal AC bisects the angle at A).

(b) The diagonal AC is a line of symmetry.

ANSWER

Angle properties of polygons

You can find the angles in any polygon if you know the following:

The sum of the angles in a triangle:

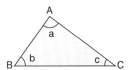

$a + b + c = 180°$.

The sum of the angles in a quadrilateral

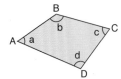

$a + b + c + d = 360°$.

You can find the sum of the interior angles for any polygon by splitting it into triangles:

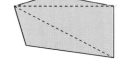

The sum of the angles in all 3 triangles equals the sum of the 5 interior angles in the pentagon.

So, the sum of the interior angles in any pentagon is $3 \times 180° = 540°$. In the same way any hexagon can be split into 4 triangles, so that the sum of the interior angles of a hexagon is $4 \times 180° = 720°$.
For any n-sided polygon, the sum of its interior angles, S, can be found by using the formula:

$$S = 180(n - 2)°.$$

**Geometrical
properties of shapes**

Interior and exterior angles of polygons

A pentagon has 5 interior angles which add
up to 540°. The diagram shows the 5
exterior angles of the pentagon. From the
diagram, a + b = 180°. This is true for all
angles in polygons.

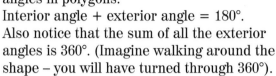

Interior angle + exterior angle = 180°.
Also notice that the sum of all the exterior
angles is 360°. (Imagine walking around the
shape – you will have turned through 360°).

A regular hexagon has 6 equal exterior angles
(marked x on the diagram). The sum of the
exterior angles is 360°. So, $6x = 360°$, and
$x=60°$. Therefore each of the interior angles is
120°. This is the quick way of finding the
interior and exterior angles for any n-sided
regular polygon:

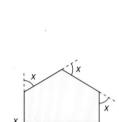

$$\text{Exterior angle} = \frac{360°}{n} \qquad\qquad \text{Interior angle} = 180° - \frac{360°}{n}$$

EXAMPLE **3** Calculate the missing angle in each of the following diagrams:

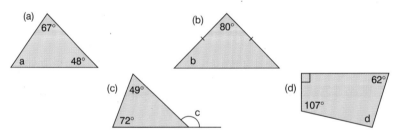

ANSWER

(a) $a + 67° + 48° = 180°$
      $a + 115° = 180°$
      $a = 65°$

(b) For an isosceles triangle
      $2b + 80° = 180°$
      $2b = 100°$
      $b = 50°$

(c) Let 3rd interior angle = x
      $x = 180° - (49° + 72°) = 59°$
      $c = 180° - x$
      $c = 121°$

(d) $d + 90° + 107° + 62° = 360°$
      $d + 259° = 360°$
      $d = 101°$

EXAMPLE **4** (a) Calculate the sum of the interior angles in an octagon.

(b) In an octagon, 3 interior angles are 132°, 158° and 124° and 3
      exterior angles are 45°, 71° and 18°. The remaining 2 interior
      angles have the same value. Calculate the size of each of the
      remaining interior angles.

**Geometrical
properties of shapes**

(a) Use $S = 180° (n - 2)$ with $n = 8$. $S = 180° \times 6 = 1080°$

(b) The other 3 known interior angles are 135°, 109° and 162°.
Let each remaining interior angle $= x$.
So, $2x + 132° + 158° + 124° + 135° + 109° + 162° = 1080°$
$$2x + 820° = 1080°$$
$$2x = 260°$$
$$x = 130°$$

ANSWER

Intersecting lines and parallel lines

When 2 lines **intersect**, 4 angles are formed: a and b are vertically
opposite angles or opposite angles and are equal. c and d are also
opposite angles. In the diagram $a = b$ and $c = d$.

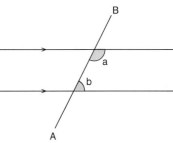

When the line AB crosses a pair of parallel lines, it is known as a
transversal. You need to know the following facts:

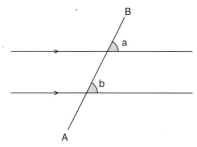

$a = b$
a and b are corresponding
angles
(Look for the letter F)

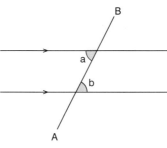

$a = b$
a and b are alternate angles

(Look for the letter Z)

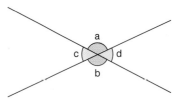

$a + b = 180°$
a and b are allied or interior
angles
(Look for the letter U)

5 Calculate the missing angles in each of the following diagrams:

EXAMPLE

(a)
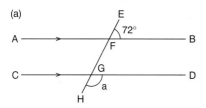

(b)
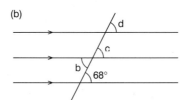

(c)
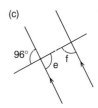

(a) $\widehat{FGD} = 72°$ (corresponding angles).
$a = 180° - 72° = 108°$ (angles on a line).

ANSWER

(b) $b = 68°$ (alternate angles); $c = 68°$ (opposite angles); $d = 68°$
(corresponding angles).

(c) $e = 96°$ (opposite angles); $f = 180° - 96° = 84°$ (allied angles).

Check yourself

ANSWERS AND TUTORIAL

A1 (a) **78°** (b) **58°** (c) **30°**
(d) **40°, 80° and 120°.**

T1 (a) Angles in a triangle = 180°;
a = 180° − (47° + 55°) = 78°.

(b) For an isosceles triangle, base angles
are equal;
b = 180° − (61° + 61°) = 58°.

(c) In first triangle, the 3rd angle = 180° −
(56° + 64°) = 60°; in second triangle,
angles are c, 90° and 60° (opposite angle).
So, c = 180° − (90° + 60°) = 30°.

(d) Angles in a quadrilateral = 360°;
d + 2d + 3d + 120° = 360°.
6d + 120° = 360°
6d = 240°,
so d = 40°.

A2 (a) **900°** (b) **290°**

T2 (a) Use S = 180° (n − 2) with n = 7;
S = 180° × 5 = 900°

(b) The 2 missing interior angles are 120° and
40°. So, x + 120° + 40° + 90° + 140° +
140° + 80° = 900°; x + 610° = 900°;
x = 290°.

A3 (a) **87°** (b) **63°**

T3 (a) Draw another parallel
line; a is the sum of
the 2 alternate angles.

(b) x = 72° (corresponding
angle); y = 45° (angles
on line);
b = 180° − (72° +
45°) = 63° (angles in
a triangle).

QUESTIONS

Q1 Calculate the missing angles in each diagram:

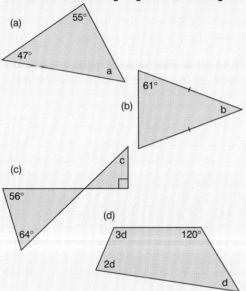

Q2 (a) Calculate the sum of the interior angles in
a heptagon.
(b) Find the missing angle x in the diagram:

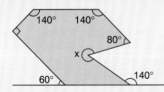

Q3 Calculate the size of the missing angle in each
diagram:

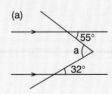

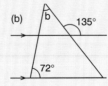

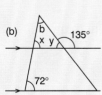

Chapter 43

Transformation geometry

You should be able to devise instructions for a computer to generate
and transform shapes and paths. You should be able to enlarge shapes
by a positive whole number scale factor.

You should already know the symmetrical properties of 2-D shapes,
how to find the exterior angle of a polygon and how to plot
co-ordinates. This chapter shows you how to draw shapes using a
computer program and how to transform shapes using **rotations** and
enlargements.

Using computer instructions to generate shapes

A computer language such as LOGO can be used to draw 2-D shapes.
You need to give a list of instructions or write a program for the
computer to follow. You need to know the instructions:

FORWARD a given distance of units.
LEFT TURN a given number of degrees.
RIGHT TURN a given number of degrees.
REPEAT an instruction a given number of times.

1 Write a LOGO program to draw a square of side 100 units.

EXAMPLE

ANSWER

FORWARD 100
RIGHT TURN 90
FORWARD 100
RIGHT TURN 90
FORWARD 100
RIGHT TURN 90
FORWARD 100

This is repeating 4 times: FORWARD 100; RIGHT TURN 90 and
can be written: REPEAT 4 [FORWARD 100 RIGHT TURN 90].

The computer drawing is shown on the right:

2 Write a LOGO program to draw the parallelogram:

EXAMPLE

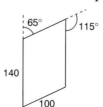

ANSWER

START
REPEAT 2 [FORWARD 140
RIGHT TURN 65
FORWARD 100
RIGHT TURN 115]

Rotation

A shape can be rotated through an angle about a centre of rotation.
You need to know how to rotate a shape clockwise or anticlockwise
through 90° or 180°. Remember that you can use tracing paper to help.

EXAMPLE

3 Rotate the flag through
90° clockwise about
the point A.

ANSWER Use tracing paper:

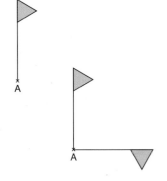

Enlargement

A shape can be enlarged to make it bigger by changing the lengths of
its sides by a scale factor. The shape is enlarged about a centre of
enlargement. You need to know how to enlarge a shape by using the
ray method or by drawing a shape on a co-ordinate grid and enlarging
it about the origin.

EXAMPLE

4 Enlarge the Triangle ABC about
the point O by a scale factor of 2.

ANSWER

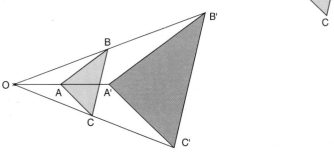

Draw rays OA, OB and OC. Measure the lengths of these 3 rays
and multiply each length by 2. Draw the rays for these 3 new
lengths as OA', OB' and OC'. Join A', B' and C' to obtain the
enlarged triangle A'B'C'.

EXAMPLE

5 Plot the points A (1, 1), B (3, 1), C (3, 2) and D (1, 2) and join
them to make a rectangle ABCD. Enlarge the rectangle about the
origin by a scale factor of 3.

LEVEL **6**
SHAPE, SPACE
AND MEASURES

**Transformation
geometry**

A N S W E R

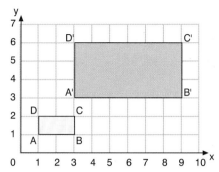

For an enlargement about the origin, the numbers in each co-ordinate are just multiplied by the scale factor. So plot the points: A' (3, 3); B' (9, 3); C' (9, 6); D' (3, 6) and join to make the enlarged rectangle A'B'C'D'.

Check yourself

QUESTIONS

Q1 Write a LOGO program to draw this shape:

```
       30
   ┌────────┐
   │        │ 20
60 │        └──────┐
   │          50   │
   │               │ 40
   │               │
   └───────────────┘
 start      80
```

ANSWERS AND TUTORIAL

A1 FORWARD 60
RIGHT TURN 90
FORWARD 30
RIGHT TURN 90
FORWARD 20
LEFT TURN 90
FORWARD 50
RIGHT TURN 90
FORWARD 40
RIGHT TURN 90
FORWARD 80

Q2 Rotate the letter T through 90° anticlockwise about the point A.

A2

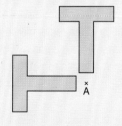

T2 Remember to use tracing paper. Put the tracing paper over the T and the point A and use a pencil point to hold the tracing paper at A. Now rotate through 90° anticlockwise.

ANSWERS AND TUTORIAL

A3

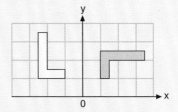

T3 Remember to use tracing paper.

A4 A' (0, 2); B' (4, –2); C' (–4, –2).

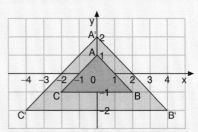

T4 Multiply the numbers in each co-ordinate by 2 and then plot these new co-ordinates.

A5

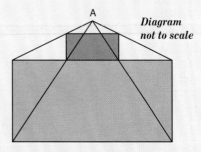

*Diagram
not to scale*

T5 Join A to the 4 vertices of the rectangle; measure these rays and multiply these lengths by 3. Draw these new rays from A and join to get the enlarged rectangle.

QUESTIONS

Q3 Rotate the letter L through 90° clockwise about the origin.

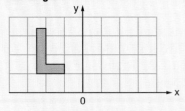

Q4 On a grid plot the points A (0, 1), B (2, –1) and C (–2, –1). Join them to make a triangle ABC. Enlarge the triangle about the origin by a scale factor of 2. Label the enlarged triangle A'B'C'. What are the co-ordinates of A', B' and C'?

Q5 Use the ray method to enlarge the rectangle about the point A by a scale factor of 3.

A

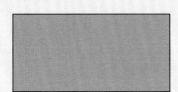

Chapter 44

Perimeter, area and volume formulae

You should understand and be able to use the formulae for finding the circumference and area of circles. You should be able to find the area of plane figures and the volumes of cuboids.

You should already understand the idea of perimeter, area and volume and know the metric units of length, area and volume. This chapter introduces the formulae that you need to be able to calculate perimeters, areas and volumes for 2-D and 3-D shapes.

Perimeter

You need to know how to use the following formulae when solving problems:

Square

$P = 4l$

Rectangle

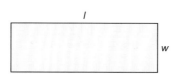

$P = 2l + 2w$ or $P = 2(l + w)$

Circle

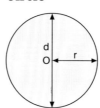

r = radius
d = diameter
perimeter = circumference (c)
$c = 2\pi r = \pi d$
$\pi = 3.14$ or 3.142 or use calculator value
$\pi = 3.141592654$.

Remember to use the correct units for perimeter: mm, cm, m, km.

---

1 Mr Peters was planting flower bulbs around the edge of a lawn 10 metres long and 8 metres wide.

(a) Find the perimeter of the lawn.

(b) How many bulbs did he need, if he planted them 50 cm apart?

EXAMPLE

(a) $P = 2(l + w) = 2 \times 18 = 36$ m.

(b) $50 \text{ cm} = \frac{1}{2}$ m. So number of bulbs $= 36 \div \frac{1}{2} = 72$.

ANSWER

---

2 Jon's mountain bike wheels have a radius of 30 cm.

(a) Find the circumference of a wheel.

(b) Jon goes on a 10 km ride. Find how many times a wheel turns.

EXAMPLE

(a) $c = 2\pi r = 2 \times \pi \times 30 = 188.5$ cm (answer to one decimal place and using calculator value for π) Remember to use the Min or Sto button on your calculator. You need this answer for the next part.

ANSWER

(b) $10 \text{ km} = 10\,000 \text{ m} = 1\,000\,000 \text{ cm}$. The wheel turns $1\,000\,000 \div 188.450 = 5305$ times (to nearest whole number). Remember to use the MR or RCL button on your calculator.

**Perimeter, area and
volume formulae**

Area

You need to know how to use the following formulae when solving area problems:

Square

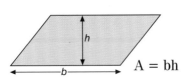

$A = l^2$

Rectangle

$A = l\text{w}$

Triangle

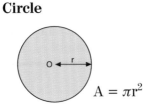

$A = \frac{1}{2}bh$

Parallelogram

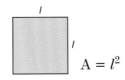

$A = bh$

Trapezium

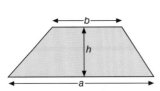

$A = \dfrac{(a+b)h}{2}$

Circle

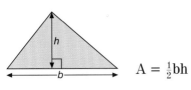

$A = \pi r^2$

Remember to use the correct units for area: mm^2, cm^2, m^2, km^2.

EXAMPLE   **3**   Find the area of the following shapes:

(a) 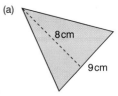   (b) 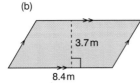   (c) 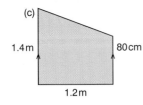   (d)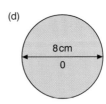

ANSWER

(a) $A = \frac{1}{2} \times 9 \times 8 = 36\,cm^2$.

(b) $A = 8.4 \times 3.7 = 31.08\,m^2$.

(c)   Change 80 cm to m. 80 cm = 0.8 m.

$$A = \frac{(1.4 + 0.8) \times 1.2}{2} \qquad A = 1.32m^2$$

(d) $d = 8\,cm$ so $r = 4cm$; $A = \pi \times 4^2 = \pi \times 16$;
$A = 50.3\ cm^2$ (to 1 decimal place).

EXAMPLE   **4**   Calculate the area of the road sign
as you enter 'Mathsville'.

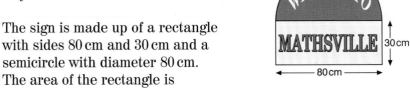

ANSWER

The sign is made up of a rectangle
with sides 80 cm and 30 cm and a
semicircle with diameter 80 cm.
The area of the rectangle is
$80 \times 30 = 2400\,cm^2$. The area of a circle with a radius of 40 cm
is $\pi \times 40^2 = \pi \times 1600 = 5026.55$. So the area of the semicircle is
$5026.55 \div 2 = 2513\,cm^2$ (to the nearest whole number). Total
area of the sign is $2400 + 2513 = 4913 = 4910\,cm^2$ (to 3
significant figures).

Volume

You need to know this formula:

Cuboid

$V = l\text{wh}$

Remember to use the correct units for volume: mm^3, cm^3, m^3.

---

5 Find the volume and total surface area of this cuboid block:

EXAMPLE

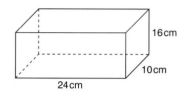

ANSWER

$V = 24 \times 10 \times 16 = 3840\,cm^3$. The area is found by adding
together the areas of the 6 faces of the cuboid. There are 3 pairs
of rectangles with equal areas. $A = 2(24 \times 10) + 2(24 \times 16) +
2(10 \times 16) = 480 + 768 + 320 = 1568\,cm^2$.

Check yourself

QUESTIONS

Q1 **Find the area of the following shapes:**

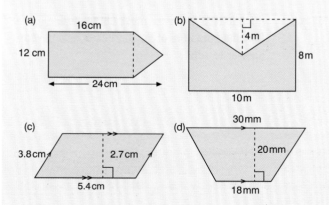

(a)

(b)

(c)

(d)

ANSWERS AND TUTORIAL

A1 (a) $240\,cm^2$
(b) $60\,m^2$
(c) $14.58\,cm^2$
(d) $480\,mm^2$

T1 (a) Area of rectangle $= 12 \times 16 = 192\,cm^2$.
Height of triangle $= 24 - 16 = 8\,cm$.
Area of triangle $= \frac{1}{2} \times 12 \times 8 = 48\,cm^2$.
Total area $= 192 + 48 = 240\,cm^2$.
(b) Area of rectangle $= 10 \times 8 = 80\,m^2$.
Area of triangle $= \frac{1}{2} \times 10 \times 4 = 20\,m^2$.
Area of shape $= 80 - 20 = 60\,m^2$.
(c) $A = bh = 5.4 \times 2.7$. Ignore slant height.
(d) $A = \frac{1}{2}(a + b)h$
$= \frac{1}{2}(30 + 18) \times 20$
$= 480\,mm^2$.

Perimeter, area and volume formulae

ANSWERS AND TUTORIAL

A2 (a) $8000\,m^2$
(b) $4000\,m^2$

T2 (a) Length of field $= 120 - 20 = 100\,m$.
Width of field $= 100 - 20 = 80\,m$.
Area of field $= 100 \times 80 = 8000\,m^2$
(b) Area of whole complex $= 120 \times 100 = 12000\,m^2$.
Area for spectators $= 12000 - 8000 = 4000\,m^2$.

A3 $3.75\ m^2$.

T3 The side is a trapezium.
$A = \frac{1}{2}(a + b)h = \frac{1}{2}(3 + 2) \times 1.5 = 3.75\,m^2$.

A4 (a) $c = 75.4\,cm$ and $A = 452.4\,cm^2$.
(b) $c = 8.2\,m$ and $A = 5.3\,m^2$.

T4 Using calculator value for π:
(a) $r = 12$; $c = 2\pi r = 2 \times \pi \times 12 = 75.4$
$A = \pi r^2 = \pi \times 144 = 452.4$.
(b) $r = 1.3$; $c = 2\pi r = 2 \times \pi \times 1.3 = 8.2$
$A = \pi r^2 = \pi \times 1.3^2 = 5.3$

A5 $397.1cm^2$

T5 Area of triangle $= \frac{1}{2} \times 20 \times 24 = 240$
Area of semicircle $= \frac{1}{2}\pi r^2 = \frac{1}{2} \times \pi \times 10^2$
$= 157.1$ (1d.p.)
Total area $= 240 + 157.1 = 397.1\ cm^2$.

QUESTIONS

Q2 The diagram shows the spectator area around a rectangular sports field:

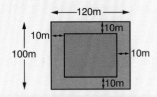

(a) Find the area of the field.
(b) Find the area for the spectators.

Q3 Mr Gleeson wanted to paint one side of his garden shed. The diagram shows the dimensions of the shed. Calculate the area Mr Gleeson will have to paint.

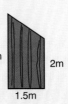

Q4 Find the circumference and area of the following circles. Give your answers to 1 decimal place.

(a)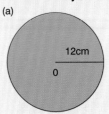

(b)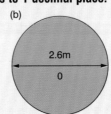

Q5 Anna makes a clown's mask out of card. Calculate the area of the card used, giving your answer to 1dp.

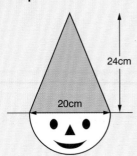

TEST QUESTIONS

Answers with examiner's comments on page 241.

1. Ursula made a solid letter U with seven plastic cubes. She drew this picture on a grid. She did not draw any edge she could not see. Ursula then turned the U so that it was upside down. Draw on a grid what the solid looks like.

    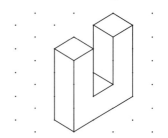

    (1995 Paper 1)

2. This is a concrete block drawn on a grid. Maya rolls it by rotating it about each 10 cm edge in turn. Draw the faces of the block you would see after the second roll. Show where the black square is.

    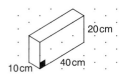

    (1994 Paper 1)

3. Shape A is an equilateral triangle.
    The instructions to draw shape A are:
    FORWARD 5
    TURN RIGHT 120
    FORWARD 5
    TURN RIGHT 120
    FORWARD 5

    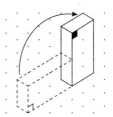

    (a) Write instructions to draw a triangle that has sides double those of shape A.

    Shape B is a parallelogram.
    (b) Complete the instructions to draw shape B.
    FORWARD 8

    ....
    ....
    ....
    ....
    ....
    ....

    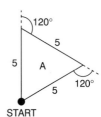

    (1995 Paper 2)

4. The California Beach leisure complex has a swimming pool.
    One whole side of the pool is a viewing window.
    The diagram is a sketch of the window.

    (a) Work out the angle w in the window.
    (b) What facts about angles did you use?
    (c) Work out the area of the window.

    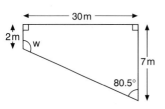

    (1992 Paper 3)

5. This is Kim's sketch of her school playground. (Units are in metres.)

(a) Work out the angle m in the diagram.
(b) What facts about angles did you use?
(c) Work out the area of the flower bed.
(d) Work out the area of the concrete.
(e) The grass is a semicircle. Work out the area of the grass.
   Use 3.14 or your calculator button for π.

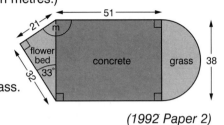

(1992 Paper 2)

6. Lucy is investigating areas and perimeters of shapes.
She makes a **square** with a perimeter of 24 cm.

(a) Calculate the area of her square.

Lucy makes a rectangle with a perimeter of 24 cm.
The **length** is **twice** the **width**.

(b) Calculate the area of her rectangle.

(1996 Paper 2)

7. Wyn and Jay are using their wheelchairs to measure distances.

(a) The large wheel on **Wyn's** wheelchair
has a **diameter** of **60 cm**.
Wyn pushes the wheel round **exactly**
once. Calculate how far Wyn has moved.
(b) The large wheel on **Jay's** wheelchair
has a **diameter** of **52 cm**.
Jay moves her wheelchair forward
950 cm. Calculate how many times the
large wheel goes round.

(1996 Paper 2)

8. What is the volume of this
standard size box of salt?

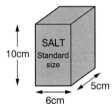

10cm

SALT
Standard
size

5cm

6cm

(1996 Paper 2)

9. One day Andrew runs along some
paths in the park.
This is his sketch of the paths.
How far does he run along the
semicircle from A to B?

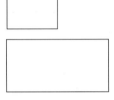

A ← 350m →

230m

B

(1992 Paper 1)

10. Robin has two round cake tins.
These circles are the bases of the tins.
Find the area of the bigger circle.
Use 3.14 or your calculator button for π.

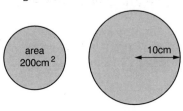

area
200cm^2

10cm

(1993 Paper 1)

Chapter 45

Frequency diagrams for continuous data

You should be able to collect and record continuous data, choosing appropriate class intervals and create frequency diagrams.

You should already know how to collect and record and how to read and interpret statistical graphs and diagrams.

Continuous data

Continuous data is data that we collect by measuring – examples are length, height, weight, time. We need to round measurements accurately and place continuous data into a **grouped frequency table** with suitable **class intervals**. These should all be of equal width with no overlap. Class intervals are usually put in the form of an **inequality** or as an **open interval**.

1 The weights of 24 boys in a Fitness Club are:

65 61 62 48 58 71 47 64 59 60 64 68

59 68 73 70 68 63 70 65 71 62 67 56

All weights are given to the nearest kilogram. Make a grouped frequency table to show the data.

EXAMPLE

The range of the weights is $73 - 47 = 36$ kg. Choose 4 class intervals of width 10 kg. Write the intervals in an open form 40- , 50- , 60- , 70- , where 40- means a weight from 40 kg up to but not including 50 kg.

ANSWER

Weight (kg)	Tally	Frequency
40–	||	2
50–	||||	4
60–	⊞⊞ ⊞⊞ |||	13
70–	⊞⊞	5

Grouped frequency diagrams

For continuous data there are two types of diagrams you need to know how to draw:

Grouped frequency diagrams. These are similar to bar charts for discrete data but the horizontal axis is labelled to show the lower and upper limits of the class interval.

Frequency polygons. These are line graphs with the points plotted in the middle of the class interval.

Frequency diagrams for continuous data

EXAMPLE

2 The grouped frequency table shows the ages of all the staff who work at Erinsburgh High School:

For the data draw:

(a) a grouped frequency diagram.

(b) a frequency polygon.

Age	Frequency
20–	14
30–	18
40–	22
50–	12
60–	6

ANSWER (a)

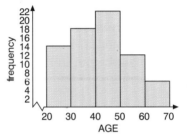

(b)

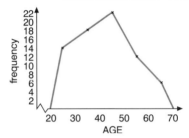

Notice the labelling of the age axis: there are no values between 0 and 20, so a jagged line is used. The numbers are the boundaries of the class intervals.

The points are plotted in the middle of the class intervals. The polygon starts and finishes on the age axis, at the lowest and highest possible age.

Check yourself

ANSWERS AND TUTORIAL

QUESTIONS

A1 (a)

Time (mins)	Frequency
$0 < t \leqslant 2$	6
$2 < t \leqslant 4$	8
$4 < t \leqslant 6$	6
$6 < t \leqslant 8$	5
$8 < t \leqslant 10$	2
$10 < t \leqslant 12$	3

(b)

frequency vs time (mins)

T1 (a) Check that the frequencies add up to 30.
(b) Notice the numbers on the time axis are the boundaries of the class intervals.

Q1 Mr Beetone's telephone bill was far more than he had expected. So during the next week he kept a record of the times that he spent on the phone and rounded all the times up to the nearest minute. The times were:

2 5 7 10 3 1 2 6 7 11 4 6 4 3 8
12 3 5 1 3 2 7 4 6 10 3 1 5 8 12

For the times given:
(a) make a grouped frequency table using class intervals $0 < t \leqslant 2, 2 < t \leqslant 4, ...$
(b) draw a grouped frequency diagram.

QUESTIONS

Q2 Constable FitzGerald was monitoring the speeds of vehicles on a dual carriageway using radar speed check equipment. The frequency table is as follows:

Speed (mph)	20–	30–	40–	50–	60–	70–
frequency	14	23	28	35	52	8

(a) Draw a grouped frequency diagram for the data.

(b) How many vehicles did he check?

(c) Can you find the mean speed for the vehicles? Explain why.

Q3 Sam was carrying out a survey on the heights of boys and girls in Year 9. He took a sample of 30 boys and 30 girls and made a grouped frequency table:

Height (cm)	No of boys	No of girls
140–	1	3
150–	6	8
160–	10	12
170–	11	7
180–	2	0

(a) Draw a frequency polygon for both sets of data on the same diagram.

(b) What is the most common height for all pupils?

(c) Compare the distribution of the heights of the boys with the heights of the girls.

ANSWERS AND TUTORIAL

A2 (a)

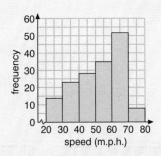

(b) **160**

(c) **No. You do not know the speed of each vehicle from the grouped frequency table. At level 7 we learn how to estimate this.**

T2 (a) Use 2 mm graph paper so that the frequencies can be plotted accurately.

(b) Add together all the frequencies.

A3 (a)

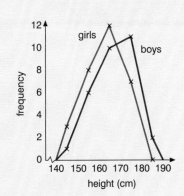

(b) **160 to 170 cm.**

(c) **The boys are generally taller than the girls.**

T3 (a) The points are plotted in the middle of the class intervals. Use a different type or colour of line for boys and girls.

(b) 22 is the highest frequency for the boys and girls added together. The most common height must be given as an interval.

Chapter 46

LEVEL **6**
HANDLING DATA

Drawing pie charts

You should be able to construct pie charts.

You should already know how to calculate fractions of a quantity, how to measure and draw angles and how to read information from a pie chart. It is not always appropriate to draw frequency diagrams to display data, particularly when there are large differences in the frequencies or when the data is only to be used for illustration purposes as in advertising. In these cases, pie charts are better. To draw a pie chart you need to be able to calculate fractional amounts of 360°. Remember that a pie chart only shows proportions and not individual frequencies.

EXAMPLE

1 Marion asked 30 pupils in her form: 'Where did you go for your last holiday?' The frequency table shows her results. Draw a pie chart to show the data.

England	Scotland	Wales	Europe	America
12	4	2	9	3

ANSWER

The table shows how to calculate the angle for each sector of the pie chart:

Place	Frequency	Calculation	Angle
England	12	$\frac{12}{30} \times 360 = 144$	144°
Scotland	4	$\frac{4}{30} \times 360 = 48$	48°
Wales	2	$\frac{2}{30} \times 360 = 24$	24°
Europe	9	$\frac{9}{30} \times 360 = 108$	108°
America	3	$\frac{3}{30} \times 360 = 36$	36°
Totals	30		360°

Draw a vertical radius and put in the 'England' sector first and then work round clockwise: the angles or frequencies do not have to be shown.

Remember to check that the angles total 360°.

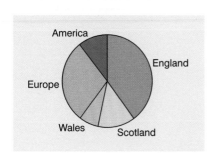

Check yourself

QUESTIONS

Q1 Form 9MP were voting for a representative to stand on the School Council.

Their voting for the four candidates was:

Z. Freeman	I. Knapp	A. Clouns	D. Best
10	7	8	11

Draw a pie chart to show how the form voted.

Q2 Sandra has saved £50 to buy Christmas presents. After a day's Christmas shopping, she found that she had spent the £50 on the following presents:

£11.00 on a table decoration for Mum
£11.50 on a pullover for Dad
£7.50 on perfume for her sister Sue
£8.00 on a model car for her brother Andrew
£12.00 on a C.D. for her boyfriend Philip.

Draw a pie chart to show the proportion she spends on each person's present.

ANSWERS AND TUTORIAL

A1

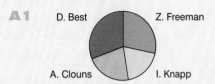

T1 The table shows how to calculate the angles:

Candidate	Frequency	Calculation	Angle
Z. Freeman	10	$\frac{10}{36} \times 360 = 100$	100°
I. Knapp	7	$\frac{7}{36} \times 360 = 70$	70°
A. Clouns	8	$\frac{8}{36} \times 360 = 80$	80°
D. Best	11	$\frac{11}{36} \times 360 = 110$	110°
Totals	36		360°

When drawing angles, you are allowed to be up to 2° out. It is not necessary to write the angles on the pie chart but you must label each sector.

A2

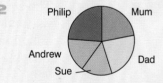

T2 The table shows how to calculate the angles.

Person	Amount	Calculation	Angle
Mum	£11.00	$\frac{11}{50} \times 360 = 79.2$	79°
Dad	£11.50	$\frac{11.5}{50} \times 360 = 82.8$	83°
Sue	£7.50	$\frac{7.5}{50} \times 360 = 54$	54°
Andrew	£8.00	$\frac{8}{50} \times 360 = 57.6$	58°
Philip	£12.00	$\frac{12}{50} \times 360 = 86.4$	86°
Totals	£50.00		360°

To make it easier to draw the pie chart, the angles have been rounded to the nearest degree.

Chapter 47

Scatter diagrams

You should be able draw scatter diagrams and understand correlation.

You should already know how to read and interpret statistical graphs and diagrams.

The statistics examples given in previous levels have considered only one set of data or used only one variable. It is sometimes useful to compare two sets of data to see if there is a connection between two variables: for example, do tall children always have tall parents? This connection is known as correlation. You need to be familiar with the terms positive correlation, negative correlation and no correlation.

A **scatter diagram** can show you if there is a connection between the two variables. Like a normal graph, it has x and y axes.

EXAMPLE

1 The scatter diagram shows the marks of 30 pupils for Paper 1 and Paper 2 in their Key Stage 3 Maths tests. Describe what the diagram tells you.

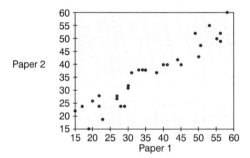

ANSWER

The scatter diagram shows a positive correlation. This means that many of the pupils who got a high mark on Paper 1 also got a high mark on Paper 2. Positive correlation tells you that as one variable increases, so does the other.

EXAMPLE

2 The scatter diagram shows the relationship between the number of hours spent on homework and the number of hours spent watching TV on a particular weekday evening for a group of Year 9 pupils.

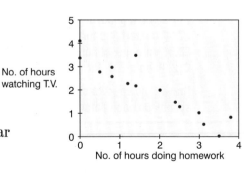

(a) Describe what the diagram tells you.

(b) Sanjay spent that evening doing $1\frac{1}{2}$ hours work on his Geography project. How much TV did he probably watch?

(a) The scatter diagram shows a negative correlation. This means that the more time pupils spend on homework, the less time they spend watching TV.

(b) Going up from the x-axis at $1\frac{1}{2}$ and looking where the points are nearby, you can see that Sanjay probably spent about $2\frac{1}{2}$ hours watching T.V.

ANSWE

3 Martha thought that the further you live from school, the earlier you needed to get up in a morning. To test this statement, she carried out a survey on 10 of her school friends and then drew the following scatter diagram:

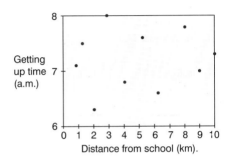

Getting up time (a.m.)

Distance from school (km).

EXAMPL

(a) Describe what the diagram tells Martha.

(b) Make another statement using distance from school with another variable which might show positive correlation.

(a) The scatter diagram shows no correlation. So there doesn't seem to be any connection between the distance from school and getting up time.

ANSWE

(b) An example to show positive correlation might be: 'The distance from school and the time it takes to get to school'

Check yourself

QUESTIONS

Q1 The scatter diagram shows the heights and weights of 12 people.

Weight (kg)

Height (cm)

(a) Describe what the diagram tells you.
(b) Eric is one of the people on the scatter diagram. He weighs 62 kg. Is he likely to be as tall as the other 11 people on the same diagram?

ANSWERS AND TUTORIAL

A1 (a) There is positive correlation.
(b) No

T1 (a) The taller you are, the more you are likely to weigh.
(b) Going across from the y-axis at 62, the points close by are for the shorter people.

ANSWERS AND TUTORIAL

A2 (a) There is a negative correlation.

(b) In warmer weather people drink fewer hot drinks.

T2 (a) As the temperature increases the number of hot drinks sold decreases.

(b) Or in cooler weather people buy more hot drinks.

A3 (a)

History mark

(scatter diagram with History mark on vertical axis from 20 to 100 and French mark on horizontal axis from 20 to 100)

French mark

(b) There is no obvious correlation.

T3 (a) Use 2 mm graph paper to make it easier to plot the points.

(b) Someone who is good at French is not necessarily good or bad at History.

QUESTIONS

Q2 Mr Reneé owns a café at Bridpool and keeps a record of the number of cups of tea and coffee he sells on certain days of the summer holidays. He also knows the midday temperature on these days. This data is shown on the scatter diagram.

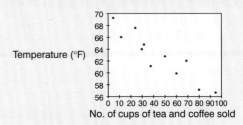

Temperature (°F)

No. of cups of tea and coffee sold

(a) Describe what the diagram tells you.

(b) Give a reason for your answer.

Q3 The table shows the end of year examination marks for French and History for 10 friends in Year 9.

Name	French mark (%)	History mark (%)
Ant	23	47
Bill	50	68
Cath	29	67
Den	60	26
Edith	85	42
Flora	68	70
Gary	34	80
Helen	88	91
Iris	55	78
Jack	95	40

(a) Plot the data on a scatter diagram.

(b) Describe what you notice from the diagram.

Chapter 48

Probability and combined events

You should know that when dealing with two experiments you can identify all the outcomes and show these in a diagrammatic or tabular form. You should know that the total probability of all the mutually exclusive events of an experiment is 1 and use this to solve problems.

You should already know how to use the formula to find the probability of an event and you should be familiar with equally likely outcomes.

When an event or experiment is carried out more than once, it is known as a **combined event**. To calculate the probability of a combined event you need to know how to use lists, tables or diagrams to identify all the possible outcomes. You can then use the probability formula:

$$P(\text{Event}) = \frac{\text{Number of favourable outcomes}}{\text{Total number of outcomes possible}}$$

1 (a) Find all the possible outcomes when throwing two coins.

EXAMPLE

(b) Find:
    (i)   P(2 Heads).
    (ii) P(1 Head).
    (iii) P(0 Heads).

(c) What do you notice about these 3 probabilities?

(a) Method 1. List all the outcomes:
HH, HT, TH, TT.

ANSWER

Method 2. Draw a sample space diagram:

In both cases there are 4 equally likely outcomes.

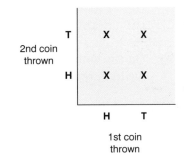

(b) Using the probability formula:
    (i)   P(2 Heads) = $\frac{1}{4}$
    (ii) P(1 Head) = $\frac{2}{4} = \frac{1}{2}$.
    (iii) P(0 Heads) = $\frac{1}{4}$.

(c) The 3 probabilities add up to 1. This is because we have included every possible outcome only once in the 3 different events. We say that the 3 events are mutually exclusive events since none of them include any common outcomes.

2 A box contains 3 differently coloured balls: red, green and blue.

EXAMPLE

A ball is drawn out at random, its colour noted and then replaced. The balls are shaken up in the box and again one is drawn at random.

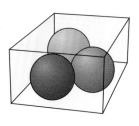

(a) Find all the possible outcomes for the colours of the 2 balls.

(b) Find:
(i) P(2 reds).
(ii) P(the 2 balls are the same colour).
(iii) P(the 2 balls are of different colours).

A N S W E R

(a) Method 1. List all the outcomes: RR, GR, BR, RG, GG, BG, RB, GB, BB.

Method 2. Draw a sample space diagram:

There are 9 equally likely outcomes.

B	X	X	X
G	X	X	X
R	X	X	X
	R	G	B

(b) (i) P(2 reds) = $\frac{1}{9}$.

(ii) P(same colour) = P(2 reds or 2 greens or 2 blues) = $\frac{3}{9}$ = $\frac{1}{3}$.

(iii) P(same colour) and P(not the same colour) are mutually exclusive events, since they do not have any common outcomes, and add up to 1. P(2 different colours) = $1 - \frac{1}{3} = \frac{2}{3}$.

E X A M P L E **3** In the game of Backgammon 2 dice are used and it is an advantage if you get a double or a high score. (A double means both dice are the same number and the score is the total of both numbers).

(a) Draw a sample space diagram to show all the possible scores when throwing 2 dice.

(b) Find:
(i) P(double 6)   (iii) P(no double)
(ii) P(any double)   (iv) P(a score of 9).

A N S W E R

(a) On the sample space you can either put 'X's for the scores or write in the scores as numbers:

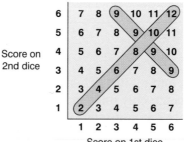

There are 36 equally likely outcomes.

(b) (i) P(double 6) = P(a score of 12) = $\frac{1}{36}$.

(ii) P(any double) = $\frac{6}{36}$ = $\frac{1}{6}$ (The 6 outcomes are ringed on the sample space diagram.)

(iii) P(no double) = $1 - \frac{1}{6} = \frac{5}{6}$ (Mutually exclusive events.)

(iv) P(A score of 9) = $\frac{4}{36}$ = $\frac{1}{9}$ (The 4 outcomes are ringed on the sample space diagram.)

4 Maggie wants to find all the outcomes when a coin is thrown three times. She decides to make a table to help her find all the possible outcomes. This is how she started the table:

(a) Complete the table.

(b) Use the table to find:
  (i)   P(3 heads)
  (ii) P(2 heads)
  (iii) P(1 head)
  (iv) P(0 heads)

(c) How can you check your answer to part (b)?

1st coin	2nd coin	3rd coin
H	H	H
H	H	T
H	T	H

(a)

1st coin	2nd coin	3rd coin
H	H	H
H	H	T
H	T	H
H	H	T
H	T	T
T	H	T
T	T	H
T	T	T

(b) There are 8 equally likely outcomes.

  (i)   P(3 heads) $= \frac{1}{8}$ (iii) P(1 head) $= \frac{3}{8}$

  (ii) P(2 heads) $= \frac{3}{8}$ (iv) P(0 heads) $= \frac{1}{8}$

(c) The 4 probabilities must add up to 1. The events are mutually exclusive and all possible outcomes have been included.

Check yourself

QUESTIONS

ANSWERS AND TUTORIAL

Q1 Stan is playing a game using the 4 letters I R O N. The letters are placed face down and shuffled. Stan takes a letter, keeps it, and then takes a second letter.
  (a) List all the possible outcomes for the 2 letters Stan can choose.
  (b) Find P(making a proper 2 letter word).

A1 (a) IR, IO. IN, RI, RO, RN, OI, OR, ON, NI, NR, NO.
  (b) $\frac{1}{3}$.

T1 (a) He cannot choose the same letter twice because he keeps the first letter.
  (b) There are 12 equally likely outcomes.
    P(2 letter word)$= \frac{4}{12} = \frac{1}{3}$. (IN, OR, ON, NO).

ANSWERS AND TUTORIAL

A2 (a) Barbara and Ian; Barbara and Linda;
    Barbara and Mike; Ian and Linda; Ian and
    Mike; Linda and Mike.

(b) $\frac{2}{3}$.

T2 (a) No names can be the same and the order of
    the names does not matter.

(b) There are 6 equally likely outcomes.

P(a boy and a girl) $= \frac{4}{6} = \frac{2}{3}$.

A3

Dice		
6	X	X
5	X	X
4	X	X
3	X	X
2	X	X
1	X	X
	H	T

Coin

T3 There are 12 possible outcomes. You could also
show the outcomes on the diagram as H1, H2, H3
etc.

A4 (a)

Number on 2nd dice				
4	4	8	12	16
3	3	6	9	12
2	2	4	6	8
1	1	2	3	4
	1	2	3	4

Number on 1st dice

(b) (i) $\frac{3}{4}$ (ii) $\frac{1}{4}$

T4 (a) It is easier to put the scores rather than 'X's
    on the sample space diagram.

(b) There are 16 equally likely outcomes.

(i) P(even) $= \frac{12}{16} = \frac{3}{4}$

(ii) P(odd) $= 1 - \frac{3}{4} = \frac{1}{4}$ (mutually exclusive
    events).

QUESTIONS

Q2 Barbara, Ian, Linda and Mike play as a team in
an Inter Form Quiz in Year 9. The team won and
two of them are then selected to play in an Inter
Year Quiz. The team decides to select the pair
by putting their names into a hat and choose the
first two names that come out.

(a) List all the possible pairs of names that can
    be chosen.

(b) Find P(the pair chosen will be a boy and
    a girl).

Q3 A coin and a dice are thrown together. Draw a
sample space diagram to show all the possible
outcomes.

Q4 In the game 'Tetra',
two four-sided dice
numbered 1 to 4
are thrown and the
numbers on the
base of each dice
are then multiplied
together to get a
score.

(a) Draw a sample space diagram to show all
    the possible scores for the game.

(b) Find:
    (i) P(the score is even)
    (ii) P(the score is odd).

T E S T   Q U E S T I O N S

Answers with examiner's comments on page 242.

1. Nikos and Sharon are planning to go on a cycling holiday in October. They are trying to choose where to go. They have the following information:

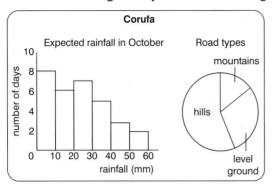
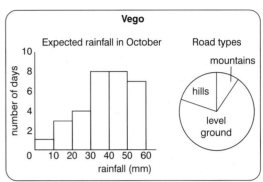

    Choose which place you would most like to go to for a cycling holiday. Use the 2 frequency diagrams and the 2 pie charts to explain your choice. It doesn't matter which place you choose to go to, but you must write something about the rainfall **and** the road types.

    (1992 Paper 1)

2. Kieron wanted to find out why people in some countries lived longer than people in other countries.

    He picked 15 countries and found out:

    ● the population;
    ● the number of doctors per million people;
    ● the life expectancy.

    He plotted these scatter graphs to help him look for links. Each cross stands for a country.

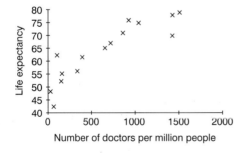
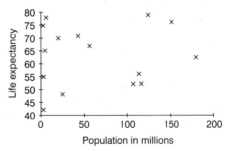

    Look at the different ways the points in the two graphs are scattered.

    (a) What does **graph 1** show about any possible links between life expectancy and the number of doctors per million people in a country?

    (b) What does **graph 2** show about any possible links between life expectancy and a country's population?

    Kieron knows these facts about another country:
    The population is roughly **80** million; it has roughly **500** doctors per million people.

    (c) Kieron does **not** know the life expectancy for this country. He wants to use one of his graphs to estimate it. Which is the better graph for Kieron to use? Use this graph to estimate the life expectancy in this country.

    (1993 Paper 1)

TEST QUESTIONS

3. Nine students were discussing their holiday jobs working on a local farm. They decided to find out if there were any relationships between the time they spent working, sleeping, watching television and the distance they had to travel to work.

The students plotted three scatter graphs:

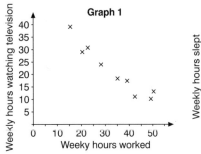 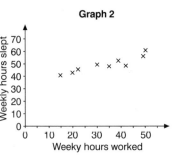 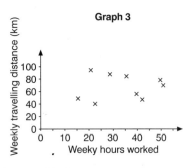

(a) What does **graph 1** show about the relationship between the weekly hours spent watching television and the weekly hours worked?

(b) What does **graph 2** show about the relationship between the weekly hours slept and the weekly hours worked?

(c) What does **graph 3** show about the relationship between the weekly travelling distance and the weekly hours worked?

(d) Another student works 30 hours per week. Use **graph 1** to estimate the weekly hours spent watching television by this student. Explain how you decided on your estimate.

(1995 Paper 2)

4. Alun has these two spinners:

Alun spins both spinners and then adds up the numbers to get a total. He starts to make a list of all the possible totals.
Complete Alun's list:

5, …

(1995 Paper 1)

5. Les, Tom, Nia and Ann are in a singing competition. To decide the order in which they will sing all four names are put into a bag. Each name is taken out of the bag, one at a time, without looking.

(a) Write down all the possible orders with **Tom** singing **second**.

(b) In a different competition there are 8 singers. The probability that Tom sings second is $\frac{1}{8}$. Work out the probability that Tom does **not** sing second.

(1996 Paper 1)

6. Gary wants to get this logo printed on a white T-shirt:

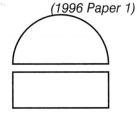

(a) One printing shop has 2 colours to choose from: red and black. He can choose one colour for the whole logo or different colours for the rectangle and the semicircle. Write **all** the possible choices of colour for the logo.

(b) Another shop has 3 colours to choose from: red, green, yellow. Gary can choose one colour for the whole logo or different colours for the rectangle and the semicircle. Write **all** the possible choices of colour for the logo.

(1994 Paper 1)

Chapter 49

Rounding off to significant figures and estimating

You should be able to round to one significant figure and multiply and divide mentally.

You should already know how to round off to the nearest 10, 100 and 1000, how to mentally multiply and divide single digit multiples of 10, how to round off decimals and how to multiply single decimals together. In this chapter we deal with **significant figures** and look at how to round off using significant figures.

Significant figures

The number 287 has three significant figures. If the digits are drawn to scale they would look like this:

2 **8** **7**

You can see that compared to the 2 the 7 does not count for very much. Rounding 287 off to the nearest 10 gives 290. This has 2 significant figures (sf). Rounding 287 off to the nearest hundred gives 300. This number has 1 sf. It might seem that the rule about significant figures is just count the digits other than zero but zero itself can be significant if it is between two numbers. The number 307, for example, has 3 significant figures.

EXAMPLE

1   How many significant figures do these numbers have?

(a)   458   (c)   203   (e)   304500

(b)   3400   (d)   1000

ANSWER

(a)   3 sf

(b)   2 sf (zeros do not count).

(c)   3 sf (the zero does count because it is between two other digits).

(d)   1 sf.

(e)   4 sf (the first zero counts but the last two do not).

Decimals and significant figures

The number 0.00546 has three significant figures. The number 0.067 has 2 sf. The number 0.9006 has 4 sf. Once again zeros, at the front or end of a number do not count but zeros between numbers do count as significant figures.

EXAMPLE

2   How many significant figures do these numbers have?

(a)   0.0045   (b)   0.2045   (c)   0.8900

(d)   0.07009

ANSWER

(a)   2 sf. (zeros do not count)   (b)   4 sf.

(c)   2 sf. (Zeros at end are not necessary, although we do not actually know if they are there for a reason so it may be that they are significant, so the answer could be 4 sf.)

(d)   4 sf.

Rounding off to significant figures

Most of the time you only have to round off to 1 sf. This is so you can make estimates of the answers to sums. However, numbers can be rounded to any number of significant figures. For example 3783 would be 4000 to 1 sf, 3800 to 2 sf and 3780 to 3 sf. 0.0906 would be 0.09 to 1 sf and 0.091 to 2 sf.

EXAMPLE   **3**   Round these numbers off to the number of significant figures given in the bracket:

(a)   3567 (2 sf)   (b)   0.0965 (2 sf)   (c)   0.599 (2 sf)

ANSWER   (a)   3600   (b)   0.097   (c)   0.60

Part (c) is unusual because 0.599 rounds off to 0.60. We need to write down the extra zero here as it counts as a significant figure. This is why the answer to part (c) of the last example could have been 2 sf or 4 sf. Halfway numbers like part (b) round upwards.

Estimating

We have met estimating before. This is where numbers must be rounded to values so that you can work them out in your head (ie, without a calculator). One significant figure is usually good enough.

EXAMPLE   **4**   Estimate the answer to these questions:

(a) $\dfrac{325.7 + 40.7}{24.9}$ (b) $\dfrac{52.1 \times 0.783}{(53.6 + 17.6)}$

ANSWER   (a)   Round off the numbers to 1 sf (or 2 sf if it an easy number like 25).

$$\frac{300 + 40}{25} \approx \frac{340}{25} \approx \frac{350}{25} = 14$$

Change 340 to 350 to make the sum easy to do in your head.

(b) $\dfrac{50 \times 0.8}{50 + 20} \approx \dfrac{40}{70} \approx \dfrac{40}{80} = \dfrac{1}{2}$

Check yourself

QUESTIONS

Q1 How many significant figures are there in these numbers?
(a) 246   (c) 3204
(b) 3567   (d) 9700

Q2 How many significant figures are there in these numbers?
(a) 0.06   (c) 30.04
(b) 0.567   (d) 0.0320

Q3 Round these numbers off to 1 significant figure:
(a) 246   (c) 3204
(b) 3967   (d) 0.0804

Q4 Round these numbers off to 2 significant figures:
(a) 246   (c) 2294
(b) 2417   (d) 0.0842

Q5 Round these numbers off to 3 significant figures:
(a) 2462   (c) 2294
(b) 2417   (d) 0.08427

Q6 Estimate the answers to:
(a) 0.72×53 (c) 612×0.63
(b) 0.076×489 (d) 72×0.087

Q7 First class stamps are 24p. About how many can you get for £10.00?

Q8 Petrol is 56.7 p per litre. About how much will 51 litres cost?

Q9 An athlete can run a mile in 6 minutes and 10 seconds.
(a) About how long will it take her to run a marathon of 26 miles?
(b) Is your answer going to be an overestimate or an underestimate? Explain your answer.

ANSWERS AND TUTORIAL

A1 (a) 3   (b) 4   (c) 4   (d) 2

T1 Count all the digits except zero. Only count zero if it is between other digits.

A2 (a) 1   (b) 3   (c) 4   (d) 3

T2 You might have said 2 for the answer to (d). You should count the last zero.

A3 (a) 200   (b) 4000   (c) 3000   (d) 0.08

A4 (a) 250   (b) 2400   (c) 2300   (d) 0.084

A5 (a) 2460   (b) 2420   (c) 2290   (d) 0.0843

A6 (a) 35 – 50   (c) 360 – 600
(b) 40 – 50   (d) 6 – 10

T6 Answers can be within a range.

A7 About 4 per pound so about 40 stamps

T7 24 is about 25. This is not 1 sf but it is a nice number to work with particularly with pounds.

A8 A litre is about 60p so about £30. (50×60)

A9 (a) $6 \times 30 = 180$ mins = 3 hours
(b) Probably over as 30 is 4 miles longer

T9 She might not run at the same pace in a marathon, so you could say under. Either would be accepted as long as your reasoning was correct.

Multiplying by numbers between 0 and 1

You should understand the effects of multiplying by a number between 0 and 1.

You should know how to multiply and divide with decimals. If you want to catch someone out ask them to do a half times a half. They will usually say 1. But if you ask them what a half of a half is they will say a quarter. Most people think that when you multiply something it has to get bigger and that when you divide something it has to get smaller. This is only true if you multiply and divide by numbers bigger than 1.

When you multiply by numbers between 0 and 1 things get smaller. When you divide by numbers between 0 and 1 things get bigger! 1 itself is a special number because multiplying and dividing any number by 1 does not change the value of the number.

EXAMPLE

1 Choose 5 numbers bigger than 1. Put them through each of the function machines below:

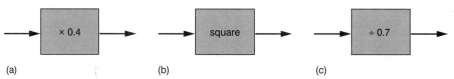

(a)   (b)   (c)

For each function decide if it:

- always makes the number you start with bigger
- always makes the number you start with smaller.
- leaves the number the same.
- does none of the above.

ANSWER

(a)   This function always makes any number bigger than 1 smaller.

(b)   This function always makes any number bigger than 1 bigger.

(c)   This function always makes any number bigger than 1 bigger.

EXAMPLE

2 Repeat Example 1 for the number 1.

ANSWER

(a)   This function makes 1 smaller.

(b)   This function makes 1 stay the same.

(c)   This function makes 1 bigger.

EXAMPLE

3 Repeat Example 1 for 5 numbers between 0 and 1.

ANSWER

(a)   This function always makes any number between 0 and 1 smaller.

(b)   This function always makes any number between 0 and 1 smaller.

(c)   This function always makes any number between 0 and 1 bigger.

Check yourself

QUESTIONS

Q1 You have the following expressions:

$0.5n$, n^2, $\sqrt{n}$, $n \div 0.5$ and $\dfrac{1}{n}$

(a) If $n = 3$, which give a value greater than 3?
(b) If $n = 5$, which give a value less than 5?
(c) If $n = 0.4$, which give a value greater than 0.4?
(d) If $n = 0.7$, which give a value less than 0.7?

Q2 Using the same expressions as Question 1 and taking n as a positive number.
(a) Which of them always gives a value greater than n?
(b) Which of them always gives a value less than n?

Q3 Complete the table using Always > n, Always < n, or Always = n (n is positive)

	n>1	n<1	n=1
n^3	Always > n		
$\sqrt{n}$			Always = n
$\dfrac{1}{n}$			

ANSWERS AND TUTORIAL

A1 (a) n^2, and $n \div 0.5$

(b) $0.5n$, $\sqrt{n}$ and $\dfrac{1}{n}$

(c) $\sqrt{n}$, $n \div 0.5$ and $\dfrac{1}{n}$

(d) $0.5n$ and n^2

T1 (a) and (b) Just substitute numbers into each expression. (c) and (d) Use your calculator to work these out.

A2 (a) $n \div 0.5$ (b) $0.5n$

T2 Squaring (n^2) , square root ($\sqrt{n}$) and reciprocal ($\dfrac{1}{n}$) depend on whether n is greater than 1 or less than 1.

A3

	n>1	n<1	n=1
n^3	Always > n	Always < n	Always = n
$\sqrt{n}$	Always < n	Always > n	Always = n
$\dfrac{1}{n}$	Always < n	Always > n	Always = n

T3 Work a few out on a calculator.

Chapter 51

Efficient use of a calculator

You should be able to solve numerical problems involving multiplication and division with numbers of any size and use a calculator efficiently and appropriately.

You should already know what a **bracket** does in a sum and you should understand how to use the **square root** and **square** button on your calculator.

Calculators do very complicated sums instantly. Unfortunately they only do the sums they are told to do. They will not do a sum correctly if the person putting the sum into the calculator (**you**) enter it in wrongly. It is important that you know how sums are structured and how to use your calculator to do them.

The order of operations

You should have heard of **BODMAS**. This word stands for Brackets, Of (pOwer), Division, Multiply, Addition and Subtraction. This is the order in which parts of sums should be done: brackets should be done first, then powers, then multiplications and so on.

Work out the sum $2 + 3 \times 4$ in your head. Ask others to do the same. You will find that a lot of people say the answer is 20. In fact it is 14. (Check with a scientific calculator). According to BODMAS, the multiplication should be done first. This means 3×4 is done before $2+$ so the sum becomes $2 + 12$ which is 14.

EXAMPLE

1 The sum below has four operations in it (and a bracket). The operations are square, add, times and subtract. What order should they be done in? Do them and check that you get an answer of 91.

$(2 + 3)^2 \times 4 - 9$

ANSWER

Do the bracket first (addition): $5^2 \times 4 - 9$

Do the power second: $25 \times 4 - 9$

Do the multiplication third: $100 - 9$

Do the subtraction fourth: 91

EXAMPLE

2 Put brackets into these sums to make them true:

(a) $2 + 4^2 \div 3 - 2 = 10$ (b) $2 + 4^2 \div 3 - 2 = 18$

ANSWER

(a) $(2 + 4)^2 \div 3 - 2 = 10$ (b) $2 + 4^2 \div (3 - 2) = 18$

Try brackets in various places until you get it right.

The bracket keys

Brackets are used to make sure we know (and the calculator knows) to work out that bit before the others. Scientific calculators all have bracket keys. There is a left hand bracket (and a right hand bracket) . You can have more than one bracket operation going on at once. (This is known as **nesting brackets**).There must always be the same number of left hand as right hand brackets in a sum or you will get an error message. Mostly you can just type in sums that have brackets 'as they read' on the page. For example to work out $(3 + 5) \times (9 - 2)$, type in:

(3   +   5   )   ×   (9   –   2   )   =

You might see some funny things on your display – this is just the calculator setting up another set of brackets.

The bracket works as an equals sign and as soon as a left hand bracket is joined by a right hand bracket everything in between them is worked out. On some calculators it is possible to type 2 (3 + 4). On others you may need to type 2 × (3 + 4). Check your calculator. If you are not sure, put the times sign in anyway.

3   Work out these sums using the bracket keys on your calculator.

(a) $(16 + (8 - 3)) \div 7$ (b) $(3^2 + 7) \div 4$

(a)   3   (b)   4

The memory keys

If you use brackets properly, you shouldn't need to write down parts of sums as you go along. Sometimes, though, you might need to keep a number to use later. You can do this using the memory keys.

The memory keys on your calculator should:

- Put a number into the memory, replacing anything already in the memory. This is Min or STO on most calculators.

- Add (or subtract) the number in the display to the number in the memory. This is M+ (M–) on most calculators.

- Recall the number from the memory and put it in the display. This is usually MR or RCL .

Some calculators have a key that swaps the number in the display for the number in the memory and vice versa. This is usually marked X⇔M .

Efficient use of a calculator

The dividing line

This has two purposes. Firstly it means *divide* the top by the bottom. Secondly it acts as a *bracket* for both the expressions on the top and the bottom. So the expression $\frac{63 + 57}{26 - 16}$ can be read as $\frac{(63 + 57)}{(26 - 16)}$ or $(63 + 57) \div (26 - 16)$.

Sums like this can be done using the bracket keys or the memory keys.

EXAMPLE

4 Do the sum $\frac{36.8 + 57.7}{17.9 - 7.4}$ using (a) brackets keys and (b) memory keys.

ANSWER

(a)

(b)

Common errors

Calculate the mean of 3 ,5 ,6 ,7, 8. You should get 5.8. If a whole class did the sum, some people would get an answer of 22.6. This is because they typed in $3 + 5 + 6 + 7 + 8 \div 5 =$ and so did not add up all the numbers before they divided by 5. They should have used a bracket or pressed = after the 8.

Another common error is forgetting to press = at the end of the sum. For example, $3 \times (22 - 6) = 48$ but if you only type in $3 \times (22 - 6)$ but forget to press =, the display will say 16. You need to press = to get the correct answer of 48.

EXAMPLE

5 What errors has been made in calculating these sums? Work out the correct answer.

(a) $6 + 9 \div 3 = 5$ (b) $(6 + 4) \times (2 + 5) = 7$

ANSWER

(a) The equals sign has been pressed after 9, giving the answer 15, which has then been divided by 3 to give 5. To do the sum correctly, you need to use brackets and press $6 + (9 \div 3) =$. This should give you the correct answer of 9.

(b) The equals sign has not been pressed after the second bracket, so 7 is shown in the display. To do the sum correctly, you need to press $(6 + 4) \times (2 + 5) =$. This should give the correct answer of 70.

Check yourself

QUESTIONS

Q1 Circle the operation that you do first in these sums, then work them out:
(a) $5 + 5 \times 3 =$
(b) $8 + 6 \div 2 =$
(c) $3 + 4^2 =$
(d) $(3 + 4)^2 =$
(e) $2 \times 5^2 =$
(f) $4 \times 3 - 6 =$

Q2 Put brackets into these sums to make them true.
(a) $4 + 4 \times 4 \div 4 = 8$
(b) $4 \div 4 + 4 + 4 = 4.5$
(c) $4 + 4 \div 4 + 4 = 1$
(d) $4 + 4 + 4 \div 4 = 3$

Q3 Write down the order of operations for these sums and then work them out:
(a) $2 + 3^2 \times 4 - 9 \div 3$
(b) $(2 + 4)^2 \div (3 - 2)$

Q4 Work these sums out using the brackets keys on your calculator:
(a) $\dfrac{87.3 - 21.9}{4.7 - 1.7}$
(b) $\dfrac{17.2 + (98.5 - 16.9)}{3.4 + 0.6}$

Q5 Work these sums out using the memory keys on your calculator:
(a) $\dfrac{37.6 - 18.4}{3.2 + 1.8}$
(b) $\dfrac{8 + (98.5 - 18.5)^2}{98.5 - 18.5}$

Q6 Work out this sum using (a) bracket keys and (b) memory keys:
$$\dfrac{12.4 \times 4.5}{3.3 - 1.8}$$

ANSWERS AND TUTORIAL

A1 (a) $5 + 5 \;\textcircled{\times}\; 3 = 20$
(b) $8 + 6 \;\textcircled{\div}\; 2 = 11$
(c) $3 + 4\textcircled{\scriptsize 2} = 19$
(d) $(3\textcircled{+}4)^2 = 49$
(e) $2 \times 5\textcircled{\scriptsize 2} = 50$
(f) $4\textcircled{\times}3 - 6 = 6$

T1 Use BODMAS to decide which to do first.

A2 (a) $4 + 4 \times (4 \div 4) = 8$
(b) $4 \div (4 + 4) + 4 = 4.5$
(c) $(4 + 4) \div (4 + 4) = 1$
(d) $(4 + 4 + 4) \div 4 = 3$

T2 Try brackets in different places until it works.

A3 (a) square, $\div$, $\times$, $+$, $-$. Answer is 35
(b) $+$ in (), $-$ in (), square, $\div$. Answer is 36

T3 Check by typing the sums into your calculator 'as they read'.

A4 (a) 21.8   (b) 24.7

T4 Either put a bracket around everything on top and bottom or press equals to work out top row. (b) may need nested brackets on top.

A5 (a) 3.84   (b) 80.1

T5 In (a) put $3.2 + 1.8$ into the memory.
In (b) put $98.5 - 18.5$ into the memory and do

A6 37.2

Chapter 52

Proportional changes

You should understand and use proportional changes.

You should already know how to solve problems using ratios and how to work out percentages of quantities. In this chapter you will see how to use **proportional changes** to solve problems such as **compound interest** and you will look at **reverse percentage** problems.

Reverse percentage

Prices of goods in the shops sometimes say: 'inc. VAT'. This means that Value Added Tax (VAT) is already included in the price. Some companies (and schools) do not pay VAT on everything they buy so they may want to know the price before VAT was added. This is called a **reverse percentage** problem or 'working backwards'.

EXAMPLE **1** The price of a cooker is listed as £446.50, including 17.5% VAT. What is the price of the cooker without VAT?

ANSWER There are many ways to do this. Two are shown here:

Method 1. Set up a table comparing percentage and price.

100% + 17.5% = 117.5%. The price of the cooker is therefore equivalent to 117.5%. Work out 1% by dividing by 117.5. This gives 3.8. Work out 100% by multiplying by 100. This gives £380 as the price without VAT.

%	Price
117.5	446.50
1	3.8
100	380

Method 2. Divide by 117.5 and multiply by 100.
446.5 ÷ 117.5 × 100 = 380.

Method 2 is actually exactly the same as Method 1, but Method 1 goes through the calculation more slowly, so use this at first.

EXAMPLE **2** The price of a burger meal is reduced by 15%. It now costs £2.72. What did it cost before?

ANSWER £2.72 is a reduction of 15%, so it represents 85%. Divide by 85 to get 1%.

2.72 ÷ 85 = 0.032. Multiply by 100 to get 100%.
0.032 × 100 = 3.20. Original price was £3.20.

Compound interest

When you put money into a saving account you get **interest** on your money. The amount you get varies but is always expressed as a percentage. This is known as the **interest rate**. The interest is paid at regular intervals (usually every 6 or 12 months). After a year you will have the money you originally put in *and the extra interest*. This *total* amount is then used to calculate the interest for the next year and so on. This is called **compound interest**.

3 I put £300 into a bank that pays 7% interest each year (called **per annum** or **p.a.**).

(a) If I leave my money there and don't take any out, how much will I have after (i) 1 year (ii) 3 years?

(b) How many years will it be before I have over £400 in the bank?

(a) (i) £321. The interest for the first year is 7% of £300 = £21 (Sum is 7 × 300 ÷ 100). The amount in the bank after 1 year is £300 + £21 = £321.

(ii) £367.51. The interest for the second year is 7% of £321 = £22.47. The amount in the bank after 2 years is £321 + £22.47 = £343.47. The interest for the second year is 7% of £343.47 = £24.04 (nearest penny). The amount in the bank after 3 years is £343.47 + £24.04 = £367.51.

Note that these can also be done using decimals. 7% is 0.07, which when added to the original amount (100%) gives 1.07. 300 × 1.07 = 321, 321 × 1.07 = 343.47, 343.07 × 1.07 = 367.51 (nearest penny). This sum can be done as $300 \times (1.07)^3$

(b) 5 years. We could use the first method and see how many years it takes to get to over £400 but if we use the decimal method we get: $300 \times (1.07)^4 = 393.24$, $300 \times (1.07)^5 = 420.76$.

Check yourself

QUESTIONS

Q1 Find the original quantity (100%) if:
(a) 40% is £60
(b) 23% is £57.50
(c) 117.5% is £305.50
(d) 120% is 78 kg

Q2 Last year 16 pupils at a school got level 8 in their SATs. This represents 6.4% of the year. How many were in the year group?

ANSWERS AND TUTORIAL

A1 (a) £150   (c) £260
(b) £250   (d) 65 kg

T1 Find 1% in each case, then 100%: (a) is divide by 40, multiply by 100.

A2 250 pupils

T2 Sum is 16 ÷ 6.4 × 100.

ANSWERS AND TUTORIAL

A3 £230

T3 This time you have to include the original so divide by 103.2 first.

A4 50 trees

T4 Find 100% which is 250 then do 20% of 250.

A5 Yes. The final cost is £960

T5 This is not really a reverse percentage. 20% increase on £1000 gives £1200, and a 20% decrease of £1200 gives £960.

A6 (a) £270.40 (b) £2621.59

T6 This is best done using decimals. In (a) multiply by 1.04 twice and in (b) multiply by 1.07 four times.

A7 (a) (i) 27 cm (ii) 49.21 cm
(b) 6 weeks

T7 The decimal is 1.35.

A8 (a) (i) £9600 (ii) £4915.20
(b) 7 years (Between 6 and 7 years)

T8 The decimal for this sum is 0.8 because it is a 20% decrease.

A9 £4140.56

T9 As the number of years is so big you would probably lose count so do the sum 1000×1.07^{21} as each year is 1.07 times the value of the last year.

QUESTIONS

Q3 After a pay rise of 3.2%, Brian's pay went up to £237.36 a week. How much did he get before the pay rise?

Q4 In a garden 24% of the plants are shrubs, 56% are flowers and the remaining 20% are trees. There are 60 shrubs in the garden. How many trees are there?

Q5 I saved up to buy a computer that was £1000. Just as I had saved enough the price **went up by 20%**. The company then had a sale and **reduced** the price of the computer by **20%**. Did I have enough money to buy the computer?

Q6 Find the amount of money in the bank if:
(a) £250 is invested for 2 years at 4% interest pa.
(b) £2000 is invested for 4 years at 7% interest pa.

Q7 Ivy grows by 35% per week. I planted an ivy that was 20 cm tall.
(a) How tall was it after (I) 1 week (ii) 3 weeks?
(b) How many weeks did it take to reach a height of 1 metre?

Q8 I want to buy a new car that costs £12 000. My buyers guide tells me that it will lose 20% of its value each year.
(a) How much is it worth after (i) 1 year (ii) 4 years?
(b) Once the value of the car gets below £3000 I will sell it. How many years will this take?

Q9 A grandmother puts £1000 in the bank on the birth of her granddaughter. She gets 7% pa interest. The money will be paid over when the granddaughter is 21 years old. How much will she get?

T E S T   Q U E S T I O N S

Answers with examiner's comments on page 242.

1. Rectangles with length and width in the special ratio $1:\dfrac{2}{1+\sqrt5}$ are called golden rectangles. Some artists use them because the proportions look attractive.

   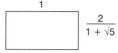

   (a) Work out $\dfrac{2}{1+\sqrt5}$. Write this using all the decimal places your calculator shows.

   (b) Ramesh used his calculator efficiently to work out $\dfrac{2}{1+\sqrt5}$. He did not have to write down any numbers and then key them back into his calculator. Show the steps he might have used with his calculator.

   (c) Four faces of this cuboid are golden rectangles.

   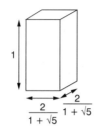

   The volume of the cuboid is $\left(\dfrac{2}{1+\sqrt5}\right)\times\left(\dfrac{2}{1+\sqrt5}\right)\times 1$

   Use a **short** and **accurate** method on your calculator to calculate this. Write the volume using all the decimal places your calculator shows.

   (d) Show the steps you used to make your method **short** and **accurate**.

   (1994 Paper 1)

2. Erica is writing a report for a newspaper. She says: 'I want to give the approximate distance from Britain to Australia; I think it is 12 400 miles so I will write 12 000 miles; I will give the distance to the nearest 1000 miles.'

   For each of the measurements below say how accurate you would need to be if you were writing a report for a newspaper.

   (a) The height of a single-decker bus in a report about different forms of transport.
   (b) The time it takes to drive 400 miles in a report about British holidays.
   (c) The length of the baby in a report about a film star's new baby.

   (1993 Paper 1)

3. Bryn wants to use the formulae $P = s + t + \dfrac{5\sqrt{s^2+t^2}}{3}$

   and $A = \frac{1}{2}st + \dfrac{(s^2+t^2)}{9}$ to work out the perimeter (P) and

   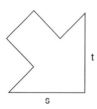

   area (A) of shapes like this:
   (a) Bryn substitutes $s = 4.5$ and $t = 6$ into the formulae:

   Work out the values of $P = 4.5 + 6 + \dfrac{5\sqrt{4.5^2+6^2}}{3}$ and $A = \frac{1}{2}\times 4.5\times 6 + \dfrac{(4.5^2+6^2)}{9}$.

   (b) Bryn substitutes $s = 1.7$ and $t = 0.9$ into the formulae:

   Work out the values of $P = 1.7 + 0.9 + \dfrac{5\sqrt{1.7^2+0.9^2}}{3}$ and $A = \frac{1}{2}\times 1.7\times 0.9 + \dfrac{(1.7^2+0.9^2)}{9}$.

   (1995 Paper 2)

4. A clothes shop had a closing down sale. The sale started on Tuesday and finished on Saturday. For each day of the sale, prices were reduced by 15% of the prices on the day before.

   (a) A shirt had a price of £19.95 on Monday. Kevin bought it on Wednesday. How much did he pay?
   (b) Ghita bought a dress on Tuesday for £41.48. What was its price on Monday?
   (c) A jacket had a price of £49.95 on Monday. What was its price on Friday?
   (d) Another shop is reducing its prices each day by 12% of the prices on the day before. How many days would it take for its original prices to be reduced by more that 50%?

   (1996 Paper 2)

5. Margaret and Nicky each measure a **different** leaf. They both say their leaf is 8 cm to the nearest cm. Does this mean that their leaves are the same length? Explain your answer.

(1993 Paper 3)

6. David is studying blood cells through a microscope. The diameter of a red cell is 0.000 714 cm and the diameter of a white cell is 0.001 243 cm.

(a) Use a calculator to work out the difference between the diameter of a red cell and the diameter of a white cell. Give your answer in **millimetres**.

(b) David wants to explain how small the cells are. He calculates how many white cells would fit across a full stop which has a diameter of 0.65 mm. How many whole white cells would fit across the full stop?

(1995 Paper 1)

7. This table shows information about some countries in Europe.

Country	Area in km^2	Population		Country	Number of people for each km^2
France	543 965	57 456 000			
Netherlands	41 785	15 129 000	Most people for each km^2		
Spain	504 782	39 952 000	Fewest people for each km^2		
United Kingdom	244 103	57 561 000			

(a) Which country has the most people for each km^2? Which country has the fewest people for each km^2? Write down these countries and their values for the 'number of people for each km^2', in the table.

(b) Look at the information for the United Kingdom. Imagine that the area of land was shared out equally amongst all the people. Calculate how much land, in m^2, each person would get. (1 km^2 = 1 000 000 m^2)

(1996 Paper 1)

8. (a) Leela has to use brackets to find the answer to: $\dfrac{7.84}{4.41 - 1.74}$

Write down the keys you would use to do this on a calculator, using the brackets keys.

(b) Jim has to use the memory to find the answer to: $\dfrac{4.56}{13.2 - 4.56}$.

Write down the keys you would use to do this on a calculator, using the memory keys.

(1993 Paper 1)

9. An engineer has labelled tubes A, B, C, D and E with their lengths, measured to the nearest hundredth of a centimetre. She keeps the tubes in 2 different boxes. Box 1 has tubes that are 8cm to the nearest cm. Box 2 has tubes that are 9 cm to the nearest cm.

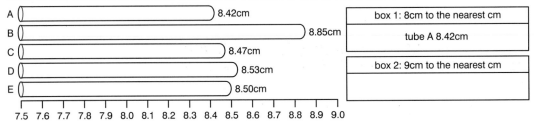

(a) Put tubes B, C, D and E in the correct box.

(b) She puts more tubes in the boxes. What is the largest possible length of a tube in Box 1?

(c) What is the smallest possible length of a tube in Box 2?

(1993 Paper 2)

Chapter 53

Finding the nth term when the rule is quadratic

> You should be able to give a rule for the next term or the nth term of a number pattern where the rule is quadratic.

You should know how to find the nth term of a linear sequence and how to substitute into formulae that use powers.

You have seen in previous levels how number patterns build up and how to find the nth terms. Most of the ones you have looked at went up by a fixed amount each time. This made rules fairly easy to find. Such rules are **linear rules** and have the form $an \pm b$. When patterns do not go up by the same amount each time we need to find **quadratic rules**.

$$2, 6, 12, 20, 30$$

This series goes up by 4, then by 6 then by 8, then by 10, then by 12 and so on. Series that increase this way have a rule that involves a term in n^2. There are two ways to try to find the pattern.

Finding a multiplication sum

Often series like that above can be written as a series of multiplication sums. For example you could write the series as:

$$1 \times 2, 2 \times 3, 3 \times 4, 4 \times 5, 5 \times 6, \ldots\ldots$$

Each part of the multiplication can be expressed as a linear series in n. The first part of each multiplication is 1, 2, 3, 4, 5 .... which is just n. The second part is 2, 3, 4, 5, 6 .... which is just $n + 1$.

This gives the nth term as $n(n + 1)$. This can also be written as $n^2 + n$.

Differencing

$$3, 7, 12, 18, 25 \ldots.$$

If you try to write this series as a set of multiplications you cannot find one that gives any sort of pattern. When this happens you can use **differencing**.

The series above can be written as a list and the differences between each term calculated.

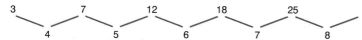

From this we can see that the differences go up by 1 each time. If we do the differences of the differences (called the second difference) then we get

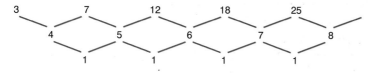

**Finding the nth term
when the rule is
quadratic**

Try this trick. As the second difference is **odd** multiply the original series by **2**. This gives 6, 14, 24, 36, 50, ... Now look for a series of multiplication sums. Try:

$$1 \times 6, 2 \times 7, 3 \times 8, 4 \times 9, 5 \times 10$$

This is a nth term of n(n + 5). Remembering that we doubled the original series we can write down the nth term as $\frac{1}{2}$n(n + 5). Check it and see if it works!

EXAMPLE **1** Find the nth term of the series:

6, 12, 20, 30, 42, 56 ....

ANSWER First look for a series of times sums. We can soon find

$$2 \times 3, 3 \times 4, 4 \times 5, 5 \times 6, 6 \times 7$$

Each part of this can be expressed as a linear series in n. For example, the first part of each multiplication is 2, 3, 4, 5, 6 .... which is n + 1. The second part is 3, 4, 5, 6, 7 .... which is the series n + 2. This gives the nth term as (n + 1)(n + 2) which can be written as $n^2 + 3n + 2$.

EXAMPLE **2** Martin is making triangles with marbles. These are his first 4 pictures:

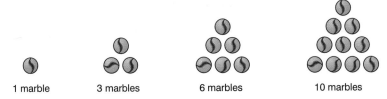

1 marble   3 marbles   6 marbles   10 marbles

How many marbles will there be in the nth triangle ?

ANSWER Write the pattern out as a list and carry it on a bit if you want to

1, 3, 6, 10, 15, 21, 28, 36, ...

The second difference is odd (1) so double the series

2, 6, 12, 20, 30, 42, 56, 72, ...

Now look for a multiplication series:

$$1 \times 2, 2 \times 3, 3 \times 4, 4 \times 5, 5 \times 6, 6 \times 7, 7 \times 8, 8 \times 9 ....$$

It should be easy to see that this series is n(n + 1). So, the nth term of the original series is $\frac{1}{2}$n(n+1).

LEVEL **7**
ALGEBRA

**Finding the nth term
when the rule is
quadratic**

Check yourself

QUESTIONS

Q1 Find the nth term of each of these number patterns: (you will be able to find a multiplication sum for each of them)
(a) 3, 8, 15, 24, 35, ...
(b) 2, 6, 12, 20, 30, ...
(c) 0, 3, 8, 15, 24, ...
(d) 4, 12, 24, 40, 60, ...

Q2 4, 11, 21, 34, 50, 69, ...
(a) Work out the second difference for the series above.
(b) Multiply the original series by 2.
(c) Find a multiplication series for your answer to (b). Hint: it starts 1×8, 2×11.
(d) Write down the nth term of the series 8, 11, 14, 17, 20, ...
(e) Write down the nth term of the original series.

Q3 Find the nth term of each of these number patterns. You will need to double each series and look for a multiplication sum of the doubled series.
(a) 2, 5, 9, 14, 20, ...
(b) 7, 12, 18, 25, 33, ...

Q4 For the series of pictures below, find how many matches are needed for the nth pattern:

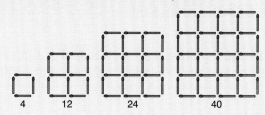

4   12   24   40

ANSWERS AND TUTORIAL

A1 (a) $n(n + 2)$ (c) $(n - 1)(n + 1)$
     (b) $n(n + 1)$ (d) $2n(n + 1)$

T1 (a) is $1 \times 3, 2 \times 4, 3 \times 5, 4 \times 6, 5 \times 7$, ...
     (b) is $1 \times 2, 2 \times 3, 3 \times 4, 4 \times 5, 5 \times 6$, ...
     (c) is $0 \times 2, 1 \times 3, 2 \times 4, 3 \times 5, 4 \times 6$, ...
     (d) is $2 \times 2, 4 \times 3, 6 \times 4, 8 \times 5, 10 \times 6$, ...

A2 (a) Second difference is 3
     (b) 8, 22, 42, 68, 100, 138
     (c) $1 \times 8, 2 \times 11, 3 \times 14, 4 \times 217, 5 \times 20,$
         6×24
     (d) $3n + 5$
     (e) $\frac{1}{2}n (3n + 5)$

T2 The trick of multiplying by 2 sometimes works. You will usually be given a big hint when to use it. Don't forget to divide by 2 for the final answer.

A3 (a) $\frac{1}{2}n(n + 3)$ (b) $\frac{1}{2}(n + 1)(n + 6)$

T3 (a) The doubled series is: $1 \times 4, 2 \times 5, 3 \times 6,$
         4×7, ...
     (b) The doubled series is: $2 \times 7, 3 \times 8, 4 \times 9,$
         5×10, ...

A4 $2n(n + 1)$

T4 Same as 1(d).

Chapter 54

Solving simultaneous equations by algebra

You should be able to solve simultaneous equations algebraically.

You should already know how to solve a linear equation and how to substitute into algebraic expressions and do some simple algebraic operations such as $2 \times 3x = 6x$ and $6y - 4y = 2y$.

The equation $2x + y = 5$ has an infinite number of solutions. For example $x = 2$, $y = 1$ is a solution; $x = -1$, $y = 7$ is another. The equation $3x - 2y = 4$ also has an infinite number of solutions. For example $x = 2$, $y = 1$ and $x = 6$, $y = 7$ both work. However only one solution fits both equations at the same time (simultaneously). This chapter looks at the ways of solving **simultaneous equations** using algebra.

The six steps

To solve simultaneous equations we need to work through 6 steps. These are **Balancing**, **Eliminating**, **Solving**, **Substituting**, **Solve Again** and **Checking**.

EXAMPLE

1 Solve: $2x + 3y = 30$
$\qquad 5x + 7y = 71$

ANSWER

Step 1: Balancing. Multiply equation 1 (1) by 5 and equation 2 (2) by 2. This will give the same coefficient for x. This gives two more equations which we call (3) and (4).

$2x + 3y = 30 \qquad (1)$
$5x + 7y = 71 \qquad (2)$

Step 2: Elimination. Equation (3) and equation (4) now have the same number of x s and they are both positive. **Subtract** equation 4 from equation 3. This will eliminate the x terms.

$(1) \times 5$
$10x + 15y = 150 \qquad (3)$
$(2) \times 2$
$10x + 14y = 142 \qquad (4)$

Step 3. Solving. You are left with a simple equation involving y. Solve this to find y. (This is already done!)

$(3) - (4)$
$10x + 15y = 150$
$\underline{10x + 14y = 142} \; -$
$\qquad 1y = \quad 8$

Step 4. Substituting. Substitute the value of y into one of the original equations.

Substitute in (1)
$2x + 3 \times 8 = 30$

Step 5. Solve Again. You have a linear equation in x. Solve this to find x.

$2x = 6$ (subtract 24)
$\quad x = 3$ (divide by 2)

Step 6. Checking. Put the values of x and y into **both** of the original equations to check that they work.

$2 \times 3 + 3 \times 8 = 30 \checkmark$
$5 \times 3 + 7 \times 8 = 71 \checkmark$

Solving problems

Solving simultaneous equations is useful in real-life situations.

2 When Mr. Walsh goes to the garage he always buys petrol and some cans of Cola. Last week he bought 4 gallons of petrol and 3 cans of Cola. His bill was £11.75. Yesterday he bought 5 gallons of petrol and 4 cans of Cola. His bill was £14.80. Today he has just bought 2 gallons of petrol and 1 can of Cola. Assuming the prices of petrol and Cola haven't changed what is his bill today?

EXAMPLE

Call the cost of each gallon of petrol p and each can of Cola c and work in pence. This gives the two equations:

ANSWER

$$4p + 3c = 1175 \quad (1)$$

$$5p + 4c = 1480 \quad (2)$$

$(1) \times 5 \quad 20p + 15c = 5875 \quad (3)$

$(2) \times 4 \quad 20p + 16c = 5920 \quad (4)$

$(4) - (3) \quad\quad\quad 1c = 45 \quad (4) - (3)$ keeps everything positive.

Substitute in (1) $\quad 4p + 3 \times 45 = 1175$

(Subtract 135) $\quad\quad\quad 4p = 1040$

(Divide by 4) $\quad\quad\quad p = 260$

Check: $4 \times 260 + 3 \times 45 = 1175$ ✓
$\quad\quad\quad 5 \times 260 + 4 \times 45 = 1480$ ✓

His bill today will be $2 \times £2.60 + £0.45 = £5.65$.

Check yourself

QUESTIONS

Q1 Solve the following simultaneous equations.
(These equations are already balanced.)
(a) $x - y = 8$
$x + 2y = 14$
(b) $2x + 3y = 1$
$2x + y = 3$
(c) $3x - y = 7$
$2x + y = 8$
(d) $4a + 5b = 6$
$7a + 5b = 3$

ANSWERS AND TUTORIAL

A1 (a) $x = 10, y = 2$ (c) $x = 3, y = 2$
(b) $x = 2, y = -1$ (d) $a = -1, b = 2$

T1 In (a) do equation (2) minus equation (1).
In (b) (1) minus (2). In (c) (1) add (2) and in (d) (2) minus (1) or (1) minus (2).

Solving simultaneous equations by algebra

ANSWERS AND TUTORIAL

A2 (a) x = 3, y = 1   (c) x = 5, y = 2
  (b) x = 2, y = –1   (d) a = 7, b = –8

T2 In (a) multiply (1) by 2 and add. In (b) multiply (2) by 3 and add. In (c) multiply (1) by 3 and subtract. In (d) multiply (1) by 5 and subtract.

A3 (a) x = 3, y = –1
  (b) x = 2, y = –1
  (c) x = 5, y = 3
  (d) a = 6, b = –4

T3 In every case you can balance the x s by multiplying an equation by the coefficient of x in the other equation. For example, in (a) multiply equation (1) by 3 and equation (2) by 5.

A4 (a) 2t + 7d = 1310
      3t + 4d = 990
  (b) d = 150, t = 130

T4 multiply (1) by 3, (2) by 2
  6t + 21d = 3930
  6t + 8d = 1980
      13d = 1950

A5 The Wests pay £3.00. Tea costs 60p and buns are 90p

T5 3t + 5s = 630
  4t + 3s = 510

A6 6x + 48y = 138
  5x + 22y = 70
  3x + 35y = £96.50

T6 You should find that x = £3.00 and y = £2.50.

QUESTIONS

Q2 Solve the following simultaneous equations. (You first need to multiply one of them to balance the equations.)
  (a) 3x – y = 8   (c) 3x – 4y = 7
      2x + 2y = 8   x + 2y = 9
  (b) 5x + 3y = 7   (d) 3a + b = 13
      4x – y = 9   7a + 5b = 9

Q3 Solve the following simultaneous equations. (You need to first multiply both of these equations to balance them.)
  (a) 5x – 3y = 18   (c) 3x – 5y = 0
      3x + 2y = 7   2x + 7y = 31
  (b) 2x + 3y = 1   (d) 4a + 5b = 4
      5x + 2y = 8   6a + 4b = 20

Q4 Mr. Wilson needs some bulbs for his garden. He buys two packets of tulips and 7 packets of daffodils which cost him £13.10. His neighbour buys 3 packets of tulips and 4 packets of daffodils. She pays £9.90.
  (a) Set up a pair of simultaneous equations to represent this situation. (Use t for tulips and d for daffodil packets).
  (b) Use your equations to find the cost of each packet.

Q5 The Wilsons buy 3 cups of tea and 5 sticky buns. They pay £6.30. The Watsons buy 4 cups of tea and 3 sticky buns. They pay £5.10. The Wests buy 2 cups of tea and 2 sticky buns. How much do they pay?

Q6 6 teachers and 48 pupils from a school pay £138 to see Romeo and Juliet. Another school party of 5 teachers and 22 pupils pay £70. Teacher's tickets cost £x and pupil tickets cost £y. Set up a pair of simultaneous equations and solve them to find the cost for 3 teachers and 35 pupils.

Chapter 55

Solving simultaneous equations using graphs

You should be able to solve simultaneous equations graphically.

You should already know how to solve simultaneous equations using algebra and how to draw straight line graphs. This chapter looks at solving simultaneous equations using graphs.

The point of intersection

Equations like $y = 2x + 3$ and $2x - y = 4$ can be represented by **linear** (straight line) graphs. Each point on each line represents one of the infinite number of solutions. Unless two lines are parallel they must cross at some point. This **point of intersection** is the solution of both lines. In other words it is the one solution that is true for both lines **simultaneously**. The point of intersection is the solution to the problem.

1 Use a graph to solve $y = 2x - 1$
$\qquad\qquad\qquad x + y = 8$

EXAMPLE

ANSWER

The first graph is drawn using the gradient-intercept method. It crosses the y-axis at –1 and has a gradient of 2.

The second is drawn using the cover up method. It crosses the x-axis at 8 and the y-axis at 8.

The two graphs cross at $x = 3$, $y = 5$ so the solution of the original equations is $x = 3$ and $y = 5$.

Check these in the original equations

$5 = 2 \times 3 - 1$ ✓
$3 + 5 = 8$ ✓

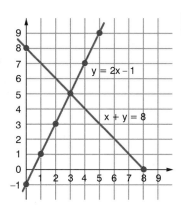

2 Use a graph to solve $2x + y = 5$
$\qquad\qquad\qquad 3x - 2y = 4$

EXAMPLE

ANSWER

Both of these graphs should be drawn using the 'cover-up' method. The first graph crosses the x-axis at 2.5 and the y-axis at 5. The second graph crosses the x-axis at 1.33 and the y-axis at –2.

They cross at $x = 2$, $y = 1$, giving the solution:

$x = 2$ and $y = 1$.

Check these values in the original equation.

$2 \times 2 + 1 = 5$ ✓
$3 \times 2 - 2 \times 1 = 4$ ✓

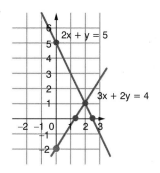

EXAMPLE

ANSWER

3 By using a graph solve $y = \dfrac{x}{2} - 3$

$$y = 2x - 5$$

Both of these are drawn by the gradient intercept method:

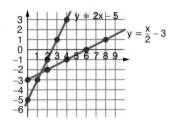

They appear to cross at (1.3, –2.3)

Check: $-2.3 = 1.3 \div 2 - 3 = -2.35$ (Close)
$-2.3 = 2 \times 1.3 - 5 = -2.4$ (Close)

This is good enough for reading off a graph.

The actual answer is $x = 1\dfrac{1}{3}$, $y = -2\dfrac{2}{3}$.

Check yourself

ANSWERS AND TUTORIAL

A1 (a) $x = 3$, $y = 2$

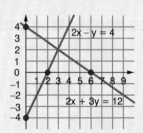

(b) $x = 3$, $y = 2$

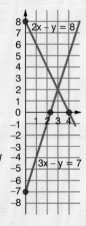

T1 (a) Draw both lines by cover-up rule and don't forget to check.
(b) The first is not easy to draw by the cover-up rule as the x value is a fraction $2\dfrac{1}{3}$. So you must check the answer.

QUESTIONS

Q1 Draw graphs to solve:
(a) $2x + 3y = 12$
    $2x - y = 4$
(b) $3x - y = 7$
    $2x + y = 8$

Check yourself

QUESTIONS

Q2 The line y = x is already drawn on the grid.
    (a) Use the table below to help you draw the line y = 2x – 1.

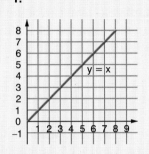

    (b) Solve the pair of simultaneous equations y = x and y = 2x – 1.

Q3 Draw graphs to solve:
    y = 2x + 1
    x – 2y = 1

Q4 The line y = $\frac{1}{2}$x – 3 is drawn on the grid below:

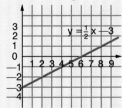

    (a) On the same grid draw the line x + y = 4.
    (b) Find the point of intersection of the graph. Check that your answer works for both lines.

ANSWERS AND TUTORIAL

A2 **(a)**

x	0	1	–2
y	–1	1	3

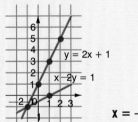

    (b) x = 1, y = 1

T2 You can use the gradient intercept method to draw the second graph.

A3

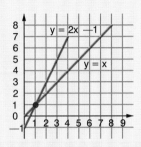

        x = –1, y = –1

T3 First line use gradient intercept. Second line use cover up.

A4 **(a)**

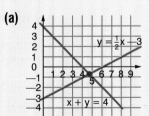

    (b) x = 4.7, y = –0.7
    Check: 4 × 4.7 – 3 = –0.65 (almost 0.7)
    4.7 + –0.7 = 4 (spot on)

T4 You can be a bit out as you would not be expected to read a graph to more than 1 decimal. (The actual answer is 4$\frac{2}{3}$, –$\frac{2}{3}$).

Chapter 56

Solving inequalities

You should be able to solve simple inequalities.

You should already know how to solve simple linear equations. You met some **inequalities** when we used expressions like $-3 \leqslant x \leqslant 3$ when drawing linear graphs. This expression means x is bigger than or equal to -3 but smaller to or equal to 3. In this chapter, will look at inequalities in more detail.

Types of inequality

There are two types of inequality:

- **Strict inequalities** have the signs < (less than) and > (greater than). **Inclusive inequalities** have the signs $\leqslant$ (less than or equal to) and $\geqslant$ (greater than or equal to). In inclusive inequalities, the **limiting number** or **boundary** is included.

EXAMPLE

ANSWER

1 x is an integer. What values can x take if $-3 < x \leqslant 2$?

Integers are positive or negative whole numbers. -3 is not included as x is greater than -3. 2 is included as x is less than or equal to 2. So, x can take the values $-2, -1, 0, 1$ and 2.

The number line

Inequalities can be represented on a number line. Strict inequalities are shown by an open circle to indicate that the boundary is not included. Inclusive inequalities are shown by a solid circle to indicate that the limiting point is included.

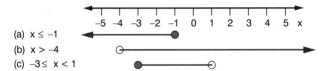

(a) $x \leqslant -1$
(b) $x > -4$
(c) $-3 \leqslant x < 1$

Solving inequalities

If $x + 4 < 6$, then x can take a range of values up to but not including 2. For example, $1 + 4 = 5 < 6, -5 + 4 = -1 < 6, 1.99 + 4 = 5.99 < 6$.

The solution would be written as $x < 2$ and could be shown on a number line as:

A useful rule to remember is 'Treat an inequality like an equation'.

2 Solve the following inequalities:

(a) $\frac{x}{2} - 3 > 5$

(b) $5x - 3 \leqslant 2x + 9$

(a) $\frac{x}{2} > 8$ (add 3)

$x > 16$ (times 2)

(b) $3x - 3 \leqslant 9$ (subtract 2x)
$3x \leqslant 12$ (add 3)
$x \leqslant 4$ (divide by 3)

Negative coefficients for the variable

The rule we have just used does not work when negatives are involved. There are two ways round this:

- The first is to move the letter term over the inequality to make it positive.
- The second is to change the sign to a plus, change all the signs and then reverse the inequality sign.

3 Solve the inequalities:

(a) $3 - 2x < 7$

(b) $4 - \frac{x}{3} \geqslant 2$

(a) Move x term across inequality sign:
$3 < 7 + 2x$ (add 2x)
$-4 < 2x$ (subtract 7)
$-2 < x$ (divide by 2)
$x > -2$ (write 'backwards')

(b) $-\frac{x}{3} \geqslant -2$ (subtract 4)

$-x \geqslant -6$ (times 3)

$x \leqslant 6$ (change all signs, including the inequality sign)

Check yourself

QUESTIONS

ANSWERS AND TUTORIAL

Q1 n is an integer. What values can n take if:
(a) $-2 < n < 5$?
(b) $0 \leqslant n < 6$?
(c) $-3 \leqslant n \leqslant 4$?

A1 (a) $-1, 0, 1, 2, 3, 4$
(b) $0, 1, 2, 3, 4, 5$
(c) $-3, -2, -1, 0, 1, 2, 3, 4$

T1 You must understand the difference between strict inequalities and inclusive inequalities.

Solving inequalities

ANSWERS AND TUTORIAL

A2
(a)
(b)
(c)

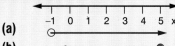

T2 Remember open circles are strict inequalities.

A3 (a) $x \leqslant 3$
(b) $x > 1$
(c) $-3 \leqslant x < 5$

A4 (a) $x < 13$ (b) $x \geqslant 8$

T4 Solve these just like you solve an equation, eg in (b) $x = 2 \times 4 = 8$

A5 (a) $x \leqslant -9$ (b) $x \geqslant 2$

T5 Move the smallest x term over the inequality, eg in (b) $3x - 2 \geqslant 20 - 8x$, $11x - 2 \geqslant 20$, $11x \geqslant 22$

A6 (a) $x > -6$ (b) $x \geqslant -16$

T6 These have a minus x term so need to have the signs changed at some stage.

A7 When a negative number is squared the answer is positive.

T7 Don't forget that all squares are positive. You will probably not get a square at level 7.

A8 (a) $-4, -3, -2, -1, 0, 1, 2$
(b) 16

T8 Squaring a negative gives a positive.

QUESTIONS

Q2 Draw the following inequalities on a number line:
(a) $x > -1$
(b) $x \leqslant 5$
(c) $-1 \leqslant x < 4$

Q3 What inequalities are represented on the number lines below:

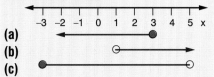

(a)
(b)
(c)

Q4 Solve the inequalities:

(a) $x - 6 < 7$ (b) $\dfrac{x}{2} \geqslant 4$

Q5 Solve the inequalities:
(a) $2x + 4 \leqslant x - 5$
(b) $3x - 2 \geqslant 4(5 - 2x)$

Q6 Solve the inequalities:

(a) $3 - x < 9$ (b) $2 - \dfrac{x}{4} \leqslant 6$

Q7 If $x^2 \leqslant 9$ explain why x can take any value between -3 and 3 inclusive.

Q8 (a) What integers obey the following inequality: $-4 \leqslant x < 3$?
(b) What is the largest value x^2 can take?

1. Magic squares were used to tell fortunes long ago in China. They contain whole numbers starting from 1. The numbers in each row add up to the magic number. Eleri's magic square has 3 rows.

magic number 15

The magic number is 15. The size is 3 × 3.

Tony made a magic square with more rows. The magic number is 2925.

We do not know the size of his square.

(a) When the size of a magic square is n × n, the magic number is $\frac{n(n^2 + 1)}{2}$. Use n = 3 to check that this works for Eleri's magic square.

magic number 2925

(b) Find the size of Tony's magic square. You may use trial and improvement.

(1994 Paper 2)

2. (a) The first five diagrams in a sequence are:

   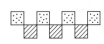 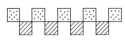

1st n=1   2nd n=2   3rd n=3   4th n=4   5th n=5

The total number of squares in the nth diagram is n + (n - 1). Which **part** of n + (n − 1) shows the number of **dotted** squares? Which **part** of n + (n − 1) shows the number of **striped** squares?

(b) Gerard put ● or ✕ on each of the corners to help him find a number pattern.

   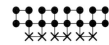 

1st n=1   2nd n=2   3rd n=3   4th n=4   5th n=5

Gerard said 'In the nth diagram there are n squares in the top row. There are 4 ● on each square in the top row so 4n stands for the number of ● in the nth diagram'

2(n − 1) stands for the number of ✕ in the nth diagram.

Explain how you can see this by looking at the diagrams.

(1994 Paper 1)

3. The equation $n^2 + n = 11$ has two roots. The roots are the values of n which make the equation correct. Kapil finds that 2 and 3 are the closest **whole numbers** to one of the roots. Then he tries **1 decimal place** numbers.

n	$n^2 + n$
2	6
3	12

He finds that 2.8 and 2.9 are the **1 decimal place** numbers closest to the root.

(a) Find the **3 decimal place numbers** which are closest to the root. Show **all** your trials in a table.

(b) Write down the two **3 decimal place** numbers you found in part (a).

n	$n^2 + n$
2.5	6
2.8	10.64
2.9	11.31

(1993 Paper 3)

4. Richard makes a square get bigger using black and white counters.

stage 1   stage 2   stage 3   stage 4

Total number of counters	1	4	9	16		100
Stage	1	2	3	4		
number of counters added	1	3	5	7		

1 counter added   3 counters added   5 counters added   7 counters added

Stage	1	2	3	4		n
number of counters added	1	3	5	7		3n + 2

(a) Fill in **both** missing numbers.

(b) Richard writes 3n + 2 in the table.
He is **wrong**. What should he have written?

(1993 Paper 2)

5. Lucy makes a rectangle with an area of 34 cm². The sides of Lucy's rectangle are x cm and (12 – x) cm.

She wants to find a value of x so that x(12 – x) = 34. Between which **one decimal place** numbers does x lie? You may use a table to help you.

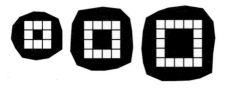

x	12 – x	area
3	9	27

(1996 Paper 2)

6. Indira, David and Lisa used square white tiles to explore this pattern.

They did not seem to agree about the **number of tiles**.
They wrote their rules for the nth shape in different ways.

Indira wrote: David wrote:

4 × 2   4 × 3   4 × 4   4 × 1 + 4   4 × 2 + 4   4 × 3 + 4

The nth shape is 4(n + 1)   The nth shape is ....

What did David write for the number of tiles in the nth shape at the bottom of his diagram?

(1993 Paper 1)

7. t and q are two numbers which fit both

     q + 2t = 17
     6 + q = 2t

Solve the equations. Show your working.

(1993 Paper 2)

Chapter 57

Pythagoras' theorem

You should understand and be able to apply Pythagoras' theorem when solving problems in two dimensions.

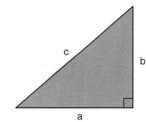

You should already know how to find squares and square roots of numbers and how to round numbers using decimal places or significant figures.

Pythagoras' theorem: for any right-angled triangle: $a^2 + b^2 = c^2$.

This chapter will show you how to use this important formula. It will help you calculate the third side in a right-angled triangle if you know the other two sides. The longest side c is called the **hypotenuse**.

Before you start working through this chapter make sure that you are familiar with the 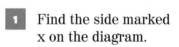 buttons on your calculator.

This table may also help you when you use Pythagoras' theorem to solve problems.

To calculate the hypotenuse	To calculate a short side
1. Square both numbers.	1. Square both numbers.
2. Add the two numbers together.	2. Subtract the smaller number from the larger number.
3. Take the square root.	3. Take the square root.

1 Find the side marked x on the diagram.

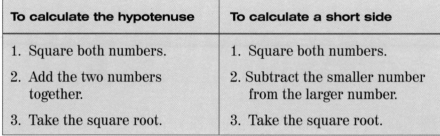

x is the hypotenuse.
$$x^2 = 3^2 + 4^2$$
$$x^2 = 9 + 16 = 25$$
$$x = \sqrt{25}$$
$$x = 5 \text{ cm}$$

Try this sequence of operations on your calculator:

You may not have to press the 2nd 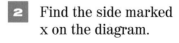 button.

You should get the answer 5.

2 Find the side marked x on the diagram.

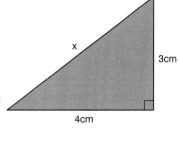

ANSWER

x is one of the shorter sides. $x^2 = 13^2 - 5^2$.

$$= 169 - 25$$
$$= 144$$
$$x = \sqrt{144}$$
$$x = 12 \text{ cm}$$

Try this sequence of operations on your calculator:

You may not have to press the 2nd $=$ button. You should get the answer 12.

EXAMPLE 3

Calculate the length of the missing side in each of the following right-angled triangles. Give your answers correct to 3 significant figures.

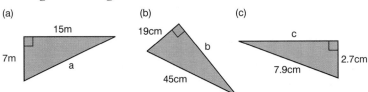

(a)   15m
7m   a

(b) 19cm
          b
    45cm

(c)   c
         2.7cm
    7.9cm

ANSWER

(a) a is the hypotenuse

$$a^2 = 15^2 + 7^2 = 274$$
$$a = \sqrt{274}$$
$$a = 16.6 \text{ m (to 3 sf)}$$

(b) b is a short side

$$b^2 = 45^2 - 19^2 = 1664$$
$$b = \sqrt{1664}$$
$$b = 40.8 \text{ cm (to 3 sf)}$$

(c) c is a short side

$$c^2 = 7.9^2 - 2.7^2 = 55.12$$
$$c = \sqrt{55.12}$$
$$c = 7.42 \text{ cm (to 3 sf)}$$

EXAMPLE 4

Abigail and Simon are on a day's hike over the moors. They set off from the car park and walk 7 km due east before stopping for a coffee break. They then continue walking due North for a further 6.5 km when they stop for lunch. After lunch they decide to go directly back to the car park. How far will they have to walk? Give your answer to a suitable degree of accuracy.

ANSWER

Draw a sensible diagram which includes the right angle and the distances. Label the unknown distance x. Using Pythagoras' theorem:

$$x^2 = 7^2 + 6.5^2 = 91.25$$

$$x = \sqrt{91.25}$$

$$x = 9.6 \text{ km (to 1 dp)}$$

Since the original distances are no more accurate than 1 decimal place, it makes sense to give the answer to the same degree of accuracy.

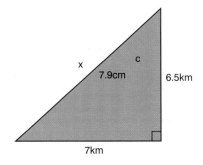

x   c
   7.9cm   6.5km

7km

Check yourself

QUESTIONS

Q 1 Calculate the length of the missing side in each of the following right-angled triangles. Give your answers correct to 2 decimal places.

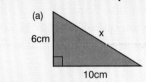

(a)
6cm x
10cm

(b)
y
5.8m
8.1m

(c)
z
5cm 5cm

Q 2 ABCD is a rectangle. Calculate the length of the diagonal AC. Give your answer correct to 2 significant figures.

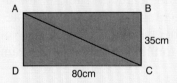

A   B
35cm
D   80cm   C

Q 3 XYZ is an isosceles triangle with XY = XZ = 16 cm and YZ = 12 cm.

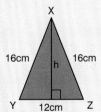

X
16cm h 16cm
Y   12cm   Z

(a) Calculate the perpendicular height h. Give your answer to the nearest centimetre.
(b) Hence calculate the area of triangle XYZ.

ANSWERS AND TUTORIAL

A 1 (a) **11.66 cm**   (c) **7.07 cm**
(b) **5.65 m**

T 1 (a) x is the hypotenuse.
$$x^2 = 10^2 + 6^2$$
$$= 136$$
$$x = \sqrt{136}$$
$$x = 11.66 \text{ (2 dp)}$$

(b) y is a short side.
$$y^2 = 8.1^2 - 5.8^2$$
$$= 31.97$$
$$y = \sqrt{31.97}$$
$$y = 5.65 \text{ (2 dp)}$$

(c) z is the hypotenuse.
$$z^2 = 5^2 + 5^2$$
$$= 50$$
$$z = \sqrt{50}$$
$$z = 7.07 \text{ (2 dp).}$$

A 2 **87 cm**

T 2 AC is the hypotenuse in the triangle ACD.
Let AC = x.
$$x^2 = 80^2 + 35^2$$
$$= 7625$$
$$x = \sqrt{7625}$$
$$x = 87 \text{ (2 sf)}$$

A 3 (a) **15 cm**   (b) **89 cm^2**

T 3 (a) The perpendicular bisects YZ.
Draw a sensible diagram:
h is a short side.
$$h^2 = 16^2 - 6^2$$
$$= 220$$
$$h = \sqrt{220}$$
$$h = 14.8 \text{ cm}$$
$$= 15 \text{ cm to nearest cm.}$$

h   16
6cm

(b) $A = \frac{1}{2}bh = \frac{1}{2} \times 12 \times 14.8 = 89 \text{ cm}^2$

Chapter 58

Areas of compound shapes and volumes of prisms

> You should be able to calculate lengths areas and volumes in plane shapes and right prisms.

You should already know the formulae for finding areas of 2-D shapes, the formula for finding the volume of a cuboid and how to enlarge a shape about the origin using a scale factor.

Finding areas of compound shapes

A **compound shape** is any shape made up from a different number of basic shapes. This chapter shows how to find the area of a compound shape by breaking the shape down into basic shapes and then using the standard area formulae for each one. Finding the total area of the compound shape may then involve addition or subtraction.

EXAMPLE

1 Mr. Slack wanted to find the area of his new garden patio so that he could pave it. He drew a sketch first and made the measurements shown. He then realised that he needed to know the length x on the diagram.

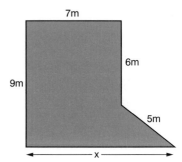

(a) Why does Mr Slack need this measurement?

(b) Calculate the length x.

(c) Find the area of the patio.

ANSWER

(a) The shape is made from a rectangle and a triangle. You need to know the dimensions of the rectangle to find its area: these are 9 m and 7 m. You can find the height of the triangle but you need to know the length of its base to find its area: the diagram does not tell you this information.

(b) The height of the triangle = 9 – 6 = 3 m.

Let the base of the triangle = y.
It is a right-angled triangle,
so use Pythagoras' theorem:
$$y^2 = 5^2 - 3^2$$
$$= 25 - 9 = 16$$
$$y = 4 \text{ m}.$$
$$x = 7 + y = 11 \text{ m}.$$

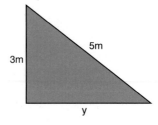

(c) The area of the rectangle = $9 \times 7 = 63 \text{ m}^2$. The area of the triangle = $\frac{1}{2} \times 4 \times 3 = 6 \text{ m}^2$. The area of the patio = $63 + 6 = 69 \text{ m}^2$.

**Areas of compound
shapes and volumes
of prisms**

2 Draw a grid with x and y axes going from 0 to 10. Plot the points
A(6, 2), B(7, 4), C(7, 8), D(8, 10), E(9, 8), F(9, 4), G(10, 2). Join the
points to get a 'rocket' shape.

(a) Find the area of the rocket.

(b) Enlarge the rocket by a scale factor $\frac{1}{2}$ about the origin.

(c) Find the area of the enlarged rocket.

(d) Find the ratio of the areas of the 2 rockets.

EXAMPLE

ANSWER

(a)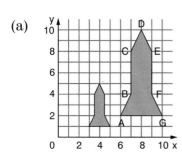

The rocket is made of 3 shapes.

Area of triangle $= \frac{1}{2} \times 2 \times 2 = 2$.

Area of rectangle $= 4 \times 2 = 8$

Area of trapezium $= \frac{1}{2}(4 + 2) \times 2 = 6$.

Area of rocket $= 16$.

(b) To enlarge a shape about the origin, you multiply each number in
the coordinates by the scale factor. If the scale factor is $\frac{1}{2}$, this
will mean halving all the numbers. So the new coordinates to be
plotted are: (3, 1), ($3\frac{1}{2}$, 2), ($3\frac{1}{2}$, 4), (4, 5), ($4\frac{1}{2}$, 4), ($4\frac{1}{2}$, 2), (5, 1).

Notice that the enlarged shape is $\frac{1}{2}$ the size of the original and so is
actually made smaller. We still call this an 'enlargement' in maths.

(c) Area of small triangle $= \frac{1}{2} \times 1 \times 1 = \frac{1}{2}$

Area of small rectangle $= 2 \times 1 = 2$

Area of small trapezium $= \frac{1}{2}(2 + 1) \times 1 = 1\frac{1}{2}$

Area of 'enlarged' rocket $= 4$.

(d) Ratio of areas of rockets $= 16 : 4 = 4 : 1$

Volume of a prism

A prism is a 3-D shape with a uniform cross-section. This
means that both ends of a prism are the same shape. You
need to know how to find the volume of prisms by using
the formula V=Al, where A = the area of the cross-
section and l is the length or height of the prism.

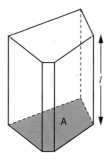

You need to know how to use the formulae for the
volumes of the following prisms:

The triangular prism   The trapezoidal prism   The cylinder

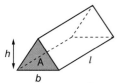 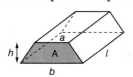

$V = A l = \frac{1}{2}bh l$ $V = A l = \frac{1}{2}(a+b)h l$ $V = A l = \pi r^2 l$

Areas of compound shapes and volumes of prisms

EXAMPLE

ANSWER

3 The diagram shows the dimensions of a doorstop in the shape of a wedge. Find its volume.

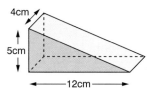

The cross-section of the wedge is a right-angled triangle with an area:

$A = \frac{1}{2} \times 12 \times 5 = 30$.

The length of the wedge is 4 cm.
The volume of the wedge = $V = 30 \times 4 = 120$ cm^3.

EXAMPLE

4 A waste skip is used for removing rubble from a building site. The diagram shows the dimensions of a skip whose cross-section is a trapezium. Find its volume.

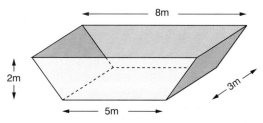

ANSWER

The area of the trapezium = $A = \frac{1}{2}(5 + 8) \times 2 = 13$. The length

of the skip is 3 m. The volume of the skip = $V = 13 \times 3 = 39$ m^3.

EXAMPLE

5 Joey has been on holiday to Torquay. The diagram shows a stick of rock he brought back as a present. Its length is 30 cm and its diameter is 3 cm. Calculate the volume of the stick of rock. Give your answer to 1 decimal place. (Use calculator value for π).

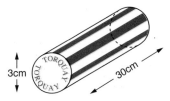

ANSWER

The diameter of the stick of rock is 3 cm and so its radius is 1.5 cm.

Using the formula $V = \pi r^2 l$,

$V = \pi \times 1.5^2 \times 30 = 212.058$.

The volume of the stick of rock = 212.1 cm^3. (1 dp).

**Areas of compound
shapes and volumes
of prisms**

Check yourself

QUESTIONS

Q1 Calculate the areas of the following compound shapes:

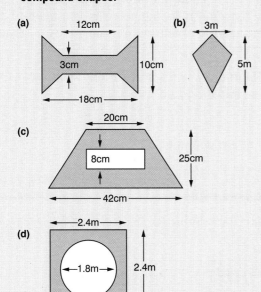

(a) 12cm / 3cm / 10cm / 18cm

(b) 3m / 5m

(c) 20cm / 8cm / 25cm / 42cm

(d) 2.4m / 1.8m / 2.4m

Q2 Find the volume of the tent in the diagram.

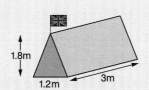

1.8m / 1.2m / 3m

Q3 The diagram shows the dimensions of a swimming pool.

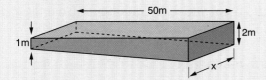

50m / 1m / 2m / x

When full the pool holds 900 m³ of water. Find the width x.

ANSWERS AND TUTORIAL

A1 (a) **75 cm²** (c) **615 cm²**
     (b) **7.5 m²** (d) **3.2 m²**

T1 (a) Use symmetry to help. The 2 trapezia have the same area. The height of each one is 3 cm.
The area of each trapezium = $\frac{1}{2}(10 + 3) \times 3$ = $19\frac{1}{2}$.
So the area of both is 39 cm².
Area of rectangle = 36.
Total area = 39 + 36 = 75 cm².

(b) Area = Product of diagonals ÷ 2 = 15 ÷ 2 = 7.5 m².

(c) Area of trapezium = $\frac{1}{2}(20 + 42) \times 25 = 775$

Area of rectangle = 20 × 8 = 160
Area of shape = 775 − 160 = 615 cm².

(d) Area of square = 2.4 × 2.4 = 5.76
Radius of circle = 0.9
Area of circle = $\pi \times 0.9^2 = 2.545$
Area of shape = 5.76 − 2.545
             = 3.2 m² (1 dp).

A2 **3.24 m³**

T2 Area of triangle = $\frac{1}{2} \times 1.2 \times 1.8 = 1.08$
Volume of tent = 1.08 × 3 = 3.24 m³.

A3 **12 m**

T3 The side of the pool is a trapezium.
Area of trapezium = $\frac{1}{2}(1 + 2) \times 50 = 75$.
The volume of the pool = Ax = 75x.
75x = 900
  x = 900 ÷ 75 = 12.

Chapter 59

Loci

You should be able to determine the locus of an object moving according to some rule.

You should already know how to draw circles with a pair of compasses and how to draw scale diagrams.

The locus of a set of points

A **locus** (plural = **loci**) is a way of showing all the points on a diagram which satisfy a certain description or rule. For example, a jet aircraft leaves a vapour trail in the sky. This trail is the locus of the aircraft as it moves in the atmosphere. This chapter shows that this idea helps to explain all mathematical loci. You will also see why you need to show boundary lines accurately and to shade regions correctly. A good tip to remember is:

If you want to include a boundary, use a *solid* line. If you don't want to include a boundary, use a *dotted* line.

EXAMPLE

1 Draw the locus of a point which is:

(a)   exactly 5 cm from a fixed point A.

(b)   5 cm or less from a fixed point A.

(c)   less than 5 cm from a fixed point A.

ANSWER

(a)  (b)   (c)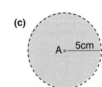

The circles must be accurately drawn with a pair of compasses.

(a)   All the points on the circle are exactly 5 cm from A.

(b)   All the points inside and on the circle are 5 cm or less from A. Use a solid line for the boundary.

(c)   Only the points which are all inside the circle are less than 5 cm from A. Points on the boundary are not, so use a dotted line.

EXAMPLE

2 Draw the locus of a point which is equidistant from the 2 points A and B if A and B are 8 cm apart.

A ——————————— 8cm ——————————— B

All the points on the line XY are the same distance or equidistant from the points A and B. The line XY bisects the line AB at right angles (and is infinitely long!). The line XY is usually referred to as the perpendicular bisector of AB and is easy to construct with a pair of compasses.

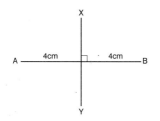

3 Draw the locus of a point which is always less than 3 cm from the line AB:

A —————————————— B

The drawing must be accurate: the 2 semicircles must have a radius of 3 cm. The shaded region shows the locus of all the points that are less than 3 cm from AB. The boundary line should not be included and so draw it as a dotted line.

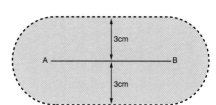

4 Lighthouse A and Lighthouse B are 10 miles apart on the coast. Lighthouse A can be seen by ships for up to 6 miles away and Lighthouse B can be seen by ships for up to 8 miles away.

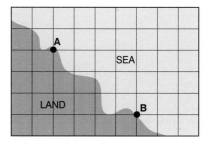

Draw a scale diagram to show the region for which a ship can see both lighthouses. Use a scale of 1 cm to represent 2 miles.

The diagram must be accurately drawn.

Draw a circle with radius 3 cm at A and a circle with radius 4 cm at B.

The locus is the region that lies *inside* both circles but *does not include* the land. The boundary lines should be included.

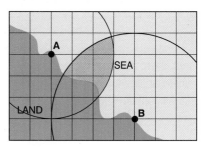

Check yourself

ANSWERS AND TUTORIAL

A1

A $\longrightarrow$ B

T1 The line AB is the required locus. It is parallel to the other 2 lines and is exactly half way between them.

A2 (a) (b)

T2 (a) All points lie on a circle which has a radius of 3 cm.
(b) All points lie in the region between 2 circles with radii 3 cm and 5 cm. The boundary lines are not included.

A3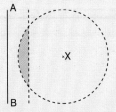

T3 The diagram must be accurately drawn. The boundary lines should be dotted. All the points to the left of the dotted line are less than 2 m from AB and the points inside the circle are less than 4 m from X. The shaded region satisfies both conditions.

A4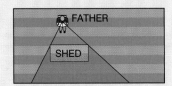

T4 The shaded region shows the area where the boy cannot be seen. The boundary lines should be included. Notice that it is not just the area directly behind the shed.

QUESTIONS

Q1 Draw the locus of a point which is equidistant from a pair of parallel lines.

Q2 Draw the locus of a point which is:
(a) exactly 3 cm from a fixed point A
(b) between 3 cm and 5 cm from a fixed point A.

Q3 In a game of bowls, the ideal position for the jack to stop is less than 2 m from the line AB and less than 4 m from the point X which is itself 5 m from AB. Draw a scale diagram to show the ideal region for the jack to stop. Use a scale of 1 cm to represent 1 m.

Q4 Johnny is hiding from his father who is reading his newspaper in the garden:

Show the region in the garden where Johnny cannot be seen by his father.

Chapter 60

Accuracy of measurement and compound measures

You should know that measurement is continuous and that measures given to the nearest whole number can be in error by up to one half a unit. You should be able to use compound measures such as speed.

You should already know how to round off numbers.

Upper and lower bounds for measurement

When you measure quantities such as height, weight, distance and time, the measurement is often given to the nearest unit. You need to know that the answer you give is inaccurate by up to half a unit in either direction. If you say that your height is 162 cm to the nearest centimetre, the smallest number that can be rounded up to 162 is 161.5 and the largest number that can be rounded down to 162 is just less than 162.5 (since 162.5 would be rounded up to 163). These measurements can be shown on a number line:

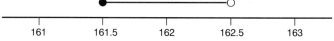

| 161 | 161.5 | 162 | 162.5 | 163 |

● means that 161.5 is included and is the lower bound for the measurement and ○ means that 162.5 is not included and is called the upper bound for the measurement. The interval in which the true height, h, can lie is a number between 161.5 and 162.5 and includes 161.5. This can be written as 161.5 cm $\leq$ h $<$ 162.5 cm.

1 Helen says that her weight is 58 kg to the nearest kilogram. Write down the interval in which her true weight, w, must lie.

EXAMPLE

The lower bound for her weight is 57.5 kg and the upper bound for her weight is 58.5 kg. Her true weight must lie in the interval 57.5 kg $\leq$ w $<$ 58.5 kg.

ANSWER

2 Steve runs a 100 m race in 15.2 seconds, to the nearest tenth of a second. Write down the interval in which his true time, t, must lie.

EXAMPLE

The lower bound for his time is 15.15 s and the upper bound for his time is 15.25 s. His true time must lie in the interval 15.15 s $\leq$ t $<$ 15.25 s.

ANSWER

3 The sides of this rectangle have been rounded to the nearest centimetre:

8cm

5cm

EXAMPLE

(a) Find the interval in which the true length, l, must lie.

(b) Find the interval in which the true width, w, must lie.

(c) Find the interval in which the true area, A, must lie.

(a) The lower bound for l is 7.5 and the upper bound is 8.5. The interval is $7.5\,\text{cm} \leqslant l < 8.5\,\text{cm}$.

(b) The lower bound for w is 4.5 and the upper bound is 5.5. The interval is $4.5\,\text{cm} \leqslant w < 5.5\,\text{cm}$.

(c) The lower bound for the area is the product of the lower bounds for l and w. This is $7.5 \times 4.5 = 33.75$. The upper bound for the area is the product of the upper bounds for l and w. This is $8.5 \times 5.5 = 46.75$.

The true area must lie in the interval $33.75\,\text{cm}^2 \leqslant A < 46.75\,\text{cm}^2$.

Compound measures

Sometimes you need to take two measurements to be able to express a quantity correctly. At this level, you need to know how to use the compound measures of speed and density.

Speed is a measure of distance and time. The units of speed are:

- miles per hour (m.p.h.),
- kilometres per hour (km/h)
- metres per second (m/s).

Density is a measure of mass and volume. The units of density are:

- kilograms per metre cubed (kg/m^3)
- grams per centimetre cubed (g/cm^3).

The formula connecting speed (s), distance (d) and time (t) is:

$$d = st.$$

This is best remembered by using the formula triangle:

From this you can see that:

$$d = st \qquad s = \frac{d}{t} \qquad t = \frac{d}{s}$$

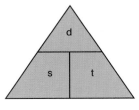

The formula connecting density (D), mass (M) and volume (V) is:

$$M = DV.$$

This is best remembered by using the formula triangle:

From this you can see that:

$$M = DV \qquad D = \frac{M}{V} \qquad V = \frac{M}{D}$$

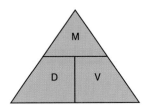

**Accuracy of
measurement and
compound measures**

4 A train leaves London Euston at 8.00 am. and arrives at Manchester Piccadilly at 10.30 am. Find the average speed of the train if the distance travelled by the train is 200 miles.

Using the formula $s = \dfrac{d}{t}$ with d = 200 and t = $2\frac{1}{2}$:

$s = 200 \div 2\frac{1}{2} = 80$ mph.

5 A Jumbo Jet travels at an average speed of 420 km/h. Find the distance it travels on a $3\frac{1}{2}$ hour flight.

Using the formula d = st with s = 420 and t = $3\frac{1}{2}$:

$d = 420 \times 3\frac{1}{2} = 1470$ km.

6 A 1 kg bag of sugar has a volume of 880 cm^3. Find the density of the sugar in g/cm^3.

Using the formula $D = \dfrac{M}{V}$ with M = 1000 g and V = 880 cm^3:

$D = 1000 \div 880 = 1.1$ g/cm^3 (to 1 dp).

7 The wooden block has a density of 0.8 g/cm^3.

(a) Find the volume of the block.

(b) Hence calculate the mass of the block in grams.

12cm

5cm

6cm

(a) V = 12 × 6 × 5 = 360 cm^3.

(b) Using the formula M = DV with D = 0.8 and V = 360:

M = 0.8 × 360 = 288 g.

Check yourself

QUESTIONS

Q1 The distance by road between London and Edinburgh is given as 410 miles to the nearest 10 miles. Write down the interval in which the true distance, d, must lie.

ANSWERS AND TUTORIAL

A1 405 miles ≤ d < 415 miles

T1 Since the number is rounded to the nearest 10 miles, half a unit is 5 miles.

**Accuracy of
measurement and
compound measures**

ANSWERS AND TUTORIAL

A2 $69.5\,cl \leqslant V < 70.5\,cl$

A3 1.6 m/s

T3 Use the formula $s = \dfrac{d}{t}$.

Change 4 mins 10 s into s to give 250 s. $d = 400\,m$
and $t = 250\,s$, so $s = 400 \div 250 = 1.6$.

A4 16 070 400 000 miles

T4 Use the formula $d = st$. Change 1 day into
seconds. 1 day $= 60 \times 60 \times 24 = 86400\,s$.
$d = 186\,000 \times 86\,400 = 16\,070\,400\,000$ miles.
(Your calculator may not show this answer, but
remember that you can ignore the zeros before
you multiply).

A5 5.79 kg

T5 Use the formula $M = DV$.
$M = 19.3 \times 300 = 5790\,g = 5.79\,kg$.

A6 2.7 g/cm^3

T6 Use the formula $D = \dfrac{M}{V}$.

Find the volume of the sheet in cm^3.
Length $= 10\,m = 1000\,cm$. Width $= 45\,cm$.
Thickness $= 0.08\,mm = 0.008\,cm$.
So volume of sheet $= 1000 \times 45 \times 0.008$
                    $= 360\,cm^3$.
$D = 972 \div 360 = 2.7\,g/cm^3$.

QUESTIONS

Q2 The volume of a bottle of wine is 70 cl to the
nearest cl. Write down the interval in which the
true volume, V, must lie.

Q3 Andy is taking part in a swimming gala and his
time for the 400 m freestyle is timed at 4
minutes and 10 seconds. Calculate his average
speed in m/s.

Q4 In outer space, light travels at 186 000 miles
per second. How far does a ray of light travel
in a day?

Q5 An ingot of gold has a volume of 300 cm^3. Find
the mass of the ingot in kilograms if the density
of gold is 19.3 g/cm^3.

Q6 A sheet of aluminium foil on a kitchen roll is
10 m long, 45 cm wide and 0.08 mm thick.
Calculate the density of aluminium in g/cm^3 if
the sheet has a mass of 972 g.

T E S T   Q U E S T I O N S

Answers with examiner's comments on page 243.

1. A boat sails from the harbour to the buoy. The buoy is 6 km to the east and 4 km to the north of the harbour.

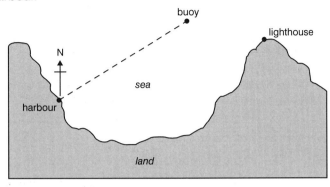

(a) **Calculate** the shortest distance between the buoy and the harbour. Give your answer to 1 decimal place.

(b) The buoy is 1.2 km to the north of the lighthouse. The shortest distance from the lighthouse to the buoy is 2.5 km.
Calculate how far the buoy is to the west of the lighthouse. Give your answer to 1 decimal place.

(1996 Paper 1)

2. A cupboard needs to be strengthened by putting a strut on the back of it like this.

(a) Calculate the length of the diagonal strut.
(b) In a small room the cupboard is in this position.

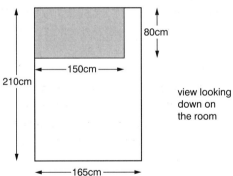

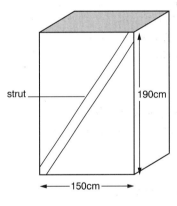

view looking down on the room

Calculate if the room is wide enough to turn the cupboard like this and put it in its new position.

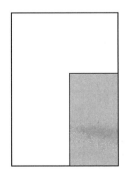

new position

(1995 Paper 1)

209

3. TJ's cat food is sold in tins shaped like this.

Each tin has an internal height of 5 cm.

(a) The area of the lid of the tin is 35 cm². Work out the volume of cat food that the tin contains.

(b) The label that goes around the tin overlaps by 1 cm. The area of the label is 134 cm². Work out the distance around the tin.

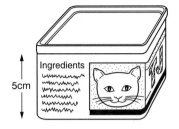

(c) TJ's plans to use tins that are the shape of cylinders. The internal measurements of a tin are shown.
Work out the volume of cat food that the tin contains.

(1995 Paper 2)

4. Two goats, A and B, are tied to opposite sides of a shed. They both have chains 5 m long.

(a) On this plan, sketch the area that **goat A** can reach.

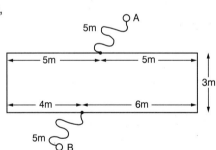

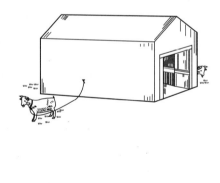

(b) On the same plan, sketch the area that **goat B** can reach.

(1993 Paper 3)

5. (a) At an athletics meeting, the discus throws are measured to the nearest centimetre.
Viv's best throw was measured as 35.42 m. Could Viv's throw actually have been more than 35.42 m?
Explain your answer.

(b) Chris won the hurdles race in a time of 14.6 seconds measured to the nearest tenth of a second.
Between what two values does Chris's time actually lie?

(1995 Paper 1)

6. The space probe Viking 1 travelled from Earth to Mars. It travelled 35 million miles. The journey took approximately 8000 hours. What was the speed of Viking 1?

(1993 Paper 2)

Chapter 61

Designing questionnaires

> You should be able to specify an hypothesis and test it by designing an appropriate survey sheet or experiment that takes into account bias.

You should already know how to collect data and construct frequency tables. In this chapter you will see how to collect data by designing appropriate questionnaires.

Questionnaires

Data is always collected for a purpose, whether it's to test an idea or to check if a particular theory is true or false. Before you collect any data you need to know what you hope to achieve: you make a statement that you want to test. This statement is called a **hypothesis.** Examples of hypotheses are:

" Boys do better than girls in science at school",
" Young people do not listen to classical music",
" Parents prefer to send their children to a school which has a uniform".

Once you have decided on your hypothesis, you are ready to design a suitable **questionnaire**. Remember, any questions you ask should help you come to a decision about your hypothesis. You can then use the data you collect to draw diagrams or produce averages to support your decision. For your data to be reliable, you should always be prepared to give your questionnaire to a random sample of at least 30 people.

When designing your questionnaire, remember the following points:

- It should not have too many questions – a maximum of 10 is about right.
- All questions should be relevant.
- Questions should be easy to understand and they should require only one answer.
- Provide alternative answers where possible, for example YES/NO or ✔ ✗ or Male ☐ Female ☐. You can also use multi-choice answers to cover all possibilities:

  0 ☐ 1 ☐ 2 ☐ 3 ☐ 4 ☐ more than 4 ☐.
- Avoid vague, misleading or embarrassing questions.
- Avoid bias in your questions – people may not always want to tell you the truth.
- If possible use a computer database to store your data. It can then be regularly amended or updated.
- Questionnaires look better if they are done on a word processor.

Designing questionnaires

1 These are poor questions to give on a questionnaire. Replace them by more suitable questions:

(a) How old are you?

(b) How many girl/boy friends do you have?

(c) Have you read a magazine recently?

(d) Do you like fast cars?

These are all sample answers: there are many more correct possibilities.

(a) Which age group are you in? Put a ✔ in the box.

Under 21 ☐ 21-30 ☐ 31-40 ☐ 41-50 ☐ over 50 ☐

(b) Do you have a girl/boy friend at the moment? YES ☐ NO ☐

(c) How many magazines have you read in the last week?

None ☐ 1 ☐ 2 ☐ 3 ☐ 4 ☐ more than 4 ☐.

(d) What type of car do you drive?

Saloon ☐ Hatch-back ☐ Estate ☐ 4-wheel drive ☐ Sports ☐ Other ☐

2 Design a questionnaire to test the hypothesis: "Tall pupils tend to weigh more than short pupils".

A sample questionnaire follows:

Please answer the following questions by putting a ✔ in the correct box:
Sex: Male ☐ Female ☐
Year Group: 7 ☐ 8 ☐ 9 ☐ 10 ☐ 11 ☐
Height: Less than 140 cm ☐ 140–149 cm ☐   150–159 cm ☐ 160–169 cm ☐ 170–179 cm ☐   180–189 cm ☐ Over 189 cm ☐
Weight: Less than 30 kg ☐ 30–39 kg ☐   40–49 kg ☐ 50–59 kg ☐ 60–69 kg ☐   70–79 kg ☐ 80–89 kg ☐ Over 89 kg ☐

**Designing
questionnaires**

3 Dennis wanted to know people's views on adverts on TV for a maths investigation. He gave the following questionnaire to 20 pupils in his class. The questions he chose were poorly worded and ambiguous. Rewrite the questionnaire in a more suitable format.

NAME: _____ FORM: _____

1. Do you think there are too many adverts on TV?

2. Do you find some of the adverts amusing?

3. What do you do when the adverts are on?

4. Do you ever buy any of the products which are advertised? Which ones?

5. Do you think that advertising on TV is a waste of money?

For more reliable results, Dennis should ask at least 30 people from a wider age range. Also, the person completing the questionnaire usually remains anonymous.

A sample questionnaire to find people's views on adverts on TV:

Which age group are you in? Under 21 ☐ 21–30 ☐ 31–40 ☐
41–50 ☐ over 50 ☐

Please underline the response or responses that are closest to your views.

1. What do you think about the amount of time that is devoted to adverts on TV? Is there: far too much / should be more / about right / should be less / far too little

2. Why do you watch adverts on TV? Because they: are informative / introduce new products / promote offers / are amusing / never watch / other.

3. What do you usually do when the adverts are on the TV? Do you: always watch them / do odd jobs / read / change channels / ignore them / other.

4. Do you ever buy any of the products that are advertised on TV? Always / frequently / sometimes / rarely / never.

5. Adverts are a waste of a company's money. Do you agree with this statement? Strongly agree / agree / no comment / disagree / strongly disagree.

Check yourself

ANSWERS AND TUTORIAL

QUESTIONS

A1 (a) **How often do you go to restaurants in a month?**
Never ☐ once ☐ 2 or 3 times ☐
more than 3 times ☐
What type of restaurant do you prefer?
English / Chinese / Indian / Italian /
French / Other.

(b) **Did you do your Maths homework last night?**
Yes ☐ No ☐
How long do you usually spend on the homework?
up to 30 mins ☐ 30 mins to 1 hour ☐
more than 1 hour ☐

T1 For time intervals, all possible values should be covered and with no overlap.

A2 **Questionnaire for Year 9 pupils.**
1. **Which form are you in?**
9A ☐ 9B ☐ 9C ☐ 9D ☐ 9E ☐ 9F ☐
2. **Would you like to go on a Year 9 visit?**
Yes ☐ No ☐ Don't know ☐
3. **Which day would you prefer for the visit?**
Mo ☐ Tu ☐ Wed ☐ Thur ☐ Fr ☐
Sat ☐ Sun ☐
4. **If you had the choice, where would you like to go?**
Blackpool ☐ London ☐ Theme park ☐
Outdoor pursuit centre ☐ Other ☐
5. **How much are you prepared to spend?**
less than £5 ☐ £5 –£10 ☐
more than £10 ☐

T2 For price intervals, all possible values should be covered and with no overlap.

Q1 Write more suitable questions for the following:
(a) Do you like going to exotic restaurants?
(b) Do you do your Maths homework when it is set?

Q2 Year 9 are planning to go on a school visit at the end of the year. Mrs White, their Year Head, decides to give 50 pupils a questionnaire to find out where they would like to go. Design a suitable questionnaire for Mrs White.

Chapter 62

Finding averages for grouped data

You should be able to find the modal class and estimate the mean, median and range of sets of grouped data. You should be able to select the most appropriate statistic for your line of enquiry. You should be able to compare two distributions using the measures of average and range and draw the associated frequency polygons.

You should already know how to find the mean, median, mode and range for a set of data and how to record continuous data using class intervals. In many everyday situations, calculating averages takes time because there is a lot of data to deal with. In this chapter you will find out how to estimate averages for **grouped frequency distributions**.

Finding averages for a frequency distribution

You know that the mean, which can also be written as

$$\bar{x} = \frac{\text{the sum of all the values}}{\text{the total number of values}}$$

For a frequency distribution, the mean can be calculated using the formula:

$$\bar{x} = \frac{\Sigma fx}{\Sigma f}$$

Σ is the Greek letter sigma; it means sum or add up all the values.

1 The frequency table shows the number of people in 20 families:

No. (x)	Frequency (f)	fx
3	9	27
4	8	32
5	3	15
Totals	20	74

EXAMPLE

(a) Find the mean.

(b) Find the mode.

(c) Find the median.

(d) Which of the three averages is it best to use? Why?

ANSWER

(a) Add up all the numbers in the fx column and all the numbers in the frequency column and put the numbers into the formula:

$$\bar{x} = \frac{\Sigma fx}{\Sigma f} = \frac{74}{20} = 3.7$$

You can also work this out on a scientific calculator by first setting the calculator in the STAT mode or SD mode.

Then enter 3 × 9 DATA 4 × 8 DATA 5 × 3 DATA

On some calculators DATA is *x* .

To find the mean press INV $\bar{x}$. The answers should be 3.7.

(b) The mode is the value with the highest frequency. The mode is 3.

Finding averages for grouped data

(c) The median is the exact middle value. This is the number between the 10th and 11th value when put in order. The 9th value is 3 and the 10th and 11th values are both 4. The median is therefore 4.

(d) The mean is the best average to use here since it takes all the values into account.

Estimating averages for a grouped frequency distribution

When data is collected using a grouped frequency table, the mean cannot be calculated exactly because all the individual values are not known. In this case the mean can be estimated by finding the mid-point value for each class interval and then use the above formula with x as the mid-point value.

It is sometimes useful to find the modal class for a grouped frequency distribution. This is the class interval which has the highest frequency.

EXAMPLE **2** The grouped frequency table shows the ages of 100 people in the village of Sumton. Calculate an estimate for the mean age and write down the modal class.

Age. (A)	$0 < A \le 20$	$20 < A \le 40$	$40 < A \le 60$	$60 < A \le 80$	$80 < A \le 100$
frequency	12	18	35	28	7

ANSWER

Age. (A)	frequency f	mid-point x	fx
$0 < A \le 20$	12	10	120
$20 < A \le 40$	18	30	540
$40 < A \le 60$	35	50	1750
$60 < A \le 80$	28	70	1960
$80 < A \le 100$	7	90	630
Totals	100		5000

$$\bar{x} = \frac{\Sigma fx}{\Sigma f} = \frac{5000}{100} = 50$$

The modal class is 40–60.

EXAMPLE **3** The frequency diagram shows the time it takes 50 employees to get to work in the morning. Estimate the range and the mean of the distribution.

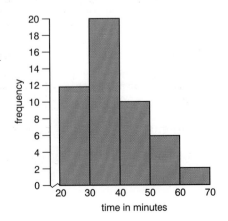

Construct a grouped frequency table first:

Time	frequency f	mid-point x	fx
$20 < t \le 30$	12	25	300
$30 < t \le 40$	20	35	700
$40 < t \le 50$	10	45	450
$50 < t \le 60$	6	55	330
$60 < t \le 70$	2	65	130
Totals	50		1910

The range is the highest time possible – lowest time possible = 70 – 20 = 50 minutes.

ANSWER

$$\bar{x} = \frac{\Sigma fx}{\Sigma f} = \frac{1910}{50}$$

$$= 38.2 \text{ minutes}$$

4 The grouped frequency table shows the marks and levels awarded to two Year 9 classes in their SATs maths test papers:

EXAMPLE

Level	Level 5	Level 6	Level 7	Level 8
Mark Range	23–29	30–44	45–79	80–120
Class 9AZ	4	10	16	6
Class 9BY	0	16	14	2

(a) How many pupils are there in each class?

(b) Estimate the range and mean mark for each class.

(c) Draw a frequency polygon for each class on the same diagram.

(d) Which class obtained the better results? Explain why.

(a) 36 pupils in Class 9AZ and 32 pupils in Class 9BY.

ANSWER

(b) Construct a grouped frequency table for each class. The marks are discrete data and so there is no need to put the class intervals into continuous data format. The mid point x can be found by adding the marks at the end of each mark range and dividing the answer by 2:

Class 9AZ

Mark Range	frequency f	mid-point x	fx
23–29	4	26	104
30–44	10	37	370
45–79	16	62	992
80–120	6	100	600
Totals	36		2066

Class 9BY

Mark Range	frequency f	mid-point x	fx
30–44	16	37	592
45–79	14	62	868
80–120	2	100	200
Totals	32		1660

Range = 120 – 23 = 97 marks

$$\bar{x} = \frac{\Sigma fx}{\Sigma f} = \frac{2066}{36} = 57.4 \text{ marks}$$

Range = 120 – 30 = 90 marks

$$\bar{x} = \frac{\Sigma fx}{\Sigma f} = \frac{1660}{32} = 51.9 \text{ marks}$$

**Finding averages for
grouped data**

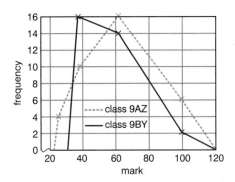

(c) Remember to plot the
points at the mid-point of
each class interval.

(d) Although the range for
9AZ is wider, showing a
greater spread of results,
the mean is higher than
the mean for 9BY. Class
9AZ therefore obtained
slightly better results.

Check yourself

ANSWERS AND TUTORIAL

QUESTIONS

A1

Score (x)	Frequency (f)	fx
1	8	8
2	11	22
3	9	27
4	12	48
5	9	45
6	11	66
Totals	60	216

$$\bar{x} = \frac{\Sigma fx}{\Sigma f} = \frac{216}{60} = 3.6$$

T1 Remember it is usual to give the mean to 1 dp.

Q1 Josh threw a dice
60 times in an
investigation at
school. His table
of results is
shown on the right:

Calculate the
mean score.

Score (x)	Frequency (f)
1	8
2	11
3	9
4	12
5	9
6	11

A2

(a)

Annual salary	frequency f	mid-point x	fx
£10000–	37	12500	462500
£15000–	30	17500	525000
£20000–	8	22500	180000
£25000–	3	27500	82500
£30000–	2	32500	65000
Totals	80		1315000

$$\bar{x} = \frac{\Sigma fx}{\Sigma f} = \frac{1\,315\,000}{80}$$

$$= £16\,400 \text{ (to 3 sf)}$$

(b) The median. It does not take into account
the few high wages which inflate the mean.

T2 Take the last interval to be £30 000 – £35 000.

Q2 The annual wage of 80 people who work at a
local supermarket is given in the frequency
table below:

Annual salary	£10 000–	£15 000–	£20 000–	£25 000–	£30 000–
frequency	37	30	8	3	2

(a) Calculate an estimate for the mean wage
(to 3 sf).

(b) An estimate for the median wage is £15 500.
Which average best reflects the average
wage of the employees? Give a reason.

QUESTIONS

Q3 The frequency diagram shows the life span of 100 'Photon' light bulbs:

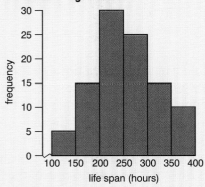

Calculate an estimate for the mean. Write down the modal class.

Q4 The following data gives the marks of 50 pupils in the Year 9 French exam:

47	61	38	36	82	74
65	48	40	42	70	63
18	59	53	87	52	25
68	55	32	25	33	54
35	21	70	14	61	80
77	89	40	93	60	82
64	71	58	16	29	57
49	68	68	71	61	90
66	20				

(a) Calculate the exact mean for the data.
(b) Construct a grouped frequency table for the data, taking equal class intervals 1–20, 21–40, ..., 81–100. Hence calculate an estimate for the mean.
(c) Comment on your answers.

ANSWERS AND TUTORIAL

A3 $\bar{x} = \dfrac{\Sigma fx}{\Sigma f} = \dfrac{26750}{100} = 267.5$ hours

The modal class is 200–250 hours

T3

Lifespan (hours)	frequency f	mid-point x	fx
100<t≤ 150	5	125	625
150<t≤ 200	15	175	2625
200<t≤ 250	30	225	6750
250<t≤ 300	25	275	8125
300<t≤ 350	15	325	4875
250<t≤ 400	10	375	3750
Totals	100		26750

The modal class is the one with the highest frequency.

A4 (a) $\bar{x} = \dfrac{2737}{50} = 54.7$ marks (1 dp)

(b) $\bar{x} = \dfrac{\Sigma fx}{\Sigma f} = \dfrac{2685}{50} = 53.7$ marks

(c) The estimate for the mean is very close to the exact mean. It is much quicker to find the estimate.

T4 Notice that the mid-point of the class intervals uses $\frac{1}{2}$ marks. The grouped frequency table is:

Marks	frequency f	mid-point x	fx
1–20	4	10.5	42
21–40	12	30.5	366
41–60	11	50.5	555.5
61–80	18	70.5	1269
81–100	5	90.5	452.5
Totals	50		2685

An easy way of finding the mid-point is to add together the two end points of the interval and divide by 2.

Chapter 63

Lines of best fit

You should be able to draw a line of best fit on a scatter diagram by eye.

You should already know how to draw scatter diagrams and you should understand correlation. When given 2 sets of data, you can recognise whether there is correlation between them by drawing a scatter diagram. If there is good correlation between the 2 sets of data, then it is usual to draw a **line of best fit** on the diagram. This chapter will show you how to draw a line of best fit and how to use it to solve problems.

Drawing a line of best fit

A line of best fit is a straight line which is drawn through the middle of all the points on a scatter diagram, passing as close to as many points as possible. You can draw the line by eye, making sure that there are roughly an equal number of points on both sides of the line and with the line passing through some of the points if possible. If you can calculate the mean for both sets of data, then the line of best fit will be more accurate if it also passes through the point representing both means on the scatter diagram. Always make sure your line touches at least one of the axes if possible – the line does not necessarily have to pass through the origin or go through the extreme points.

EXAMPLE

1   The scatter diagram shows the masses of 15 children against their age:

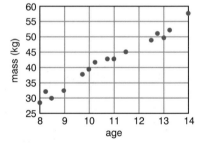

(a)   What does the diagram tell you?

(b)   Draw a line of best fit on the scatter diagram.

(c)   Use the line of best fit to estimate the mass of a child who is 12.

ANSWER

(a)   There is positive correlation.

(b)

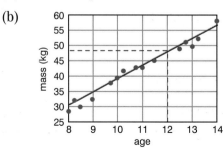

(c)   The child's mass is about 48 kg. The dotted lines are useful to put on the diagram to help find the mass for any given age.

Lines of best fit

2 The table shows the population (in millions) of a large city over a 10 year period.

Year	1980	1982	1984	1986	1988	1990
Population (m)	3.5	3.3	3.2	2.9	2.8	2.6

(a) Show the data on a scatter diagram and draw on a line of best fit.

(b) What can you deduce from the diagram?

(c) Estimate the population of the city in 1985.

(a)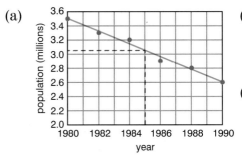

(b) The diagram shows negative correlation. The population has been decreasing over the 10 years.

(c) The population was just less than 3.1 million in 1985. The dotted lines will help you work out this answer.

Check yourself

QUESTIONS

Q1 Shaun was carrying out an experiment to find out if there was a relationship between the length of the extension of a spring when different masses were hung from it. He decided to do the experiment 6 times using different masses. His results are recorded in the table.

Mass (g)	50	100	150	200	250	300
Extension (cm)	1.7	3.8	5.8	8.2	10.1	11.8

(a) Calculate the mean for the masses and for the extensions.

(b) Show the data on a scatter diagram and draw a line of best fit.

(c) Estimate the length of the extension if a mass of 120 g was hung from the spring.

ANSWERS AND TUTORIAL

A1 (a) Mean for the masses = 175 g
Mean for the extensions = 6.9 cm

(b)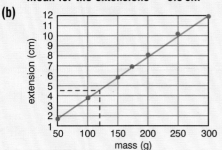

(c) The extension is about 4.5 cm

T1 (a) For masses: mean = 1050 ÷ 6 = 175
For extensions: mean = 41.4 ÷ 6 = 6.9

(b) Remember to plot the point for the means. Using 2 mm graph paper will make your answers more accurate. The diagram shows positive correlation.

(c) Draw on the dotted lines to help.

Chapter 64

Relative frequency and probability

You should understand relative frequency as an estimate of probability and use this to compare the outcomes of experiments.

You should already know how to find the probability of an event using equally likely outcomes. So far you have been able to calculate probability by finding all the equally outcomes by using lists or diagrams. In this chapter you will see how to use relative frequency as an estimate of probability and use it to compare outcomes of experiments.

Relative frequency

Sometimes, because it is not possible to use equally likely outcomes, you can only estimate probability. You can repeat an experiment to estimate the probability for an event: each experiment is called a trial.

$$\text{Relative frequency} = \frac{\text{the number of trials for the event}}{\text{total number of trials}}$$

This gives an *estimate* for the theoretical probability. The more trials conducted, the closer the estimate will be to the theoretical probability.

EXAMPLE

1 Dana throws a dice 120 times. Her results are given in the table:

Score	1	2	3	4	5	6
frequency	18	19	20	17	24	22

Use relative frequency to estimate the probability of getting a 6.

ANSWER

There are 120 trials. Relative frequency $= \frac{22}{120} = \frac{11}{60}$.
(Theoretical probability $= \frac{1}{6}$)

EXAMPLE

2 Graham, James, Ruth and Tim want to find the probability that a drawing pin will land point up. Each of them decides to carry out a different number of trials by dropping a number of pins onto the floor. Their results are shown in the table:

	No of trials	No of trials with point up
Graham	100	63
James	120	72
Ruth	200	122
Tim	50	37

(a) Complete the table to show the relative frequency for each person.

(b) Whose answer will give a better estimate for the probability of a pin landing point up? Explain why.

(c) If someone who worked in an office dropped a box of 288 drawing pins on the floor, estimate how many of them would land point up.

(a)

	No of trials	No of trials with point up	Relative frequency
Graham	100	63	0.63
James	120	72	0.6
Ruth	200	122	0.61
Tim	50	37	0.74

(b) Ruth because she conducted more trials.

(c) Estimated probability for point up $= \dfrac{122}{200} = 0.61$.

The number landing point up $= 288 \times 0.61 = 175.68$.
So approximately 176 would land point up.

Check yourself

QUESTIONS

Q1 A sampling bottle contains 100 black and white balls. [A sampling bottle is a sealed tube containing coloured balls which cannot be seen. After shaking it, a ball descends into a clear tube at one end]. Samantha wants to find out how many black balls there are in the bottle. To do this she conducts a number of trials as shown in the table:

No of trials	No of black balls	Relative frequency
10	3	0.3
50	9	0.18
100	24	0.24
200	38	0.19

How many black balls did Samantha estimate were in the bottle?

ANSWERS AND TUTORIAL

A1 **19 or 20**

T1 Use the data with the most trials. Estimated probability for getting a black ball = 0.19. Estimated no. of black balls = 0.19 × 100 = 19. Since this is an estimate, an answer of 20 is acceptable.

ANSWERS AND TUTORIAL

QUESTIONS

A2 (a)

	Total no. of trials	No of trials for each colour	Relative frequency
Blue	200	46	0.23
Green	200	62	0.31
Red	200	37	0.185
Yellow	200	55	0.275

Yes. The relative frequencies should all be about the same.
(b) P(blue) = 0.23
P(green) = 0.31
P(red) = 0.185
P(yellow) = 0.275

T2 (b) Check that the answers add up to 1.

A3 (a) 120
(b)

Month	Number of pupils	Relative frequency (to 3dp)
Jan	9	0.075
Feb	8	0.067
Mar	12	0.1
Apr	10	0.083
May	11	0.092
Jun	9	0.075
Jul	10	0.083
Aug	7	0.058
Sep	11	0.092
Oct	14	0.117
Nov	9	0.075
Dec	10	0.083

(c) (i) 0.083   (ii) 0.9   (d) 4

T3 (a) Add the frequencies: 9 + 8 + 12 + 10 + 11 + 9 + 10 + 7 + 11 + 14 + 9 + 10
(b) relative frequency = Number in month ÷ 120
(c) (i) Read the value from the table.
(ii) 1 – 0.1 = 0.9
(d) 30 × 0.117 = 3.51, so 4 pupils.

Q2 A four sided dice used in a game has one blue, one green, one red and one yellow face. Four people playing the game think that the dice is biased. To check this, they kept a record of the colour each got during a game. Their results are shown in the table.

	No. of throws	Blue	Green	Red	Yellow
Albert	45	10	15	8	12
Beatrix	60	14	18	12	16
Charles	40	9	11	7	13
Dot	55	13	18	10	14

(a) By putting all their results together, draw a relative frequency table. Do you think that the dice is biased? Explain why.
(b) Work out an estimate for the probability of getting each colour.

Q3 Clifford and Derek were conducting a survey to find out in which month pupils in Year 9 had their birthdays. To illustrate their data, they drew the following chart:

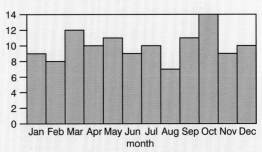

(a) Find the total number of pupils in the survey.
(b) Draw a relative frequency table to show the data.
(c) Estimate:
(i) P(A pupil has a birthday in July)
(ii) P(A pupil's birthday is not in March)
(d) There are 30 pupils in Clifford and Derek's form. Estimate how many of them will have a birthday in October.

TEST QUESTIONS

Answers with examiner's comments on page 243.

1. Tony, Ben, Sally and Chitra want to find out what people think and do about animal welfare. They are writing a questionnaire. Here are some questions they suggest:

Tony	Are you a member of an animal welfare organisation?	yes/no
Ben	Are animals important?	yes/no
Chitra	Don't you agree that experimenting on live animals is very, very cruel?	yes/no
Sally	Do you buy products that have been tested on animals?	yes/no/don't know

(a) Choose **two** questions which **you** think should **not** be used. Whose questions are they?

(b) Explain why you think these two questions should not be used.

(c) Write an extra question **you** would use. People must be able to answer your question with yes or no.

(1993 Paper 3)

2. A survey asked 100 women and 100 men how much money they earned in a week. These are the results:

Women's weekly wages

Men's weekly wages

Weekly wage (£)		Mid-point men's weekly wages	Frequency (men)	Mid-point × Frequency
at least	below			
0	100	50	3	
100	200	150	14	
200	300	250	38	
300	400	350	16	
400	500	450	29	

(a) Calculate the mean of men's weekly wages.

(b) What is the modal class for women's weekly wages?

(c) Put your answers to (a) and (b) into the table.

(d) Look at the differences between women's and men's wages shown in the graph and table. Explain which average in the table in part (c) represents the data most fairly.

	Women	Men
median	266	280
modal class		200–300
mean	265	

(1992 Paper 3)

225

3. A school has 5 Year groups. 80 pupils from the school took part in a sponsored swim. Lara and Jack drew these graphs.

number of lengths swum by each year group

Lara's graph:

number of lengths — year group:
- 7: 150
- 8: 210
- 9: 230
- 10: 170
- 11: 70

number of pupils who swam different numbers of lengths

Jack's graph:

number of pupils — number of lengths:
- 1 to 5: 12
- 6 to 10: 33
- 11 to 15: 27
- 16 to 20: 6
- 21 to 25: 2

(a) Look at **Lara's** graph. Did Year 10 have **fewer** pupils taking part in the swim than **Year 7**? Tick the correct box. Yes ☐ No ☐ Cannot tell ☐. Explain your answer.
(b) Use **Lara's graph** to work out the mean number of lengths swum by each of the 80 pupils.
(c) Use **Jack's graph** to work out the mean number of lengths swum by each of the 80 pupils.
(d) Explain why the means calculated from Lara's graph and Jack's graph are different.

(1996 Paper 2)

4. A company has 10 pizza shops. All the shops sell the same types of pizza at the same prices. Mr. Bal asked: "Is there a **relationship** between the **number of pizzas sold** and the **number of people who live within 3 miles** of a shop?". He then looked at this graph:

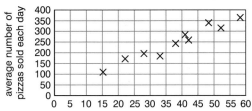

number of people who live within 3 miles (thousands)

(a) What does the graph show?
(b) The company opens a new shop and 35 thousand people live within 3 miles of it. Use the graph to estimate the average number of pizzas the shop is likely to sell each day. Explain how you made your estimate.

(1996 Paper 1)

5. The probability of getting a 2 with this spinner is 0.125.

Leena, Alun, Petra and Roy did an experiment with the spinner. They each spun it a different number of times. They wrote down the number of times they got a 2.

One of them made a mistake and wrote down the wrong number of times they got a 2. Who do you think it was? Explain how you made your decision.

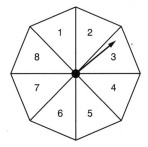

	Number of spins	Number of times I got a 2	Relative frequency
Leena	10	3	0.30
Alun	50	7	0.14
Petra	100	28	0.28
Roy	1000	120	0.12

(1993 Paper 3)

Introduction

A few pupils sit SATs that cover level 8. If you have found the work in this book straightforward then you might be able to take the tier 6-8 paper. This is usually something that your teachers decide. You should know what tier paper you will be sitting. If not ask your teacher.

The following four sections list the National Curriculum descriptors for level 8 in Number, Algebra, Shape, space and measures and Handling data. Each of the descriptors is linked to a past National Test question. The answers to the National Test questions, together with examiner's comments, are on page 244.

LEVEL 8 NUMBER

- You should be able to solve problems using powers or roots with numbers expressed in standard form, checking that the answers are of the correct order of magnitude. (Question 1).

- You should be able to choose fractions or percentages to solve problems involving repeated proportional changes or the calculation of the original quantity given the result of a proportional change. (Question 2).

- You should be able to evaluate algebraic formulae, substituting fractions, decimals and negative numbers. (Question 3).

- You should be able to calculate one variable, given the others in formulae such as $V = \pi r^2 h$. (Question 4 and Question 5).

---

1 Johann Bode was a mathematician and astronomer. In 1772 he made calculations which suggested that there was an unknown planet. His work led to the discovery of the asteroids, which are pieces of rock moving around the Sun.

QUESTION

Vanessa copied some of his methods. She recorded the average distance in kilometres of some planets from the sun.

Planet	Distance from Sun
Venus	1.082×10^8 km
Earth	1.496×10^8 km
Mars	2.279×10^8 km
Jupiter	7.783×10^8 km
Saturn	1.427×10^9 km

Vanessa said:

> Saturn is about 1200 million km further away from the Sun than Mars.

(a) Is Vanessa right? Show the calculation you did to help you decide. Give a reason for your decision.

(b)   Vanessa calculated the ratio: $\dfrac{\text{distance of planet from the Sun}}{\text{distance of Earth from the Sun}}$

Work out the ratio for Jupiter and Saturn, correct to 2 decimal places. Complete the table.

Planet	Venus	Earth	Mars	Jupiter	Saturn
ratio	0.72	1	1.52	………	………

(c)   Johann Bode noticed that the ratios were similar to some of the numbers in this pattern:

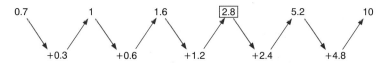

If there was an unknown planet, the ratio for it would be approximately 2.8. Use the ratio 2.8 to calculate approximately how far the unknown planet would be from the Sun.

(d)   You can use a formula to find the average distance of an object from the Sun in kilometres.

The formula is $R = \dfrac{Gm}{V^2}$

R = the average distance of an object from the Sun in kilometres

V = the speed of the object in kilometres per second

G = gravitational constant = 6.67×10^{-20}

m = mass of Sun = $1.993 \times 10^{30}\,\text{kg}$

Pieces of rock are moving round the Sun with a speed of 17.5 km/s. Use the formula to find out how far they are from the Sun. Show your working.

(e)   Could these pieces of rock be parts of the missing planet between Mars and Jupiter? Explain why or why not.

(1994 Paper 1)

QUESTION **2**   There are about 9000 MegaBurger restaurants in America. Each restaurant serves about 2000 people every day. There are about 250 million Americans. A newspaper had this headline:

> **Every day 7% of
> Americans eat at
> Megaburger restaurants.**

Is the newspaper report fair? Make your method and working clear.

(1992 Paper 3)

3 Use the formula $d = \dfrac{m^2 - s^2}{2g}$ to find d when $g = -8.9$, $m = 0$, $s = 27.0$. Show your working.

(1992 Paper 3)

4 A robot accelerates at a constant rate. It can move backwards or forwards. When the robot moves, three equations connect the following:

u its initial speed in m/s
v its final speed in m/s
a its acceleration in m/s^2
s the distance travelled in m
t the time taken in seconds

The equations are:

$v = u + at$
$v^2 = u^2 + 2as$
$s = ut + \frac{1}{2}at^2$

For a journey made by the robot:

$u = 0.25\,\text{m/s}$
$t = 3.5$ seconds
$a = -0.05\,\text{m/s}^2$

Use the appropriate equation to find:

(a) The distance travelled. Show your working.

(b) The robot's final speed. Show your working.

(1995 Paper 2)

5 This formula can be used to find the rate (r) at which yeast cells are growing after a time (t):

$$p = s + rt$$

Find the value of r when:

$p = 48.46$
$s = 2.7$
$t = 5.5$

Show your working.

(1992 Paper 2)

LEVEL 8 ALGEBRA

- You should be able to manipulate algebraic formulae, equations and expressions, finding common factors and multiplying two linear expressions. (Questions 6, 7, 8 and 9).

- You should be able to solve inequalities in two variables. (Question 10).

- You should be able to sketch and interpret graphs of linear, quadratic, cubic and reciprocal functions, and graphs that model real situations. (Question 11).

QUESTION 6 The volume of milk in a full bottle is $3d^3 - 3d$. The volume of milk in a full glass jug is $3d^3 - (3d - d^2)$. d is the thickness in millimetres of the glass. Which has more milk, the bottle or the jug?

Write the volume of the milk in the jug in a different way to help you explain your decision.

(1993 Paper 3)

QUESTION 7 Elaine wants to change $A = \frac{1}{2}st + \frac{s^2 + t^2}{9}$ so that she has a new formula to work out the area (A) when $s = 2t$.

Substitute $s = 2t$ into $A = \frac{1}{2}st + \frac{s^2 + t^2}{9}$ to get a new formula. Write this formula as simply as possible.

(1995 Paper 2)

QUESTION 8 Multiply out the brackets in the expressions to see that the expressions are equivalent:

$4n + 2(n - 1)$ **and** $6 + 4(n - 1) + 2(n - 2)$

(1994 Paper 1)

QUESTION 9 Helen wants to work out $(p + 3)(2p + 7)$. She chooses to use the area of this rectangle to help her:

(a) Fill in the missing areas inside Helen's rectangle.

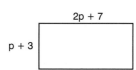

Helen writes $(p + 3)(2p + 7) = 2p^2 + 13p + 21$

(b) Use Helen's rectangle to show that she was right.

(c) Work out $(3a + 5)(a + 4)$.

(1992 Paper 3)

10 This pattern is formed by straight line graphs of equations in the first quadrant:

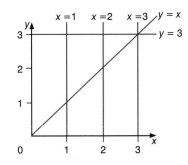

(a) One region of the pattern can be described by the inequalities:

$x \leqslant 2, x \geqslant 1, y \geqslant x, y \leqslant 3$

Put an **R** in the single region of the pattern that is described.

(b) This is another pattern formed by straight line graphs of equations in the first quadrant:

The shaded region can be described by **three** inequalities. Write down these three inequalities.

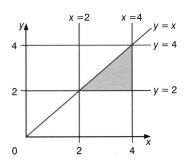

(1996 Paper 1)

11 Clare does a parachute jump. She jumps out of the plane and falls faster and faster towards the ground. After a few seconds her parachute opens. She slows down and then falls to the ground at a steady speed.

(a) Which of these graphs shows Clare's parachute jump?

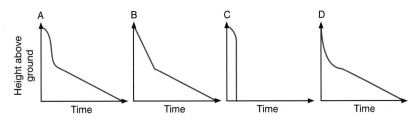

(b) Explain why each of the other graphs is wrong.

(1996 Paper 2)

LEVEL 8 SHAPE, SPACE AND MEASURES

- You should understand and be able to use mathematical similarity (Question 12).

- You should be able to use sine, cosine and tangent in right-angled triangles when solving problems in 2 dimensions (Question 13).

- You should be able to distinguish between formulae for perimeter, area and volume, by considering dimensions. (Question 14).

QUESTION | **12** Timpkins Builders make wooden frames for roofs on new houses. In the diagram of the wooden frame shown on the right PQ is parallel to BC.

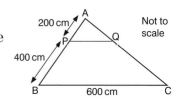

(a) Calculate length PQ using similar triangles

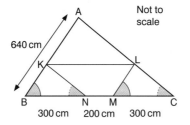

(b) In the wooden frame shown on the left, angle ABC = angle LMC, and angle ACB = angle KNB.

Calculate length LM using similar triangles.

(1995 Paper 2)

QUESTION | **13** Cassie made two similar triangles:

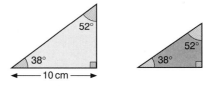

They fitted together **exactly** like this:

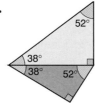

Would they also fit together **exactly** like this?

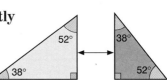

Use any of sine, cosine or tangent to find out. Use at least 2 decimal places in your working.

(1994 Paper 2)

14 These stars are all the same shape, but they are different sizes:

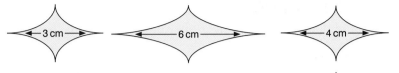

Look at these formulae:

$P = kw$
$Q = cw^2$

w stands for the width of any star.
k and c are constants.

(a) Doris wrote: P could be the height of a star. Jed wrote: P could be the distance all round a star. Write what Q could be.

(b) Mike wrote: P could be the area of a star. Why **must** Mike be wrong.

(1993 Paper 2)

LEVEL 8 HANDLING DATA

- You should be able to interpret and construct cumulative frequency tables and diagrams, using the upper boundary of the class interval, be able to estimate the median and interquartile range and use these to compare distributions and make inferences. (Question 15).

- You should understand when to apply the methods for calculating the probability of a compound event, given the probabilities of either independent events or mutually exclusive events and solve problems using these methods. (Question 16).

QUESTION **15** This graph shows the cumulative frequency for women's wages.

Women's wages

Men's wages

Weekly wage (£)		Frequency	Cumulative Frequency
at least	below		
0	100	3	
100	200	14	
200	300	38	
300	400	16	
400	500	29	

(a) Complete the table above and show the cumulative frequency for men's wages on the same graph.

(b) Complete the table on the right

	Women	Men
lower quartile	218	
upper quartile	328	
inter-quartile range	110	

(c) Use the lower and upper quartiles to comment on the difference in the overall distribution of women's and men's wages.

(1992 Paper 3)

QUESTION **16** A company makes computer disks. It tested a random sample of the disks from a large batch. The company calculated the probability of any disk being defective as 0.025.

Glenda buys two disks.

(a) Calculate the probability that both disks are defective.

(b) Calculate the probability that only one of the disks is defective.

(c) The company found 3 defective disks in the sample they tested. How many disks were likely to have been tested?

(1996 Paper 2)

Levels 4-8

Mental arithmetic test 2: Levels 4 to 8

The Questions: Time: 5 seconds

1   What is eighty-six multiplied by ten?

1	

2   Change one hundred and seventy millimetres into centimetres.

2	cm

3   What is forty-eight divided by six?

3	

4   What is seven point four multiplied by one hundred?

4	7.4

5   Write three hundredths as a decimal number.

5	

6   A line is measured as seven millimetres to the nearest millimetre. What is the minimum length that the line could be?

6	mm

The Questions: Time: 10 seconds

7   A television programme starts at ten minutes to eight. It lasts twenty-five minutes. At what time does the programme finish?

7	

8   Fifty per cent of a number is forty-five. What is the number?

8	

9   What is half of one hundred and thirty-eight?

9	

10   In a group of seventy-three children, thirty-nine are girls. How many are boys?

10	boys

11   Ten per cent of a number is sixteen. What is the number?

11	

12   Write down the number six and a half million in figures.

12	

13   Write six tenths as a decimal number.

13	

14   Jean got fifteen out of twenty on a test. What percentage did she get?

14	%

15   Two angles in a triangle are each seventy degrees. What is the size of the third angle?

15	°

16   Huw and Lynn share some money in the ratio of three to four. Huw's share is one hundred and fifty pounds. How much money is Lynn's share?

16	£	3:4 £150

17   Multiply six point nought eight by one thousand.

17	6.08

18 Two hundred and one out of two hundred and ninety-eight people said they could swim. Estimate the percentage who could swim.

| 18 | | % |

19 How many fourteenths are there in three sevenths?

| 19 | |

20 Look at your answer sheet. What is the greatest integer x can be?

| 20 | | $x^2 < 144$ |

21 What is nought point seven divided by nought point nought one?

| 21 | | 0.7   0.01 |

The Questions: Time: 15 seconds

22 What is the cost of five mugs at one pound ninety-nine pence each?

| 22 | £ |

23 Look at the angle on you answer sheet.
Estimate the size of the angle in degrees.

| 23 | ° |  |

24 Each side of a square is twenty-seven centimetres.
What is the perimeter of the square?

| 24 | | cm |

25 Look at the calculation on your answer sheet.
What is thirty-two multiplied by twenty-two?

| 25 | | $32 \times 44 = 1408$ |

26 Look at the equation on your answer sheet. If a equals eight, what is b?

| 26 | $b =$ | $b = 9a - 18$ |

27 Forty per cent of a number is sixteen. What is the number?

| 27 | | 16 |

28 Look at the calculation on your answer sheet.
What is four hundred and forty-eight divided by one point six?

| 28 | | $28 \times 16 = 448$ |

29 A square has a perimeter of twenty-four metres. What is the area of the square?

| 29 | | m^2 |

30 Look at your answer sheet. If x equals two y and y equals ten, work out x plus y, all squared.

| 30 | | $x = 2y$ $(x + y)^2$ |

31 The price of a train ticket goes up from five pounds to five pounds and twenty-five pence. What is the percentage increase?

| 31 | | % |

32 Look at the calculation on your answer sheet.
Write an approximate answer.

| 32 | | $\dfrac{80.18 \times 9.89}{1.96}$ |

In the section that follows answers are given in **bold** type, examiner's comments are given in plain type.

Level 4 – Number

1. (a) **Kate is wrong because each number is less than 200 so the total could not be more than 400.** Any valid explanation is OK but you must not actually work out the answer. You must show that you understand about the size of numbers and that you can do rough calculations in your head.

   (b) **Kate forgot to carry the tens digit to the next column when she added 4 and 7.** The minimum answer acceptable would be 'she didn't carry the ten'.

2. (a) **13 chocolate bars.**

   (b) **6 pence left over.** Multiply by 10 first, as this is straightforward: $7 \times 10 = 70$. You still have 27 pence. It's then easy to work out that there are 3 sevens in 27 with 6 left over. Or, you can do it by short division: $\underset{7\overline{)97}}{13 \quad r\,6}$

3. (a) Again, several ways of doing this:
   Tom is wrong because 200 is bigger than 50. The number of bags must be less than 50.
   Or, you could say that 4×12 is almost 50 and 12 is a lot less than 200.
   Or, 200 bags of 4 cakes is 800 cakes which is too many.
   It is not enough to say, for example, $4 \times 200 = 800$, without making a comment as well.

   (b) **12 bags of 4 cakes.**

   (c) **2 cakes left over.** This is short division or you might know your 12 times table.

   (d) **Lela needs 7 bags.** If you do this by short division, you get 6 remainder 3. However, as Lela needs to have enough cakes for everyone, she must buy 7 bags. If you said 6 bags and 3 cakes you would be wrong because Tom does not sell single cakes.

4. (a) **09:30**   (c) **08:25**
   (b) **45 minutes**   (d) **08:30, 08:45 or 09:20**
   (e) **20 minutes.** You cannot do time calculations on a calculator. You have to 'count on' to the next hour and then 'count past' the hour. Derek took a total of 20 minutes from leaving his house until the bus arrived. Ruth arrived at the bus stop at 09:00 so had to wait 20 minutes for the 09:20.

5. **Any answer from £977, £980 or £1000.** The answer must be an approximation that is bigger than £976.85. The most sensible answer is £1000 as this is what you are most likely to see in a newspaper.

6. **480 and 4800, 489 or 4890, 28 or 280, 22 or 220.**
   Unless a decimal is involved, a number tens times bigger just has a zero on the end.

7. (a) **A zero in the end space:**

7 _ 0

   You do not know what the other number is but there must be a zero at the end.

(b)

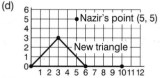

7 4 0 0

You know the first digit is 7 and the last two must both be zeros as it is multiplied by 100.

8. (a) **Either 245 or 254.** The hundreds digit must be smaller than 4 so it must start with a 2. Or, the 10s digit could be smaller than 2, which is impossible.

   (b) **542.** The hundreds digit must be as big as possible, then the 10s digit must be as big as possible.

   (c) **She should pick zero.** The number 10 times bigger is 4250.

9. **They each get $\frac{3}{4}$ of a pizza.** There are 12 slices shown in the picture. They get 3 slices each this is 3 slices out of 4 for each pizza.

Level 4 – Algebra

1. **160 °C.** You need to do each stage of the calculation and work out an answer before you move on to the next part of the sum. For example: $320 - 32 = 288$; $288 \times 5 = 1440$; $1440 \div 9 = 160$
   If you write the sum as $320 - 32 \times 5 \div 9$ and just type this into a calculator, it gives an answer of 17.78.

2. (a) **£7.00.** The sum is $220 + 8 \times 60$. Remember to change £2.20 into pence.

   (b) **£6.10.** The sum is $450 + 8 \times 20$. Remember to change £4.50 into pence.

   (c) **At the Milltown he gets 4 rides. At the Seaview he gets 2 rides.** Take off the cost of entry and divide by the cost of the rides. Convert pounds to pence. The answers on a calculator are 4.667 and 2.5. Ignore the decimal parts as you cannot have a part of a ride and just take the whole number part as the answer.

3. (a) **4 cm².** You can do this by the area of a triangle formula $\frac{1}{2} \times$ base $\times$ height or by counting squares.

   (b) **(0, 0), (3, 3) and (6, 0)**

   (c) **9 cm².** The area is the square of the number you times by.

   (d)

   (e) **5**

4. $10 \to \boxed{21}$ $5 \to \boxed{11}$ $2 \to \boxed{5}$

   You always get an example (i.e. 3 goes to 7), which will help you understand the rule.

5. (a)

   $7 \longrightarrow \boxed{28}$

   You can do this by drawing 7 tiles if necessary.

   (b) **The number of rods goes up by 8 each time, or the number of rods is 4 times the number of squares.**
   There are usually two ways to 'see' a pattern. The first is how much it goes up by each time and the second is to see what connects the 'starting number' with the 'finishing number'.

(c) **Rods = four times the number of squares: r = 4s.**

s ——→ [× 4] ——→ r

At this level you only need to give a rule in words or in a flow diagram (number machine). You can write it in symbols (r = 4s), but this is level 5 and 6 algebra.

6. (a)

number of tables	2	4	6	8	10	12	14
number of chairs	6	10	14	18	22	26	30

(b) **The numbers of chairs goes up by 4 each time.** If you spot the pattern, it is easy to fill in the table. You need to see the pattern as you won't have time to draw all the tables that you would need. Sometimes you get no marks if you have to draw pictures to get the answers.

7. (a) **The perimeter is 8 units which can be counted on the shape. Tracey's rule gives 2 × 3 + 2 = 8. So, Tracey's rule works for two tiles.**

You need to make sure you count on the diagram and also use Tracey's rule. It is not enough just to say 'It works' or to do 2 x 3 + 2 = 8. You must show that the rule works, as the question asks.

(b) **10 x 3 + 2 = 32 units.** If you need to do this by drawing a shape with 10 tiles you would not get any marks – the question is trying to test whether you can use a rule.

8. (a) **It is obvious where Mandy's cross must go.**

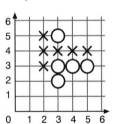

(b) **(2, 4), (3, 4), (4, 4), (5, 4).** Remember the rules. Start at the origin (0, 0) and count across first and up second.

(c) **The second (y) co-ordinate is always 4 or the second number is 4 or y = 4.** This is obvious. y = 4 is called the equation of the line and is higher level algebra but it is easy enough to see and much easier to write down.

Level 4 – Shape, Space & Measures

1. (a) **4 and 8**
   (b) **6 and 12**

2. (a) **Any 2 of the following 14 shapes.**

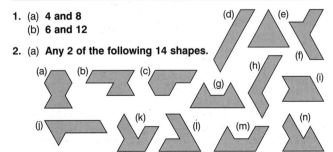

(b) **11 cm**
(c) **One of a or c or e or i (or a rotation or reflection of 1 of these).**

3.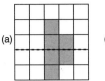

Remember that you can check by using a mirror or tracing paper.

4.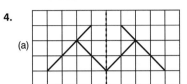

(a) (b)

5. (a) ✔ **(Order 2)**   (d) ✗ **(Order 1)**
   (b) ✗ **(Order 1)**   (e) ✔ **(Order 3)**
   (c) ✔ **(Order 5)**
   Remember that you can check by using tracing paper.

6. (a) **Order 6**   (c) **Order 8**
   (b) **Order 2**   (d) **Order 4**
   Remember that you can check by using tracing paper.

7. (a) **22 cm**
   (b) There are a number of possible shapes. Some are given here. If you are not sure you could cut out 7 hexagons, fit them together and then count the number of edges on the outside.

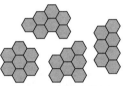

   (c) The shape is more compact because more of the edges are touching.
   (d) There are a number of possible shapes. Some are given here. Each one has a perimeter of 30 cm.
   (e) Only one edge of each hexagon touches another. This means that the maximum number of edges of each hexagon is showing.

8. (a)

   Two more examples are given.
   (b) The first has 16 squares. The second has 25 squares.
   (c) For example, any 3 numbers from **36, 49, 64, 81, 100**. These are all examples of square numbers.

Level 4 – Handling Data

1. Any of these statements would be acceptable: The Adams spend more on fresh food, the Smiths don't have a baby, the Smiths have a pet, the Adams spend more in total, the Smiths spend more on frozen food. There are many equivalent answers.

2. Add together the heights of the bars:
   10 + 8 + 6 + 5 + 1 = **30**

3. (a)

Size	Tally	Frequency
4	⫻⫽⫽	5
5	⫻⫽⫽ ⫽	6
6	⫻⫽⫽	5
7	⫻⫽⫽ ⫽⫽⫽	8
8	⫽⫽⫽	3
9	⫽⫽	2
	TOTAL	29

(b) **Size 7** (This is the mode).

(c) From the table, only 13 of the pairs sold were bigger than size 6. This is less than half of the total sold, so **Lisa is wrong**. Remember to check the total agrees with the original question.

4. (a) This is the amount most frequently spent.
(b)

Amount of money spent	5pm to 6pm	6pm to 7pm	7pm to 8pm	Total number of people who spent each amount
Under 50p	⫽⫽⫽⫽	⫽⫽⫽		7
50p to 99p	⫽⫽⫽⫽	⫽⫽⫽⫽	⫽⫽	10
£1.00 to £1.49		⫽	⫽⫽⫽	4
Over £1.49			⫽⫽⫽	3

(c) **Yes.** More people spent 50p to 99p than in any of the other intervals.

(d) The most amount of money spent is between 7 pm and 8 pm. They are more likely to be hungry later on in the evening. Or, older people with more money tend to go later in the evening.

5. Raw egg, thin glass, calculator, sock or thin glass, raw egg, calculator, sock.

6. (a) **Green.** It's the one with the highest frequency.
(b) **Blue.** It's the one with the lowest frequency.

Level 5 – Number

1. (a) **£123.50.** The sum is 26 × 4.75. This can be done as 26 × £5 and then subtract 26 lots of 25p.
(b) **15 kites.** The sum is 250 ÷ 16:
As you only want to find the whole number of kites, it does not matter what the remainder is.

$$16 \overline{)2\ 5\ {}^90} \quad \begin{array}{c} 1\ 5 \quad \text{rem }10 \end{array}$$

2. (a) **360 cm³.** 10% is 30 cm³, so 20% is 60 cm³.
300 cm³ + 60 cm³ = 360 cm³.
(b) **12 pots.** Work out how much 1 pot holds (30 cm³) and then work out how many of these can be taken from the larger box.

3. **315 calories.** The sum is $\frac{3}{8}$ of 840. $\frac{1}{8}$ is 105 so $\frac{3}{8}$ is 3 × 105 = 315.

4. (a) **10366 cm.** The sum is 142 × 73.
(b) **Length is 103.66 metres, width is 3.65 metres.** The width is 5 × 73 cm = 365 cm. You divide by 100 to convert measurements from centimetres to metres.

5. **4096 mm².** The sum is 32 × 128. Gary was wrong: the area is over 4000 mm².

6. **3 m².** The sum is 20% of 15 m². It is easy to work out $\frac{1}{5}$ of 15 (20% = $\frac{1}{5}$).

7. (a) He made the square by taking off $\frac{1}{3}$ of the rectangle. When he puts the piece back, it is still $\frac{1}{3}$ of the rectangle, but it is $\frac{1}{2}$ of the square.
(b) $\frac{1}{3}$ of shape 2 is added on.
(c) $\frac{1}{7}$ of the new shape would have to be added on to get back to the original shape. You have to spot what is happening here. The amount added back on is 1 over the fraction cut off, minus one. For example, if $\frac{1}{3}$ is cut off, $\frac{1}{3-1} = \frac{1}{2}$ is added on.

8. **324 and 3240.** Multiplying a decimal by 10 means moving all the digits one place to the left. Multiplying a decimal by 100 means moving all the digits two places to the left.

Level 5 – Algebra

1. (a) 1 joins to 2, 3 joins to 8, 5 joins to 14, 7 joins to 20, 9 joins to 26, 11 joins to 32.
Each sum is × 3 – 1, so, 3 × 3 – 1 = 8, 5 × 3 – 1 = 14, and so on.

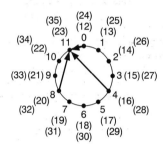

(b) 8 is joined to 3 × 8 – 1 = 23. 23 is the same dot as 11. You can see this by counting round the circle. 12 is joined to 3 × 12 – 1 = 35. This is not on the circle but if you keep on counting round 35 is also at the same dot as 11.

2. **L = D – 1, or, D = L + 1.** Check that your rule works by looking at each entry in the table.

3. **r = 4 × s.** This is better written as r = 4s.

4.

	width	length
rectangle A	3	5
rectangle B	6	8
rectangle C	12	14
rectangle D	24	26

5. (a)

	IN				OUT
Val	4 →	2 →	4 →	9
Liz	9 →	3 →	6 →	11
Huw	16 →	4 →	8 →	13
Paul	25 →	5 →	10 →	15

Remember that the square root is the number that we times by itself to give the answer.

(b) The prime numbers are **11 and 13**. Prime numbers can be divided exactly by themselves and 1 only.

6. (a) **n plum trees.**
   (b) **2n apple trees (or 2 x n).**
   (c) **n + 7**
   (d) **5n + 7.** This is 'translating' real life situations into mathematical language. The answer to (d) is n + n + 2n + n + 7 = 5n + 7.

7. (a) **Vijay is correct.**
   (b) **Karen is correct.**
   (c) They have 5 bags of n which is 5 × n or 5n and 3 extra marbles which is + 3. Put it together and you get 5 × n + 3, which is 5n + 3, which is 3 + 5n. (You can add things in any order.) Part (c) covers both answers. You only have to explain one. Remember 5 × n can be written as 5n. It cannot be written as n5.

8.

	Start	During game	End of game
Cath	1 bag	lost 2 counters	m − 2
Fiona	4 bags	won 6 counters and lost 2 counters	4m + 4

You may have written the last part as 4m + 6 − 2. This is only partly correct, because you can simplify it a bit more. In the real SAT, this answer scored 1 mark instead of 2.

Level 5 – Shape, Space & Measures

1. and 2. You need to draw accurate diagrams. Remember that your lengths need to be within 1mm and your angles need to be within 1° of the exact measurements.

3. (a) **52920 g.** 840 × 63.
   (b) **No, the tins are too heavy.** You must back up your answer by showing your working. 52920 g = 52.92 kg. This is more than 50 kg.
   (c) **8 layers.** First change 1.24 m into cm: 1.24 × 100 = 124 cm. 124 ÷ 14 = 8.857. Rounded down, this is 8.

4. **No, their total mass is too heavy.** Total mass = 508 kg. This is about 1016 lb.

5. 0.5 **litres. 20 cm** bowl: 8 × 2.5.

6. (a) About 1.5 m to 2.5 m.
   (b) About 5 m to 7 m. (An answer in Imperial units would also be accepted.)

7. (a) **1.53 metres, 5 feet;** (b) **196 kilometres, 122 miles.**

8. Lines of symmetry:
   (a) **1**; (b) **0**; (c) **1**; (d) **6**; (e) **2**.
   Order of rotational symmetry:
   (a) **1**; (b) **2**; (c) **1**; (d) **6**; (e) **2**.

Level 5 – Handling Data

1. I would choose Karen because her mean score is quite high and her range shows that she always scores about the same, **or** I would choose Jo because her mean score is quite high and her range shows she fluctuates between very high and very low scores which would make the match more exciting.

2. The low range represents more consistent portions, so they will know roughly how many chips they are going to get.

3. (a) This is the completed pie chart:

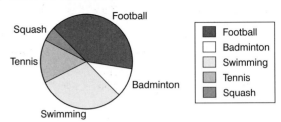

   (b) **30%** (an answer between 25% and 30% is acceptable).
   (c) **15%** (an answer between 10% and 20% is acceptable but the 2 answers for (b) and (c) **must** add up to 45%).

4. (a) This is the completed pie chart:

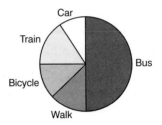

   Both sectors must be correctly labelled. The angle for the train sector should be between 54° and 66°.
   (b) **Train – 3; bicycle – 9; car – 3.**
   (c) There are 36 pupils in Sara's class but only 24 in Jim's class. The sectors show different proportions.

5. (a)

   Ed has less chance than Sue.
   P(Sue gets a black bead) = $\frac{1}{6}$.
   P(Ed gets a black bead) = $\frac{1}{9}$.
   (b) There are unequal numbers of white and black beads in the bag, so it cannot be an evens chance.
   P(Bob gets a black bead) = $\frac{1}{3}$.
   (c) See the diagram above.

Level 6 – Number

1. (a) **3000 mm² to 4500 mm².** Use 100, 130, 150 for 128 mm and 30 for 32 mm. Other answers are acceptable but you must not show any evidence of using a calculator.
   (b) **128 × 32 = 4096.** This is level 5 long multiplication. You must do this without a calculator.
   (c) **Gary pays over £1** but our estimate was OK. Gary rounded both of his answers down.

2. (a) P has side **4 mm**, R has side **24 mm**, S has side **36 mm**.
   (b) **2:3.** The ratio is 24:36, which cancels by a factor of 12.
   (c) **2:3.** The actual ratio is 96:144 which cancels by a factor of 48.
   (d) They are the same because we are comparing lengths in the same ratio.

3. (a) Round 214 to 200 and 92 to 100. 200 × 100 = **20 000**.
(b) Steve is wrong. He has missed a zero off in his multiplication.
(c) 214 × 92 = **19688**.
This is level 5 long multiplication. Do this without a calculator.

4. There many acceptable answers: 40 is only 50% of 80; A 100% decrease would leave nothing at all; It is only a 50% decrease.

5. (a) **1:4:5:9** (5:20:25:45 cancelled by a factor of 5).
(b) **47%**. He saw 45 sparrows out of 95 birds. This is the sum 45 ÷ 95 × 100 = 47.36. Round off the answer.
(c) **1:3:8:6.** 25% off of 20 (crows) is 15; 60% increase on 25 is 15; 7 of 45 is 30. The ratio is 5: 15 : 40 : 30 which cancels by 5 to give the answer. You could also work out the percentage and fractions on 1:4:5:9

6. (a) **78.49 points.** (Add 7.5 + 8 +8 = 23.5 and multiply by 3.34)
(b) The total was **26**. (82.68 ÷ 3.18)
(c) There are a lot of explanations. For example, 102.69 ÷ 3.29 = 31.5 which is more than the three judges can award. 102.69 ÷ 30 = 3.423. If all the judges gave full marks he would need a dive with a rating of 3.423 or above. 30 × 3.29 = 98.7. The most he can score is 98.7 which is not enough.

7. (a) **15000**   (b) **50p or £0.50**
(c) **15000 × 0.5 = £7500**
Use sensible numbers. Do not use a calculator.

8. (a) **62%** (sum is 1558 ÷ 2518 × 100 = 61.87). Round answer off to a sensible figure. 61.9 or 61.87 would be OK.
(b) **About 12.** The sum is 3402 ÷ 276 = 12.32 or reduce the ratio 276:3402 to the form 1:n.
(c) **About 3.** The sum is 642 ÷ 222 = 2.89 or reduce the ratio 222:642 to the form 1:n.
(d) Tick 'Yes' and say something like 'The population doubled' or tick 'Cannot tell' and say something like. 'The numbers have been rounded so it may not be an exact 13 million increase'.

Level 6 – Algebra

1. (a) **They are parallel.** You could also say 'They have the same gradient' but you do not need to be too mathematical.
(b) **The number on its own at the end.**
(c) **It will cross at (0, –20).**
(d) **Any line that is parallel to the others.** The equation you write down should be $y = \frac{1}{2}x + c$ where c is where your line crosses the y axis.

2. (a) **b = 14.** The equation is solved like this:
$$3b - 4 = 2b + 10$$
$$3b - 2b - 4 = 10 \quad \text{(move 2b across equals)}$$
$$b - 4 = 10 \quad \text{(Collect b terms together)}$$
$$b = 14 \quad \text{(Add 4)}$$
(b) Carol and Daisy because there is no answer to b + 3 = b + 4.

3. **Both Vijay and Karen are correct.** The two possible equations are 3 + 5n = 88 and 5 × n + 3 = 88. The value of n is 17

4. (a) There will be 64 grey tiles and 4 black tiles.
(b) There will be 256 grey tiles and 4 black tiles.
(c) There will be P² grey tiles and 4 black tiles.
(d) **T = P² + 4.** If you got parts (c) and (d) correct then you obviously spotted the rule.

5. (a) He should use **14 tables**.
(b) The graph shows the line through the crosses drawn out further. A line across from 30 pupils to the line and then down to the axis gives 13.5 tables but you cannot have half a table, so 14 tables are needed

6. (a) **Income is 7100p or £71.00.** F = 60 × 65 + 40 × 80 = 7100.
(b) **y = 45 tubs.** 4800 = 60 × 50 + 40 y. 4800 = 3000 + 40 y. 1800 = 40y.
(c) **46%.** The calculation is 437 ÷ 950 × 100. This is level 6 Number but Test questions can have different topics (and different levels!) mixed up in them.

7. (a) See graph
(b) **Any line of the form y = ax will do.** The only unacceptable answers are y = 3x and y = 2x. So y = x, y = 4x y = –x, y = 0 are all acceptable.
(c) See graph
(d) **y = 3x – 1.** This is y = mx + c where m is the gradient and c is the intercept on the y axis

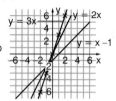

8. (a) **3m – 5 = 2m + 3**
(b) **m = 8.** The equation is solved like this:
3m – 2m – 5 = 3 (take 2m over equals sign)
m – 5 = 3 (collect letter terms together)
m = 8 (Add 5)

Level 6 – Shape, Space & Measures

1.

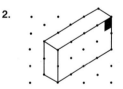

2.

3. (a) FORWARD 10   (b) TURN RIGHT 45
    TURN RIGHT 120   FORWARD 6
    FORWARD 10   TURN RIGHT 135
    TURN RIGHT 120   FORWARD 8
    FORWARD 10   TURN RIGHT 45
                            FORWARD 6

4. (a) **99.5°**
(b) w and 80.5° are allied angles and add up to 180°.
(c) **135 m².** A = $\frac{1}{2}$(7 + 2) × 30.

5. (a) **147°.**
(b) 3rd angle in triangle = **57°.** m = 57° + 90°.
(c) **336 m²;** A= $\frac{1}{2}$ × 32 × 21.
(d) **1938 m²;** A = 51 × 38.
(e) **567 m²** (nearest m²); A= $\frac{1}{2}$ x π x 19².

6. (a) **36 cm².** Each side is 6 cm.
(b) **32 cm².** The length is 8 cm and the width is 4 cm.

7. (a) **188 cm.** c = $\pi \times 60$.
   (b) **5.8 or 6 times**. $950 \div (\pi \times 52)$.

8. **300 cm³.** V= $6 \times 5 \times 10$.

9. **361 m.** d = $0.5 \times \pi \times 230$.

10. **314 cm².** A= $\pi \times 10^2$.

Level 6 – Handling Data

1. You can choose either place. A possible answer is: 'I would choose Corufa because, although it is very hilly it is less likely to rain heavily; whereas Vego is less hilly but it is likely to be very wet.'

2. (a) There is positive correlation: more doctors increase the life expectancy.
   (b) There is no correlation.
   (c) Use graph 1. An estimate is any age between 55 and 65 inclusive.

3. (a) There is negative correlation: the more hours worked, the less time spent watching television.
   (b) There is positive correlation: the more hours worked, the more time sleeping.
   (c) There is no correlation.
   (d) An estimate is any time between 20 and 25 hours. You draw a line up from 30 on the x-axis and look at points that are close to it.

4. Totals are: **5, 6, 7, 9, 10, 11, 13, 14, 15**.

5. (a) Les Tom Nia Ann   Nia Tom Ann Les
       Les Tom Ann Nia   Ann Tom Les Nia
       Nia Tom Les Ann   Ann Tom Nia Les
   (b) $\frac{7}{8}$. Mutually exclusive events: P(Tom not singing second)
       $= 1 - \frac{1}{8}$.

6. (a) RR, RB, BR, BB.
   (b) RR, RG, RY, GR, GG, GY, YR, YG, YY. or draw a sample space diagram.

Level 7 – Number

1. (a) **0.6180339888.** Your calculator may show a few less digits. You will need to use brackets to do this sum. Type in $2 \div (1 + \sqrt5)$.
   (b) One way is shown in (a). Another might be to use memory:

   (c) **0.381966013**
   (d) You can use brackets or memory.

   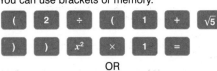

   OR

2. (a) The nearest **foot** or the nearest **metre**.
   (b) The nearest **hour** or **half hour**.
   (c) The nearest **inch** or **centimetre**.
   You could also say the nearest 10 centimetres in (a) and the nearest 15 minutes in (b). You need to have a sensible grasp of units and what they would be given to in a real-life situation.

3. (a) **23** and **19.75**
   (b) **5.805897344** ≈ 5.81 (3 sf) , and **1.043888889** ≈ 1.04 (3 sf). The answers to (a) are nice decimals which have terminating answers. In (b) the answers are recurring decimals. These have to be rounded off. In general you should not round off to much more than the accuracy given in the question, so 5.8 or 1.0 would be acceptable. Note that 1 would not be correct as this is only 1 sf.

4. (a) **£14.41.** This is a compound interest problem. After one day (Tuesday) the price is £16.96. Multiply by 0.85.
   (b) **£48.80.** This is a reverse percentage problem. £41.48 is 85%, so divide by 85 and multiply by 100.
   (c) **£26.07** This is best done by multiplying by 0.85 four times. Do 49.95×0.85^4 A common mistake is to do 5 reductions. Monday to Friday is 4 reductions.
   (d) **6 days.** One way to do this is to start with a price and reduce it. £100 is a good choice. If you multiply by 0.88 it takes 6 multiplications to get to less than £50.

5. **No:** their leaves could be any length between 7.5 and 8.5 cm. The error is half a centimetre. On a number line the leaf would have a length bigger or equal to 7.5 centimetres but less than 8.5 centimetres.

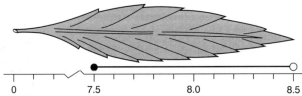

6. (a) **0.00529 millimetres.** $0.001243 - 0.000714 = 0.000529$ cm. Multiply by 10 to get an answer in millimetres.
   (b) **122 or 123.** $0.65 \div 0.00529 = 122.8733459$. Obviously this rounds to 123 but only 122 full cells will fit across the full stop.

7. (a)

	Country	Number of people for each km²
Most people for each km²	Netherlands	362
Fewest people for each km²	Spain	79

It is important to get the division the right way round. In this case divide the land by the population. A clue is given in the question. People per km² is the same as people/km², which tells you to divide people by area.
   (b) **4241 or 4240 or 4200 m².** In this case the sum is m² per person so do area divided by population. You also have to multiply the area by a million to get an answer in square metres. The answer is 4240.770661 but this must be rounded off to a sensible accuracy.

8. (a) **2.936329588 = 2.94 (3 sf)**

(b) **0.5277777778 = 0.528 (3 sf)**

9. (a)

Box 1: 8cm to the nearest cm	Box 2: 9cm to the nearest cm
Tube A 8.42cm Tube C 8.47cm	Tube B 8.85cm Tube D 8.53cm Tube E 8.50cm

(b) **8.50.** This seems like a contradiction but the length is 8.499999… (Eight point four nine recurring)

(c) **8.50**
Mathematics doesn't always make sense.
Look at this proof.
x = 0.999999… (0.9 recurring) (1)
Multiply both sides by 10
      10x = 9.999999… (2)
Subtract equation (1) from equation (2)
      9x = 9 (all the recurring bits cancel each other out)
        x = 1
So 0.9999999… = 1!

Level 7 – Algebra

1. (a) **Yes it works.** $\frac{3(3^2 + 1)}{2} = \frac{3 \times 10}{2} = \frac{30}{2} = 15$. You need to do enough of the sum to prove you can put numbers into the formula.

(b) **18.** You could try some values: 20 gets 4010 which is too big, 15 gets 1695 which is too small, so you know roughly what the answer will be.

2. (a) n shows the number of dotted squares. n-1 shows the number of striped squares. You can see this from the pattern; write out a list if you need to.

(b) The number in each diagram is 0, 2, 4, 6, 8. This is 2 less than the 2 times table. 2(n – 1) = 2n – 2 which is also 2 less than the 2 times table.

3. (a)

2.85	10.9725
2.86	11.0396
2.855	11.006025
2.854	10.999316

(b) The 2 decimal place numbers are **2.85 and 2.86**. The 3 decimal place numbers are **2.854 and 2.855**.

4. (a)

100
10
19

The numbers in row 2 are the square roots of the numbers in the top row. The numbers in row 3 are given by 2n – 1.

(b) He should have written **2n – 1**. This is level 6 Algebra.

5.

x	12 – x	Area
3	9	27
4	8	32
5	7	35
4.5	7.5	33.75
4.6	7.4	34.04

The numbers are 4.5 and 4.6.

6. David wrote **4 × n + 4**. This is the same as 4(n + 1) if you expand the bracket.

7. **q = 5.5, t = 5.75**

	q + 2t = 17	(1)
	6 + q = 2t	(2)
(1) – (2)	2t – 6 = 17 – 2t	Eliminating (already balanced)
	4t - 6 = 17	
	4t = 23	
	t = 5.75	Solving
Substitute into (1)	q + 11.5 = 17	Substituting
	q = 5.5	Solving again
	5.5 + 2 × 5.75 = 17	
	6 + 5.5 = 2 × 5.75	Checking

Level 7 – Shape, Space & Measures

1. (a) **7.2 km.** $x^2 = 6^2 + 4^2 = 52$. $x = \sqrt{52} = 7.2$ (to 1 dp).
   (b) **2.2 km.** $x^2 = 2.5^2 - 1.2^2 = 4.81$. $x = \sqrt{4.81} = 2.2$ (to 1 dp).

2. (a) **242.1 cm** (to 1 dp) or **242 cm** (to 3 sf). $x^2 = 150^2 + 190^2 = 58600$. $x = 242.074$.
   (b) The room is not wide enough for the cupboard to be turned because the length of its diagonal (170 cm) is greater than the width of the room (165 cm).
   $x^2 = 150^2 + 80^2 = 28\,900$. $x = \sqrt{28\,900} = 170$ cm.

3. (a) **175 cm³.** V = Ah = 35 × 5 = 175.
   (b) **25.8 cm.** A = lw. 134 = l × 5. l = 134 ÷ 5 = 26.8. Distance without overlap = 26.8 – 1 = 25.8.
   (c) **113.1 cm³** (to 1 dp). $V = \pi r^2 h = \pi \times 3^2 \times 4 = 113.097$.

4. (a)   (b)

5. (a) **Yes.** The upper bound for the distance is 35.425 m.
   (b) **14.55s** and **14.65s**.

6. **4375 mph.** Use $s = \frac{d}{t}$. s = 35 000 000 ÷ 8000 = 4375.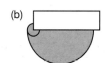

Level 7 – Handling Data

1. (a) and (b) None of the questions are really suitable for a questionnaire. Here are some reasons – you can probably think of others.
   Tony: you might care about animals but not be a member of a welfare organisation.
   Ben: the question is too vague and will give rise to many different responses.
   Chitra: she is putting across her own point of view: questions like this should always be avoided.
   Sally: you might like animals but some important medical research might need to use animals.

(c) A selection of appropriate questions could be: Have you ever had a pet animal? Do you go to zoos? Do you agree with using animals for medical research? Do you buy battery-farmed eggs? Do you buy things which you know were tested on animals? Do you have an allergy which is caused by pets?

2. (a) **The mean = £304.**

The mean $\bar{x} = \frac{\Sigma fx}{\Sigma f}$

$$= \frac{(50 \times 3) + (150 \times 14) + (250 \times 38) + (350 \times 16) + (450 \times 29)}{100}$$

$$= \frac{30400}{100} = 304$$

(b) **£200 – £300.** The modal class is the one with the highest frequency.

(c)

	Women	Men
median	266	280
modal class	**200–300**	200–300
mean	265	**304**

(d) The mean represents the data most fairly. It takes account of the large proportion of men in the highest class interval and it shows up the differences between the 2 sets of data whereas the median and modal class are too similar.

3. (a) You cannot tell because you do not know how many lengths each pupil swam. One pupil in Year 10 could have swum lots of lengths or Year 10 pupils might be stronger swimmers.

(b) The mean for Lara's graph is **10.4 lengths**.

Mean $\bar{x} = \frac{\text{total number of lengths}}{80}$

$$= \frac{150 + 210 + 230 + 170 + 70}{80} = 10.375$$

(c) The mean for Jack's graph is **10.1 lengths**. For a grouped frequency distribution you need to find the mid-points of each class interval first. These are 3, 8, 13, 18 and 23.

Mean $\bar{x} = \frac{\Sigma fx}{\Sigma f}$

$$= \frac{(12 \times 3) + (33 \times 8) + (27 \times 13) + (6 \times 18) + (2 \times 23)}{80}$$

$$= \frac{805}{80} = 10.065.$$ Your answer should be to 1dp.

(d) Lara's mean is exact because we can find the total of all the lengths swam. Jack's mean is only an estimate because he used class intervals.

4. (a) There is positive correlation: as the number of people increases, the number of pizzas sold also increases.

(b) **About 220.** Draw on a line of best fit:

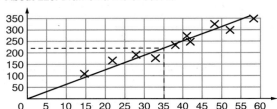

Put in the dotted lines to help read off the values on the graph.

---

5. **Petra.** The relative frequency should be close to the actual probability of 0.125 after 100 throws.

Level 8

1. (a) Yes. The sum is $1.427 \times 10^9 - 2.279 \times 10^8$
$= 1427 \times 10^6 - 227.9 \times 10^6$
$= 1200.9 \times 10^6$
$= 1200$ million.
Standard form is a way of writing very large or very small numbers. Numbers are written as a $\times 10^n$ where a is a number between 1 or 10 and n is an integer. The answer from a calculator is probably 1.2×10^9, which is 1200 million as 1 million is 10^6. To enter this on a calculator you need to use the EXP or EE button.

(b) **Jupiter is 5.20 and Saturn is 9.54.** The value for Jupiter must be given to 2 decimal places so the zero is necessary. At this level you must read the question carefully and answer what is asked for. Most pupils would give an answer of 5.2 which is only 1 dp.

(c) **41888000 = 4.189×10^8 or 4.19×10^8 or 4.2×10^8.**
4 significant figures or more would be wrong as it is only an approximate answer. In general the answer should not be more accurate than the information given in the question.

(d) **434067265.3 = 4.34×10^8 or 4.3×10^8.**
The sum is $6.67 \times 10^{-20} \times 1.993 \times 10^{30} \div (17.5^2)$.

(e) It is possible as they are both about the same distance from the Sun. You could have said no because they are not the same distance but as both answers are approximate 4.2×10^8 and 4.3×10^8 are nearly the same.

2. **The report is fair.** 7% of 250 million = 17.5 million people.
$9000 \times 2000 = 18\,000\,000 = 18$ million people.
You would need to show both calculations to get all the marks. There are other ways to do this. For example you could work out that if 18 million was 7% then the population would be 257 million, or divide 17.5 million by 9000 to get 1944.4, the number of people served in each MegaBurger restaurant. Whatever you do you should conclude that the report is fair. You could get away with saying it is not fair if you said it is half a million out. You would have to justify any conclusion you came to.

3. **d = 40.96 or 41.0 (3 sf).** The sum is $-(27^2) \div (2 \times -8.9)$.
The accuracy should not be more that 4 sf as the numbers in the sum are given to 3 sf at most (You can assume that 27.0 is 3 sf).

4. (a) **Distance = 0.56875.** The equation to use is $s = ut + \frac{1}{2}at^2$. Look at the information given. Only one of the equations involves all the given information.

(b) **Final speed = 0.075 m/s.** The equation to use is $v = u + at$ but you could use $v^2 = u^2 + 2as$ because you have the value for s from part (a) but the first is easier and doesn't use a value you may have worked out wrongly.

5. **r = 8.32**
$$48.46 = 2.7 + 5.5r$$
$$5.5r = 48.46 - 2.7$$
$$r = \frac{48.46 - 2.7}{5.5}$$
$$r = 8.32$$

6. The jug has the greater volume. $3d^3 - (3d - d^2) = 3d^3 - 3d + d^2 =$ volume of bottle plus d^2. Whatever value d is d^2 will be positive. A minus outside
a bracket can be treated as -1 times the bracket. i.e. $-1(3d - d^2) = -1 \times 3d - 1 \times -d^2 = -3d + d^2$. The effect of a minus outside a bracket is to change the sign of all the terms inside the bracket.

7. $A = \dfrac{14}{9}t^2$

Substitute 2t for s but use brackets!

$A = \dfrac{1}{2}(2t)t + \dfrac{(2t)^2 + t^2}{9}$

Work the expression out using BODMAS and you get

$t^2 + \dfrac{5t^2}{9} = \dfrac{14}{9}t^2$

8. $4n + 2(n - 1) = 4n + 2n - 2 = 6n - 2$.
$6 + 4(n - 1) + 2(n - 2) = 6 + 4n - 4 + 2n - 4 = 6n - 2$.
They are the same. This is simply the distributive law and collecting like terms. The algebra isn't too difficult but you must show all the working to get the marks.

9. (a)

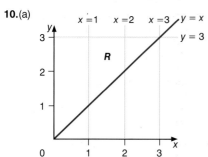

	2p	7
p	$2p^2$	$7p$
3	$6p$	21

Helen writes $(p + 3)(2p + 7) = 2p^2 + 13p + 21$
(b) $2p^2 + 7p + 6p + 21 = 2p^2 + 13p + 21$
(c) $3a^2 + 5a + 12a + 20 = \mathbf{3a^2 + 17a + 20}$
You could use a rectangle approach to do this. It is like the box method used in long multiplication at level 5.

10. (a)

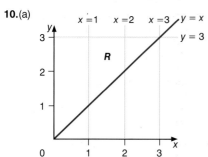

To find an inequality you have to find the boundary line and then decide which side of the line is represented by the inequality. The boundary line is the line you get when you replace the inequality sign by an equals sign. The region is greater than $x = 1$, less than $x = 2$, greater than $y = x$ and less than $y = 3$. Only the region marked obeys all four inequalities.
(b) $\mathbf{x \leqslant 4, y \geqslant 2, y \leqslant x}$. The region is less than $x = 4$, more than $y = 2$ and less than $y = x$. There are other inequalities, for example $x \geqslant 2$ but these wouldn't really be of any use in describing it as the line $x = 2$ is not a boundary.

11. (a) **Graph A.**
(b) **Graph B is wrong** because the first part of the fall is at a steady speed and she gets faster and faster.
Graph C is wrong because she falls to the ground instantly.
Graph D is wrong because the falls quickly at first then slows down before coming down at a steady speed.
These graphs are difficult to describe. A lot of people think that the graphs show how she falls out of the sky but it is a graph of her height above the ground against time. Read the axes to see what the graph is about. It is easy to lose marks on this type of question by not making your explanation relevant and precise.

12. (a) **PQ = 200 cm.** To solve a problem using similar triangles you have to identify two triangles which are similar. This means they have the same angles and their sides are in the same ratio. You will always find that you can match up two of the triangles to give a scale factor. In this part the two triangles are APQ and ABC. So PQ:BC is the same as AP:AB which means that you have to add 200 and 400 to get AB. PQ:600 = 200:600 so PQ is 200.
(b) **LM = 240 cm.** The two triangles are ABC and LMC.
LM:AB = MC : BC, so LM: 640 = 300:800
LM = 300 × 640 ÷ 800 = 240

13. **Not quite.** The side of the larger triangle is 7.81 cm and the matching side of the smaller triangle is 7.88 cm.
Trigonometry is about the ratios of sides of right angled triangles. There are three ratios, sine, cosine and tangent. Depending on the information known then one of them can be used to find the other sides and angles of the triangle. The second picture shows that the hypotenuse of the smaller triangle is 10 cm.
The vertical side of the larger triangle in the final diagram is calculated by 10 × tan 38 = 7.81.
The vertical side of the smaller triangle is calculated by 10 × cos 38 (or 10 × sin 52) = 7.88

14. (a) **Q could be the area of a star.**
(b) **P only has 1 dimension** because it has only got one letter so it is a length. (k is a number). Lengths have 1 letter, areas have two (or a square term) and volumes have three (or a cube or a square and a single letter. For example $2\pi r$ is a length, πr^2 is an area and $\pi r^2 h$ is a volume).

15. (a)

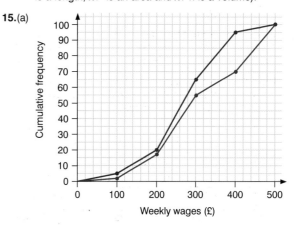

Weekly wage (£)		Frequency	Cumulative Frequency
at least	below		
0	100	3	3
100	200	14	17
200	300	38	55
300	400	16	71
400	500	29	100

The cumulative frequency is obtained by adding up the frequencies. The graph is drawn by plotting the top value of each group against the cumulative frequency. For example, (100, 3), (200, 17), etc.

(b)

	Women	Men
lower quartile	218	221
upper quartile	328	415
inter-quartile range	110	194

Quartiles are found by drawing lines across from the quarter and three-quarter values (25 and 75) to the graph and drawing lines down to the bottom axis.

(c) The lowest quarter of both men and women earn about the same amount of money but at the top end men earn a lot more than women. Any comments must refer to the quartiles. Saying men earn more than women isn't enough for full marks.

16.(a) **0.025 × 0.025 = 0.000625**. The word **'both'** means first **and** second. **'and'** suggests that you multiply the probabilities.

(b) **0.025 × 0.975 + 0.975 x 0.025 =0.04875.** One defective disk can occur if first is defective **and** the second is not defective **or** the second is not defective **and** the second is defective. **'and'** means multiply the probabilities, **'or'** means add the probabilities.

(c) **120 disks.** 1 disk is 0.025 of the sample so divide 3 by 0.025 to get the size of the sample.

Mental arithmetic test 1

1	3006	15	120
2	7	16	81
3	580	17	34
4	25	18	8
5	7	19	5903
6	13	20	17
7	470	21	130
8	64	22	4 500 000
9	9	23	0.8
10	760	24	53
11	19	25	9.95
12	8.7–8.9 inc.	26	2397
13	7.15	27	6
14	36	28	16–24 inc.

Mental arithmetic test 2

1	860	17	6080
2	17	18	65–70 inc.
3	8	19	6
4	740	20	11
5	0.03	21	70
6	6.5	22	£9.95
7	8.15	23	140–160 inc.
8	90	24	108
9	69	25	704
10	34	26	54
11	160	27	40
12	6 500 000	28	280
13	0.6	29	36
14	75	30	900
15	40	31	5
16	200	32	380–420 inc.

ACKNOWLEDGEMENTS

Published by HarperCollins*Publishers* Ltd
77–85 Fulham Palace Road
London W6 8JB

www.**Collins**Education.com
On-line support for schools and colleges

© HarperCollins*Publishers* Ltd 2001

First published 2001

ISBN 0 00 711208 4

Kevin Evans and Keith Gordon assert the moral right to be identified as the authors of this work.

British Library Cataloguing in Publication Data

A catalogue record for this book is available from the British Library.

Edited by Kathryn Senior

Production by Kathryn Botterill

Cover design by Susi Martin-Taylor

Book design by Rupert Purcell and produced by Gecko Limited

Index compiled by Laurence Errington

Printed and bound by Bath Press

Acknowledgements
The Authors and Publishers are grateful to QCA (SCAA) for permission to reproduce past Test questions: pp. 15, 16; 29, 30; 39, 40; 51, 52; 67, 68; 81, 82; 91, 92; 103, 104; 119, 120; 135, 136; 151, 152; 165, 166; 179, 180; 193, 194; 209, 210; 225, 226; 227–234.

Illustrations
Gill Bishop, Harvey Collins, Richard Deverell, Gecko Ltd, Ian Law, Dave Poole, Carl Thorney and Tony Warne

Every effort has been made to contact the holders of copyright material, but if any have been inadvertently overlooked, the Publishers will be pleased to make the necessary arrangements at the first opportunity.

You might also like to visit:
www.**fire**and**water**.com
The book lover's website

INDEX

INDEX

INDEX

obtuse angles 83
opposite (inverse) operations 69, 70-1
origin (in a grid) 26, 78

parallel lines 141
parallelograms 138, 148
percentage(s) 11-14, 64-6, 112
  interconversion
    and decimals 114
    and fractions 114-15
  probability expressed as 99
  reverse 176
perimeters 36, 147
pie charts 96-8, 156-7
place value 5
  in decimals 107
points on grids/graphs
  finding 26
  of intersection of 2 lines 187, 188
  locus of set of 202
  plotting 131-2
polygons
  angle properties 139-41
  frequency 153-4
  symmetry and 85, 86
primes 21-2
prisms, volume 199-200
probability 50, 99-102, 161-4
  calculating/estimates 100-1, 161-4, 222-4
    of compound event 233, 234
  relative frequency and 222-4
  scales of 99
proportion(s), of whole numbers 11-14
proportional change 176
protractor 83
Pythagoras' theorem 195-7

quadrant(s)
  co-ordinates in all four 78-80
  co-ordinates in first 26-8
quadratic rules, nth term in 181-3
quadrilaterals 138
questionnaires, designing 211-14

range 94-5
ratios 111, 117-18, 228
rectangles 138, 139, 147, 148
reflective (line) symmetry 33, 85
reflex angles 83
relative frequency 222-4
reverse percentage 176
rhombus 138
rotational symmetry 33-4, 86
rotations 144
rounding off 72-3, 167-9, 205,
  see also estimation
  decimals 108, 168
  to significant figures 167-9

scales
  measuring from various 35
  of probability 99
scatter diagrams 158-60
  line of best fit 220-1
shapes, 2-D (and in general) 31-4, 36-8, 137-52, 195-210, 232-3
  3-D shape represented by 2-D 31-2, 137
  area of 36, 148, 198-9
  congruent 34
  elevations of 31
  geometrical properties 138-42
  perimeter of 36, 147
  symmetry in see also symmetry
  transforming 143-6
shapes, 3-D shape see also 3-D shape
significant figures, rounding off to 167-9
simultaneous equations 184-9
speed 206, 229
square (shape) 138, 147, 148
square number 69-70
square root 70-1
statistical data in probability calculation 101
strict inequalities 190
subtraction 1, see also BODMAS
  and addition as inverse operations of each other 69

in algebra 75, 124
  decimals 8-10, 57
  negative numbers 61-3
supplementary angles 84
symmetry 33-4, 85-6
  line 33, 85
  rotational 33-4, 86

tables
  data recording in 41-4
  multiplication 1
tally 41
ten
  multiples of
    dividing 57, 109
    multiplying 57, 109
  multiplying/dividing by 5-7
    decimals 57
terms
  next, in number patterns 17
  nth see also nth term
3-D shape 31-2
  2-D representations 31-2, 137
  volume see also volume
time in speed calculations 206
transformation geometry 143-6
trapezium 138, 148
triangle 148
2-D drawing/shape see also shapes, 2-D
2-D representations of 3-D shapes 31-2, 137

units (of measurement) 35, 87-9
  for estimation, choosing 90

vertices 138
volume 37, 148
  density and 206
  prisms 199-200

x-axis 131

y-axis 131